T0354358

FROM VICTIM
TO SOLDIER

FROM VICTIM TO SOLDIER

My journey from Auschwitz to Israel

ZVI AND DANNY RITTMAN

FROM VICTIM TO SOLDIER
MY JOURNEY FROM AUSCHWITZ TO ISRAEL

iUniverse books may be ordered through booksellers or by contacting:

iUniverse
1663 Liberty Drive
Bloomington, IN 47403
www.iuniverse.com
1-800-Authors (1-800-288-4677)

ISBN: 978-1-5320-3833-4 (sc)
ISBN: 978-1-5320-3832-7 (e)

Library of Congress Control Number: 2018900621

Print information available on the last page.

iUniverse rev. date: 01/25/2018

CONTENTS

Life was good and easy, and I called life 'friend'. I'd never hidden anything from him, and he'd never hidden anything from me. Or so I thought. I knew everything. He was an awfully intelligent companion; we had the same tastes (apparently) and he was awfully fond of me. And all the time he was plotting up a mass murder.

– Wyndham Lewis

On this day, when we remember the six million victims, let us also remember two lessons: first, the Holocaust – never again. And second – an independent, strong, thriving and peaceful State of Israel is the vengeance of the dead.

– Ehud Barak

ACKNOWLEDGMENTS

T he authors would like to thank family members for sharing photographs and recollections, and Rebecca Rittman for the wonderful illustrations in this memoir.

We also thank family friend and editor of this book, Brian Downing, for inspiring support and sound advice.

PREFACE

Sometimes I wonder. If we could remember everything from the moment of birth to the present, would we better understand how we arrived at where we are? We'd see small private moments and immense world events. Some things in our control, others far beyond it. Sublime continuities and jarring derailments. This is my story – pieces of the past, from my entrance into the world in Romania to my retirement in Israel. In between there was the Second World War, the Holocaust, Israel's founding, and several wars. I had a part in them all.

Hope and innocence ended suddenly in boyhood. Europe began a descent into night, but hope persisted at odd places and for small moments. Fortune kept me from death many times and left me wondering about meaning and purpose in life. I don't know how or why I survived what we now call the Holocaust. Millions of others did not. Many of them were close to me, if only for a brief time – sometimes just before their deaths.

There were consequences. Neither religion nor spirituality resonated with anything inside me. Indeed, I disliked anything related to religion. Old age and longer shadows have softened me, but I cannot say my view has changed much.

Embarking on a new life in a new land, and changing my first name from Herman to Zvi, I found meaning in family and country. I served both. I devoted my life to Israel, a land that for centuries looked impossible, only a dream, the topic of elders' dinner conversations. But it turned into reality. Better days arrived. Days of purpose, days of beauty.

The darker period will always dwell in me. As I get on, it eddies up more and more. More than I like, and at unexpected times. I'm retired now and have plenty of time on my hands. The past takes advantage of the absence of daily routine, and demands attention.

For those of us who experienced those days, all that is left is to wait. Wait for something we can never forget, and should never forget, to at last unburden us. My son once read me a quote he'd come across. The words were said by a great spiritual leader, one of many whom I never believed in, but in whom I can now see wisdom.

Light need not combat and overpower darkness in order to displace it – where light is, darkness is not. A thimbleful of light will therefore banish a roomful of darkness.

Reading those words once, twice, and even three times made me feel their beauty and power. They are indeed wise. They encapsulate what I've experienced and why I'm here today.

My story is marked by occasional dark humor. Events conferred it upon me in late boyhood and it is an essential part of who I am to this day. It's been a close companion ever since. Dark humor can illuminate and liberate, as I hope to show.

I'd like to accomplish something more here than answering questions that I've either avoided or responded to briefly, incompletely, and above all reluctantly. I hope to *inform* people.

I also hope people will *remember.*

HOME AND SEPARATION

The story of my early days I learned in later years from family members. My father Solomon was born in 1887, my mother Hermina three years later. My father owned restaurants and cafes. Europe's economy was faring poorly in the 1930s. Markets crashed, banks failed, shops closed. Our family moved from place to place trying to improve prospects.

Two years before my birth, my family moved from a small town called Valealui Mihai, which means "the town in the valley", where my father had a cafe in the train station, to Focşani, a town with a population of about 100,000. It had factories, businesses, and vineyards in the surrounding countryside. My father worked most of the day in his restaurant. My mother took care of the family in a rented house on Bucuresti Street.

My parents had their first daughter, Viorica, in 1923, and one year later had my brother Maurizio, who was called "Motzu". My father wanted to open a restaurant in Constanza, so we moved there. In 1928, Rosy, my second sister, was born. I was born January 1 1930. New Year's Day. They called me Shuly.

That same year my family redecorated the establishment and offered better fare, but income stayed the same and we still lived day to day. The Depression was beginning and getting by was harder.

In 1935, a second brother, Lucian, was born while my family was living in Ploesti, where my father was trying another venture. My mother had another baby just before me, but he died just after birth.

It was an autumn night when my uncle Joseph Davidovich came to visit us in Focşani. He was my mother's brother and he lived in a small town a few hundred kilometers away called Alba Julia. He visited every few months and sometimes we traveled to see him and his family. He was married to a beautiful woman named Catalina. Their son Yanosh was fifteen years older than I.

Joseph Davidovich was a tall handsome man in his late thirties. He was thin, with a small neatly trimmed mustache, blue eyes with a penetrating look but always more than a trace of a gentle nature. He drove about Romania in his truck, buying and selling miscellaneous goods. The hours were long, the money pretty good. He was better off than we were.

His large suitcases were full of merchandise of all types and styles. For a child my age, the contents were exotic treasures. When he opened a suitcase, we kids would marvel at the watches, kitchenware, candlesticks, toys, and old coins from across Europe and the Levant. I didn't recognize many of the items, but I knew they were not found in local stores – at least not until Uncle Joseph came back to town.

He'd let me look through the cache and if a small toy caught my eye, he'd smile and present it to me. His travel and eye for value brought a measure of success. He owned a spacious house in Alba Julia with a large backyard. Uncle Joseph was a very special man. As a matter of fact he was like a father to me. But I'm getting ahead of myself.

"We eat stew only on weekends," Viorica said with practiced assertiveness. As the oldest sister, she liked to demonstrate her maturity. She complemented her words with an adult face, one that could last only a moment on a young girl. Although only eight years old, Viorica had the mannerisms of a young woman. That's what my mother used to say.

"I understand very well, Viorica. Are you helping your mother with the household?" Uncle Joseph sat between her and me, and smiled to her.

She nodded with pride as she thought of her importance in the family.

"Viorica, please be a darling and help your sister Rosy sit in her chair." My mother gave her a kind smile as she prepared the table.

Rosy, about five years old, expressed her hunger by tapping a fork on the table.

"Rosy, please stop that," my father gently chided.

"It's good to see the family hasn't lost its spirit!" Uncle Joseph noted.

I sat quietly in my chair. My family said I was a quiet baby who preferred to simply watch events unfold around him.

"Yes, at least we have spirit!" My mother smiled as she scurried from stove to table. "I'll serve the children first so we can eat without too many interruptions."

Uncle Joseph tousled my hair. "You are adorable, Shuly." I'm told I was his favorite.

He held a teddy bear in front of me and I instinctively reached for it. Of course, he pulled it back just as my fingers came near the bear's tummy, and he did so repeatedly. But he gave in and I became the happiest lad in all Romania.

"Now, give me back the bear," Joseph asked in comic sternness.

I clutched it to my chest.

"He'll not give it back," said Motzu, my seven-year-old brother. He returned to his bowl.

"Let's see." Uncle Joseph thought of another approach. "Shuly, *please* give me the bear. Pretty please?"

I looked at my uncle's gentle eyes and handed him the bear.

"Thank you."

Later my uncle told me years later that he was quite surprised that I relinquished the bear. I probably was as well.

Joseph held the bear for a few moments as I stared at my former possession with great interest. I wanted it back and waited patiently. But a child's patience is limited and after a few minutes I started to wiggle restlessly.

"Here is the bear, Shuly. It's all yours. Thank you for letting me hold it for a while." Joseph laughed and I felt relief as I clutched my friend to my chest again.

"Thank you for the toys, Joseph." My father sliced a generous portion of pumpernickel bread for Joseph. "How is life in Alba Julia nowadays?"

"The hours are long and I'm always on the move, but business is good."

"Good to hear. How is your wife and Yanosh?"

"They're well, thanks. Yanosh is seventeen now and he's found a job in a hardware store. He wants to go to the university one day, so he saves as much as he can."

"Good for him." My mother smiled as she held out a serving dish. "Have some potatoes, Joseph."

"And my wife is doing well at home. She likes to be there when Yanosh comes home from work. The weather is getting colder but no worse than last year."

"Oh yes, it's getting colder here also." My father said. "Did I tell you the story about what happened last winter? Ah, that was quite a day. The snow was so high one morning that we couldn't get out of the house through the doors."

"We couldn't! We couldn't!" Rosy jumped in. "We had to crawl out through the attic window."

"Indeed," continued my father, pleased with Rosy's dramatic contribution. "The snow was so thick and deep that the door simply couldn't be opened. And as you've heard, the attic was our only way out."

"Yes, and I got a nasty scratch!" Viorica said. She proudly raised her arm for all to see a red mark on her elbow.

"It's healed nicely, dear. It'll be completely gone soon." My mother's voice was soothing. "We didn't have wood for heating or cooking. We had to walk quite a way into the woods to find dry branches under the snow. The kids protested that it was too cold and the wood too heavy."

"But we made it." Rosy's cheeks reddened as she laughed. "Papa always says that we were very brave that day."

"Yes, you were." My father smiled. "We returned home, shoveled the snow from the walk, and took our wood inside. Then we gathered around the fireplace and felt the heat slowly spread into our bones. You never forget relief from the cold, the crackling wood, and the amber flames."

"Well, I'm sure my brother has raised his children to be brave and devoted." Joseph smiled to all of us and raised his glass. "To the brave Rittman children!"

"People say this winter will be just as severe." My mother didn't take any of the stew for herself yet. She was waiting for everyone to have enough before she took a single spoonful.

"And how is the household doing this year?"

Joseph's question expected. My father released a long sigh. My mother looked downward.

"Not so well, I take it."

"Not so well at all," my father sheepishly admitted, though it must have been obvious from our modest dwelling and furnishings. "The restaurant is small and not in the best location. Not many customers. We live day to day but we get by. Yes, we get by."

"Solomon, I'm sure you remember my suggestion."

"Yes…." my father's voice was weak. "But I didn't find time to discuss it with Hermina."

I'm told it was more that he avoided the matter. My mother had lost a baby boy just after Motzu, leaving her with a need to be near her children at all times – perhaps me, the youngest, above all.

"What is it?" My mother stopped eating. She looked to my father, then my uncle.

"Dear," my father started hesitantly. "Joseph and I discussed a way to help the household. Only temporarily, of course."

Joseph believed in straight talk, even at the dinner table. "Our house in Alba Julia is roomy. We have only one child and he'll be out on his own soon enough. Catalina's life will be empty. It would be no trouble. No trouble at all."

My mother didn't fully grasp where this was going, though she had suspicions.

My father placed an arm over her shoulder. "Hermina my love, times are hard right now. I'm never sure we'll have enough food on our table. Joseph's wife needs a child in her life, in her home."

The room fell silent. The children looked at one another anxiously. They thought they saw my father's eyes mist up. There was no doubt about my mother's.

"I suggest that baby Herman come to live with Catalina and me – only for a few months."

"No!" My mother frantically took me in her arms and pressed me to her heart. "Shuly doesn't go anywhere! I need him. He doesn't eat much anyway. We get by. We always do." Her lips trembled, perhaps as she realized the weakness of her arguments.

"Dear, it's only temporary. Only for a few months, until things turn around." My father's smile was clearly forced.

"No, I say! I can't give up Shuly. He needs me."

Rosy, Viorica, and Motzu remained silent. They didn't understand fully but they sensed a great change was about to come over the family.

"I'll send him to good schools. I'll take him with me to marketplaces. He'll learn the trade. My wife will take care of him like her own son. The name Catalina means *pure*. Shuly will have Yanosh watching over him like a brother."

My father spoke more firmly than before. "Remember, darling, only last week we had to get by on cabbage."

My mother rocked me in her arms, barely listening to the men's words. I was silent, enjoying the motion that reminded me of a rocking chair. My mother lifted me and looked into my eyes. I was too young to know what all the fuss was about. I at first giggled and held my teddy bear. Then I looked at my mother and was struck by her tears. I could feel her anguish. I sent my hands to her face and she burst into tears.

Uncle Joseph held a morsel of bread before me. I took it and chewed it with the few teeth I had. I'm told I was always hungry. Quiet but hungry.

"He'll always have plenty of bread, milk, fruit, and vegetables. He'll play on a wool rug in winter, a green yard in spring and summer. Hermina, I'm only suggesting this for Shuly's benefit. I'm family. Consider it an extended vacation in Alba Julia for your little boy."

"Ha!" my mother laughed bitterly. "You always had a way with words. But you are his uncle . . . and we'll visit you and Shuly."

"And you'll always be welcome. I love all of you. Right, children?"

"Yes, we want to visit Uncle Joseph too," Viorica said, with a superior face.

"Yes, me too!" Rosy added.

"What about me?" Motzu asked longingly.

"We will all visit Uncle Joseph, of course. Maybe in the spring." My father joined his brother in making the matter less trying.

"Yes, we'll all visit in the spring. Then Shuly can come home." My mother clung to this thought. Then she lifted me again to her face. "You hear me? I'll bring you home in only a few months. Do you want to go with Uncle Joseph? Do you?"

I sent my little hand to her face. She closed her eyes and treasured the touch. Tears streaked down her cheeks and I gently wiped them. I didn't know exactly what was going on, as time and distance meant little to a small child. I'm sure I felt my mother's anguish, though.

Yes, I'm told it was a very hard moment for my mother. I of course do not remember these events. I was much too young. But my brother and sister never forgot the scene and they recounted it to me many times over the years we had together. My uncle did the same once, far away from either home.

Joseph took me with him that night. It was the fall of 1931. I was not quite two. My mother didn't sleep for weeks. Although she knew that I was in good hands, her heart ached, every moment, every day. She counted the days until the visit to Alba Julia, when she would bring me home.

I had better clothes and a large yard to play in. Aunt Catalina took care of me as though I was her own. My cousin Yanosh loved me like a brother and played with me every day. My new folks took me to a baby pageant and I won first place.

The spring arrived and my family arrived. I'd become a toddler. It was decided to leave me with Uncle Joseph and Aunt Catalina for a few more months. Next visit, they'd take me home, or at least that's what they thought.

At the end of the summer Joseph and his family brought me to visit my family in Focșani and a joyful reunion followed. But my family felt it best to let me go back with the Davidoviches.

A year passed and then another. I never returned to live with my birth family until after the war. Aunt Catalina and Uncle Joseph for all practical purposes became my parents. I was a Davidovich. The Rittmans were kindly relatives in another city that I saw from time to time. There was no official adoption. The world was less bound by formal procedures then.

I never learned that Catalina and Joseph were not my true parents until many years later – in 1944, far away, on a train platform near a small town in southern Poland.

BOYHOOD

Life was good in Alba Julia. I attended a Romanian public school and from a young age enjoyed sports, especially football. My new folks spent a considerable amount of time with me, and I relished every moment. We weren't a very religious family; we only observed the high holy days such as Yom Kippur. Yanosh was much older than I, and helped his father with business. He also attended high school and started to work several hours a week in a car shop.

It was a delicately beautiful spring night in 1937 when Catalina picked me up from my violin lesson. Joseph was already home.

"What a nice surprise to find you home early, dear. I'll start dinner."

"Young man, how went your lesson today? Will you play something for us? A recital for the family!"

Joseph sat in his armchair and prepared for an impromptu concert from a young prodigy, of sorts. He enjoyed music and was pleased to hear me grind away. I'd studied violin for the past year – private lessons twice a week. My instructor was a young woman named Anka who taught at the conservatory in Alba Julia.

My violin was an old instrument that Joseph got for a good price at a trade fair. I placed the music book on the stand and opened to a Beethoven piece, which I'd played several times and mastered, at least as much as a young boy could. I didn't need the score in front of me as I knew it by heart. I placed the violin's base to my chin and the music of Beethoven and Herman Davidovich filled the room. Rich tones and timbres came from the resonant wood and reverberated off the paneled walls as my small hands darted about the strings. Music and love flowed in generous portions.

The last reverberation came to an end and I looked over to see my folks leaning lovingly against one another.

"More!"

Accustomed to calls for encores, I launched into another Beethoven sonata and once more music and love filled the room, if not the entire house.

"Come here, my boy." Joseph clasped his hands on my shoulders. "You played beautifully. I could listen to your music all day and night."

Catalina kissed me on my cheek and sighed. "You play amazingly, Shuly. I love you. I must now prepare a dinner for the young virtuoso and his audience."

I beamed with joy and pride.

Yanosh came in from work. "Did I miss a performance, Shuly?"

"I'm afraid so, but there can be another one – but after dinner."

"Good news. Shall we play checkers till then?"

I carefully returned my violin back to its case, and we opened the wooden checkerboard and placed the disks on their squares.

"I was in the library reading about airplanes. They're being built more and more in Europe."

"I hope you become a pilot."

Everyone in the neighborhood knew that Yanosh's interests had gone from cars to planes. The sound of a motor in the sky had him running outside for a look.

Catalina was an outstanding cook. She had mastered several traditional dishes of Central Europe, none more so than beef goulash with spiced potatoes and sauerkraut. The town's bakeries and grocers accented our meals. Desserts were not outside her expertise. When in season, local cherries and strawberries filled the pies. In colder days, we enjoyed cakes and cookies, often chocolate ones.

After dinner, we sat in the living room. Yanosh and I played board games while Joseph and Catalina discussed their days and events in town and beyond. I listened in and heard them speak in worried voices, though never going into detail. That night there was an especially portentous conversation, which I only partly understood.

"I think it would be wise to make the move, dear. It will be good for us. It will be good for Hungary too." Joseph drew from his cigar then blew the smoke toward the ceiling.

There'd been discussion of moving from Romania to Hungary before, but it was only talk, much like seeing Vienna – nice to talk about but unlikely to occur. Joseph wanted to move to Oradea, about 200 kilometers southeast of Budapest, where he hoped to get a commission in the Hungarian army. As a respected veteran of World War I, and one who'd been a prisoner of war in Russia, he had credentials and connections. While our lives were comfortable in Alba Julia, they would be all the better in Oradea. Besides, he sensed a war coming and wanted to help.

War. The word was strange and powerful. That night was perhaps the first time it made its presence felt in my life.

Catalina worried about the move's effect on Yanosh and me.

"They have friends and rhythms here. Taking them from here will be hard on them."

"It will be better for them in the long run." Joseph looked out the window. The night was dark and chilling autumnal winds rattled windows and shook tree branches. "War is coming and if I'm in Oradea I'll be able to rejoin the Hungarian army, probably as a major. That will mean greater pull and security than a tradesman has."

"Are you sure they'll promote you? You have no assurance."

"They need every man. That was the case in 1914. I hear from people that they accept all who show interest. Almost all."

"I worry, Joseph. It's still a war. What if something happens to you?"

"No need to worry, my dear. Bullets passed near me in the last war without touching me. I had a way with them!"

Catalina clearly didn't share his assurance. Joseph smoothed his mustache. "We've been discussing this for months now and the time has come. Tomorrow, I'll begin the process."

Catalina didn't approve, but wives accepted their husbands' decisions in those days. Later, she regretted her silence and the move to Oradea. The city would soon change from Romanian to Hungarian rule, and in time the people of Oradea would come under the administrative control of Nazi Germany. War would see to that.

I ran through the streets of Oradea with friends. My arms out to the sides, there was an uncanny resemblance to a combat airplane. I made roaring noises as we flew at great speed through busy stone streets. My two friends chased me, also making the guttural sounds of great fighter aircraft. It was 1942. Real fighters were overhead at times. A war was on and boys dreamed of glory.

It was winter break and already freezing. A dusting of snow covered Oradea. The pine trees and streets were frosted, and there was joy everywhere. You could smell the roasted chestnuts sold from pushcarts by enterprising lads on just about every corner. Some were caramel coated and their scent traveled along the breeze, filling the nostrils of passersby and persuading them to make a small purchase on the way home.

Stores stayed open late, their window fronts brightly lit by candles and decorated with sleds, elves, and wrapped gifts. Carolers entertained from doorway to doorway and enjoyed a sampling of cider. People walked home with Christmas trees in tow. Though not of that religion, I nonetheless enjoyed the holiday sights and sounds along with my friends.

The cold barely registered as we soared down cobblestone streets and engaged in dogfight after dogfight. The engagements took us down to the city center where government buildings, gracious parks, and a towering cathedral stood out from the shops and houses.

Just as we were oblivious to the cold, we were also unaware of details of the war raging only a few hundred kilometers to the east. Romania and Hungary had invaded the Soviet Union in 1941. I hasten to add they did so in concert with their ally in chief, Nazi Germany. In the last few months government buildings were draped in bright red Nazi flags, the centers of which had swastikas. I thought their size and colors looked ridiculous against the snow.

I adjusted the trim on my wings as we neared the stonework around the fountain, which was iced over, the water turned off. Nonetheless, it was an ideal landing strip after a wearying patrol accented by victorious engagement after victorious engagement.

"A perfect landing!" I exclaimed proudly. Fritz and Yuri came in shortly after I did, their landings discernibly less well executed than my own, at least in my estimation. The three of us had heard countless war stories since the conflict started and we recreated them each day and dreamed of them at night.

"I'm tired," Fritz panted.

"I'm hungry," Yuri added.

"Me too, but I don't want to go home."

We caught our breath and looked at how red our faces were. The official buildings towered above us, Hungarian and German flags billowed lazily until a sudden gust picked them up forcefully and spread them out like ship sails. The German flag struck me as having both power and evil. It was the bright red, I suppose. Their motions seemed eerie and menacing. But the day was too enjoyable to dwell on it.

Yuri wiped his nose on a coat sleeve and looked up. "I think those flags are beautiful."

"Father doesn't like German flags in our town. He says they don't belong here and they're no good for us." Fritz spoke with great seriousness, probably emulating his father's expression as he repeated his words.

"They remind me of circus banners. But there's something scary about them too." I tried to understand my jumbled thoughts. "I know my parents don't like them either."

"Why aren't they good for us?" asked Yuri, still preoccupied with his runny nose.

"I don't know. Father just says they're not."

"What is it that's bad about those German flags?" I wanted to better understand my unease.

"Father says the Germans want to control our government. They tell them what to do, and they fly their flags here." Fritz looked around for grownups.

"I heard my father talking about them," Yuri added. "He said that they're taking over all Europe. Anyway, what does it matter? It's not like they give toys and sweets to kids."

We all laughed.

"Yes, it's truly a shame that we can't get things from the Nazis." I spoke with a measure of irony I didn't fully understand.

"Then we would like them?" Fritz joked.

"No!"

"There are some Germans right now." Yuri pointed toward two soldiers coming out of a government building. "Let's go ask them." I think underlying his yen for gifts was a boyish sense of daring and mischief.

Driven by inquisitiveness, mischievousness, and abandon, we ran toward the soldiers. We ran so fast that we almost bumped into them. We soon saw swastika armbands and ambivalent sentiments coursed through me.

"Careful, little men!" One of the soldiers cautioned. "Why all the rush?"

"We're just playing. Do you guys have any candy?" I asked straightway and summoned a charming smile usually reserved for teachers. We all spoke German as well as our native Hungarian. There were German-speakers everywhere in Oradea even before the war as national and ethnic boundaries rarely coincided.

"Candy? You boys want candy?" The other soldier laughed and tousled my hair. "And why do you think we have candy? We are in the army, not the confectionery business."

"I don't know. I just thought I'd ask." I made my smile wider. My two friends took the cue.

"Boys, you know something? I happen to have a chocolate bar." He removed a bar wrapped in paper and handed it to me. "But you'll have to split it up."

"We will! Thank you very much." I broke the chocolate bar into three pieces and handed out the portions.

One of the soldiers leaned down to speak to us man-to-man. "So what brings you fellows here?"

"We're playing air combat," Yuri replied.

"Air combat? Against who?" asked the second soldier.

"I don't know. Against the *bad* guys."

"And who's winning?"

"We are!"

"Well then. We are the good guys, so you lads must serve in our *Luftwaffe*."

"Yes." The second soldier joined in the lesson. "The bad guys are the *communists*."

"And the Jews!" added the first soldier.

I remained silent. The meaning of the words hit me and although I was young I could sense malevolency. I was a Jew. I went to a Jewish school at times and we had a special family dinner on Friday nights, though we were not religious.

Fritz and Yuri attended public school, and knew I was Jewish. They too fell silent. The soldiers recognized the sudden change and it soon dawned on one of them. The moment of international benevolence was gone. One asked in an icy voice, "Are any of you communists or Jews?"

Nervous, even frightened, we all shook our heads, and that eased the tension. They became affable once more.

"All's well then." One of them laughed and concluded the meeting. "Enjoy the chocolate and always remember: stay away from communists and Jews. They're no good for Germany or Hungary."

We scurried away, our fear easing the farther away we got. We reached the frozen fountain where our planes had been refueled and rearmed for the next patrol.

"I told you the Nazis are no good. Just like my father said." Yuri looked back and saw the soldiers walk down a street away from us.

"Right, the Nazis are no good," I agreed, "but German chocolate is excellent!"

We chuckled as we ate the last of it.

"What's their problem with the Jews?" Fritz wondered.

"I don't know, but who cares? We got their chocolate. Now, let's get back to play." I spread my arms out in pre-flight.

"I am going to be a big combat plane, fighting the Nazis." Yuri spread his arms and ran into the large grass area where patches of brown grass asserted themselves from the snow.

"Me too," Fritz followed him.

"I'm with you guys!"

I returned home late that night. We got caught up in the dogfights and didn't notice the hour. When I arrived, Catalina was knitting in her rocking chair. Yanosh had married and moved out a year earlier. He had one child and another was well on the way. I sat near her and she pressed me close. Something was amiss.

"Sorry for being late."

"Oh, that's fine. Tomorrow is Saturday anyway. So tell me, Shuly, how was your afternoon? What did you do?"

Her smile barely concealed unease. I looked into her eyes and knew something was very wrong.

"I played with Fritz and Yuri in the park."

"They're fine boys, and good friends."

"The best. Could we have them for dinner again, maybe next week?" I felt a special pride with my friends over – pride for our home, the repast, and my folks.

"We can see to that." Her reply was positive yet imprecise. She continued knitting and her look of worry returned.

"Is something wrong?" I asked carefully, as a young boy wasn't supposed to inquire about adult things.

"Oh, I don't know." She shook her head and continued knitting.

"What is it?"

"You won't understand, Shuly."

"Please tell me."

"It's about work. I'm worried."

"Why?" The idea of something being wrong inside my family was completely foreign. All was well inside the dwelling. Troubles were outside and never got past the doorway.

Catalina caressed my head. "You're so caring. We're so fortunate to have you with us, Shuly."

"What's happened with father?"

She held an inward debate on what to say and not say. "He is deeply loyal to Hungary. You know he served in the Austro-Hungarian army during the last war. He was an officer then and he was hoping that here in Oradea he'd be able to obtain a commission in the Hungarian army."

"Yes. I heard him say that."

"But nothing will come of it. The Hungarian army doesn't want him."

"Why?"

It baffled me that someone so smart and fit would not be wanted in the army or any other organization. Many of my friends had fathers, uncles, and brothers in the service. Why not the head of our household?

Catalina caressed my head soothingly, at least as much to console herself as me. "It's because of the Germans. They don't like us and don't want us in the Hungarian army. They don't like Jews, Shuly. They *hate* us."

I instantly recalled the two Germans bearing gifts.

"Why?"

She just shook her head. "I don't know, love. I don't know. It's nothing new. It's been part of Europe for a long time. It's worse in other countries – Germany, Poland."

I sat silently, trying to comprehend this. Many thoughts crossed my mind. Thoughts about the past and about the future. Our future. What does it mean to be a Jew? Why don't they like us?

"So what will happen?"

"I don't know. Father's very upset and doesn't sleep at night. I hope he gets over it."

The door opened suddenly, startling us. Catalina immediately went to Joseph and took his coat. "How are you, dear? I'll start dinner."

"I'm well, thank you." He gave her a kiss and approached me. "And how are you, Shuly? How did you spend your day?" He pinched my cheek and looked lovingly into my eyes.

"We played in the park."

After dinner, my folks had a serious talk.

"Did you hear the news, dear?" Joseph sat in his chair – men had their own chairs – and opened the evening paper. "The offensive into the Soviet Union is slowing down and a major battle is building around Stalingrad."

"Yes, I heard from Bertha," Catalina answered from the kitchen, her voice a little elevated. "You know what I also heard from her?"

I sat on the couch and listened carefully, though I tried not to show it. Adults are more candid when they think children are uninterested. Bertha and her husband Rudolph were neighbors, about the same age as my folks, with two daughters. They were Roman Catholic, as were most Hungarians, and good friends of our family.

"What did Bertha have to say?" Joseph prepared his post-meal cigar – an item increasingly hard to come by.

"She wants to move out of Oradea."

"Move out?"

"She and Rudolph don't like the Germans being everywhere. They both think they're bringing ruin on Hungary and all Europe. Bad things will crash down on Oradea in coming months."

"They need not worry? They're Catholic."

I sensed Joseph was engaging in dark humor; he believed that ruin would come to all.

"They simply don't like the Germans all around. Rudolph is sure it's a very bad sign."

"I wouldn't move out, if I was them. Rudolph has a good job at the train station, and they own their home. They'll get through whatever comes."

He returned to his cigar and tried to appear unworried. It was an effort to keep me at ease, yet apprise me of what was going on outside the Davidovich home.

"Bertha thinks *we* should move far away from here," Catalina said quietly, her eyes cast downward.

"We're not going anywhere. Hatred of Jews will not last. Such things come in for a while, then go away like the tide. When it goes, I will be able to serve in the army once more. We stay."

I listened carefully to their conversation, more so than ever before. Germany, Hungary, Jews. I was beginning to understand something about the world. It was no longer far away.

"Joseph, there's talk that the Germans are treating the Jews in Poland very badly."

He listened but kept reading. I think he'd heard the talk too. And now, so was I.

"The Jews are put in work camps. I hear worse things too." Catalina's voice quavered.

I wondered what the worse things could be.

"Nonsense! The world cannot go along with this . . . this –"

"Anti-Semitism."

"It can't continue long. It has to stop at some point." Joseph was confident and a little annoyed by her display of emotion. "We need not worry. Europe is civilized, Catalina. We are educated human beings who've been taught science and reason."

Catalina didn't believe him.

Yuri and I met at a football field as a light drizzle fell. We were disappointed that there weren't other kids our age to play with us. We made the best of it and played against one another for two hours until we were soaked with rain and sweat and our shoes and socks were coated with mud. This of course was great fun.

It was Yuri's turn to challenge my goalkeeping skills on a penalty kick. He closed in, craftily faking one way than the other before booting the ball. It flew high in the air and directly toward the goal. My hands and fingers extended their fullest. The ball nonetheless sailed a centimeter or two above my outstretched fingers. As I came down, I turned to see the black and white sphere hurtle into the net. Yuri had made a masterful move, freezing me with lateral fakes, then placing the ball right above me.

"Got it!" Yuri leaped into the air, emulating the older boys on the high school team. "Now we're tied – one, one."

"Excellent move, Yuri!" We were both honing each other's skills, so there were no losers. We sat to catch our breath and didn't notice when two older boys took the ball and started to walk away.

"Hey, that's my ball!" Yuri called out.

They didn't stop.

We started toward them. "Hey guys, give us the ball. It's ours."

"Who the hell are you to tell us what to do?" The taller boy replied belligerently.

"We don't want any trouble. How about if we all play together?" I offered. "We can make two teams."

"We don't play with Jews," one of them sneered.

"I am not a Jew," Yuri snapped back but then immediately regretted his words as I remained silent.

"Then you are playing with a Jew?" The tall boy set his eyes on me. I remained quiet as my heart raced. "Are you a Jew?"

"Yes," I replied firmly.

Turning to Yuri, he said, "Then I was right. You *are* playing with a Jew." Again the sneer.

"That is none of your business. I play with anyone I want."

"No, you can't. Don't you know? No one plays with Jews. They are filthy – and *evil*."

I remained quiet. The boys were bigger and things were getting nasty. But Yuri was upset and likely to get even more so. He had a temper and was always one to stand up for a friend.

"You will not tell me who to play with! Now give me back my ball!"

Without warning one of the boys punched Yuri in the face. He fell to the ground, crying, his nose bleeding. I ran to help but the taller boy tripped me and kicked me in my stomach. I lost my breath. The older boys kicked us repeatedly. All we could do was try to fend off their kicks and call for help.

"What's going on there?" We heard an adult voice from a way off.

The two boys stopped kicking us as he approached. It was Bernard, the maintenance man who tended to the field, well-liked by kids and adults alike. In fact, we'd often ask him to try to kick past us as we played goalie, but he'd usually beg off saying he was too old.

"Leave them alone!" Bernard shouted as he trotted over to us. The boys ran away, of course. We got up and brushed the grass and mud from our shirts. "Don't ever come here again," he shouted to the boys. "If I see you here again I'll call the police."

"Thank you, Bernard. You saved us. They'd have pummeled us. They said it was because Shuly's a Jew."

"What's the world turning into. Boys doing such things." Bernard shook his head. "It's all because of our government. They allow this sort of thing. Now go home and clean up – and stay away from those crazy kids, if you can."

As we left the field we heard Bernard grumbling. "I've seen wars before." He looked at the government buildings in the distance and shook his head again. "I've seen wars before and I've seen what they do to people. Things will get worse, much worse."

The manager of the Oradea football team visited schools routinely, ever on the lookout for talent. One day he watched a scrimmage at my school. I was in top form, passing well, stymying opponents, and adroitly moving the ball toward the goal. At the end of the scrimmage, the manager asked my coach if I could play on the city's youth team. The coach approved and I was in heaven and it must have showed when I came home and shouted the news.

"This is wonderful news, Shuly." Catalina clasped her hands on my shoulders.

"My first practice is in an hour."

"Wait a moment, Shuly. Have you forgotten your violin lesson?"

I had indeed forgotten that detail, or pushed it aside. My spirits sank.

"Oh, that's fine. You can miss one violin lesson. Go play your football."

"Thank you! You understand perfectly. Off I go to get changed." I ran to my room.

Over the next weeks I practiced diligently with the Oradea team. The others were much better athletes than my friends and schoolmates, and this sharpened my skills. My passing, agility, and kicking became much better. Athleticism came at the expense of musicianship. This saddened the folks but my dedication to football compensated somewhat.

"You'll be a famous player one day," Joseph used to say, though only half-heartedly. "I was hoping more for a musician, but an athlete is good too."

"It's what he likes. That's what's important." Catalina's words were just as resigned as her husband's.

I promised them that I'd continue to practice the violin, and I did – just not nearly as often before, and not nearly as enthusiastically. My guardians attended games and were proud of my play. The football profession beckoned.

In the fall of 1943, with the war to the east moving closer, Oradea was playing the team from nearby Debrecen. At halftime I sat briefly with my folks and tried to catch my breath.

"You're playing well, my boy," Joseph smiled proudly.

"Thank you. This is a tough game. Good players. The best we've seen yet. But we'll come through in the second half. You'll see."

"I have no doubt." Catalina reached into a basket. "Here, I brought food for the three of us."

"I'll eat after the game. We have to keep light for the game – coach's orders." I hopped up and down, first on one leg, then on the other – much to their puzzlement. "I'm trying to fend off the cold, dear ones."

"Well, I hope I will not offend you if I nosh a bit. All your hopping about has made me hungry. Ah, salami!" His eyes lit up as Catalina handed him a slice wrapped in butcher shop paper.

A man in a suit approached us. People dressed well at public events back then, but there was something out of the ordinary about him.

"Are you the Davidoviches?" The man spoke gruffly and without any greeting. Even a boy could see was his suit was inexpensive and didn't fit well.

"Yes, we are. I'm Joseph Davidovich and this is my wife Catalina. This is our son, Herman. He's quite the young athlete."

Joseph extended his hand, but the man made no effort to shake it.

"Your son will no longer play on the Oradea team, as of this very moment!"

My folks looked at each other.

"May I ask why? And who are you?" Joseph was upset but controlled his emotions. He knew what was coming. I did.

"My name is Arthur Bodor. I am with the Iron Guard and am now an assistant to the mayor. Jews are not allowed in city positions." He glared at me. "You are forbidden to play another minute."

I cringed. Anti-Semitic boys were mere nuisances. This man was with the Romanian fascist group that was influential in Oradea, even though it was now under Hungarian rule. The Iron Guard, also known as the Archangel Legion, was an ultranationalist movement that hated communists, foreigners, and Jews. Bodor had the Iron Guard, city bureaucracy, and the gendarmerie behind him. And they were all increasingly hostile to Jews. The signs were there over the last few months.

"Take your son and leave."

Bodor barked his orders, added a menacing glance, then turned and walked away.

"Let's go, Joseph." Catalina was alarmed, close to tears.

Joseph was stunned. The Jewish community of Oradea had experienced anti-Semitism for the past few years, and probably more and more of it, but our family had fortunately not witnessed any. Now this Bodor fellow from the Iron Guard was coming up to people and issuing orders.

"Wait!" I protested. "I have to help the team. It's only halftime."

Joseph shook his head. Anger not far beneath the surface. "Shuly, my boy, you heard that man. I'm afraid it's over. You can no longer play for the city."

We silently stood and went to the back row.

Halftime ended and the teams went back on the field. Minus a key player, Oradea was at a disadvantage, if I do say so myself. I looked on in frustration as our offense sagged and Debrecen moved the ball closer and closer to the goal before one of our players made a defensive play. Nonetheless, a trend was clear and after twenty minutes or so, Debrecen scored. There was nothing I could do.

Our coach looked into the stands and saw me. During a penalty he came up. "Herman! Here you are. I've been looking for you. Why are you up here?"

Joseph found the words. "I'm sorry but a man from the mayor's office forbade our boy from playing anymore."

"What?" My coach was annoyed. "I don't care what that guy says. This is my team and I decide who plays and who sits."

"He's with the Iron Guard," Joseph cautioned.

The coach became silent, then angry.

"No! I'll not allow those crazy Iron Guard people to ruin my team and country. Herman, go back on the field. I'll call a time out."

My heart rejoiced. Catalina was alarmed, though.

"Do not worry, madam. This Bodor fellow is gone now and I don't care what he says anyway. Herman is playing and that's a fact." He then looked around.

"He left after he ordered us to leave," Joseph replied in an unsettled voice.

"Then all is well. Come and sit near me, in case he comes back. And Herman, get down there now!"

I returned to the field much to the appreciation of my teammates and even some people in the stands, besides Joseph and Catalina of course. Energized, I played well. Pretty sure I scored a goal.

Things were changing in the city. The war wasn't going well and people began to look warily and even angrily at Jews. Friendships ended, neighbors stopped speaking. I felt it. My family felt it. The entire Jewish community of Oradea felt it. On May 3 1944, the deputy mayor of Oradea decreed that Jews must wear the Star of David.

The atmosphere became increasingly worrisome as weeks passed. Joseph smoked more and more cigars. Catalina tried to knit but her anxiousness made her hands imprecise. Eventually she stopped.

"We have to do something, Joseph," she announced one evening. "Jews are losing their jobs, their children can no longer go to school. Fear is everywhere. I worry for us and for Yanosh and his children."

I had little real knowledge of politics but my folks did and I respected their views. I also picked up on unspoken things.

Joseph shook his head. "I can't believe this is happening. I served in the army like any other man in the last war. I was on the battlefield. I suffered with fellow soldiers. I was a prisoner in Siberia! We do not deserve this, Catalina. We do not deserve this!"

"I know, Joseph, but the government doesn't care about right and wrong or past service. Many of our friends have already left Oradea. Others worry about the old district that's been walled in. Some people from other parts of the city have already been sent there."

Joseph knew he had to protect us. It wasn't a matter for family discussion; the decision was his. He showed great concern, then announced that we were going to get away from Oradea and go to

Romania. "Tomorrow, I'll tell Yanosh. I want him and his family to come with us. We'll all move out of here by the end of the week."

Catalina wiped a tear but clearly thought it for the best. Even I felt relief. Somehow I sensed that Oradea was becoming hostile, even dangerous. Joseph was dejected. He might have had a far better idea than we did about just how ugly things could get in Hungary.

We woke up a few mornings later to loud knocks on our door. A commission of three arrived: a civilian, a government clerk, and a gendarme – a member of the national police. Their faces showed determination, and no sign of compassion.

"You're coming with us. Pack only a few things."

Joseph didn't ask any questions. He knew he had to accept the power of the authorities. He had seen the gears turning for weeks and now this – knocks at the door and stern orders.

We were being sent to the Oradea-Mare ghetto.

THE GHETTO

There wasn't time to pack much. That was by design. We filled suitcases quickly and stuffed things into bags – bedding, clothing, groceries, cooking utensils, and a kilogram or two of coal. I packed only two small bags.

Is this all that we'll be able to save? Will I be able to continue playing sports? What about my friends? When will I see them again?

As we quietly gathered our things, I saw tears in Catalina's eyes. So sad for all of us. We had to leave behind family mementoes from many happy years together. Also, family events, graduations, games, friends, and relatives had to be left behind. Joseph voiced what we all were thinking. "We'll be able to return one day and find our house just as we left it." I was able to return years later, alone.

Joseph packed books into a valise. I watched quietly. A proud, patriotic man was trying to maintain dignity and self-respect, confidence and faith. Today I know he did it for us. So we would not be afraid. So we would persevere and believe that all this would be over one day.

Disconcerting sounds came from the street. Old folks, young people, and small children, all with bundles on their backs or in their hands, slowly followed luggage-filled carts as they were herded along by gendarmes. It couldn't have been more than thirty meters from me and I saw anguish and despair on every face. There were school friends and their families. I reflexively waved to them but the dreadful occasion asserted itself on me, as it already had on them. I lowered my hand and felt the warmth drain from my face. There was a solemn crush of dispossessed people on the street in front of our house, and we were about to join them.

Catalina was distraught. Joseph returned to packing. The meaning of all this penetrated me, and I became devastated as well. Waving and smiling were parts of childhood that had to be left behind.

Two more gendarmes arrived. They rifled through our luggage then rudely told us we'd packed too much. They took inventory of the valuables left in our house – carpets, candlesticks, furniture, and the like. They ordered my folks to hand over their wallet, purse, and money. Joseph complied immediately, though not completely.

The final moment arrived. Joseph closed the door and handed the key to the gendarme, who tagged it and placed it in a box with many others. And that's how our home was taken from us. That home meant safety and security for me. I spent my childhood there. It was gone.

Would we ever be back? Would we ever see our home again? I wiped a tear, and am close to doing so now. That moment is embedded in my being as one of the hardest ones in my life.

The authorities demanded our rings, necklaces, and other jewelry. Here Joseph protested but he was shouted down by angry references to laws and decrees. Catalina could no longer keep it in; she broke into inconsolable tears. She was a frail woman.

For the first time that day I felt wrath – a powerful anger focused on the gendarmes who were humiliating my folks. But I knew that anger would worsen matters, and I held back from any rash act. Yes, it could be worse. We trudged down the street with our luggage and bags, three more people in a long line of people on their way into the unknown.

People didn't look at each other, only straight ahead – broken human beings abruptly stripped of home and hearth and pushed into the streets. One after the other, occasionally hearing words of encouragement, we followed those ahead of us, like blind men in a dense fog.

I felt better with my folks by my side. I was intermittently jarred by the thought of being separated from my family. A similar thought must have passed through the minds of everyone. There no longer were homes, belongings, laws, or decency. I imagined we were walking back into the past before there were such things. The strong took from the weak, then marched them away.

I have the strange recollection that it was a beautiful day. Spring – the spring of 1944. The scent of foliage and blossoms occasionally reached me. Such a cruel paradox.

More and more people were pushed into the march. The residents of this street and that avenue endured the same loud knocks and gruff commands. Just ahead I saw a shoddily built brick wall with a gate of wood and metal. Behind the wall was a rundown part of the city – dilapidated tenements, broken pavement, debris strewn all about. We walked out of the city and into the Oradea Mare ghetto. I shivered as I walked through the gate. I'd entered a kingdom of doom. Catalina took my hand.

The crush quietly trod down the streets of the ghetto, vigilant gendarmes alongside. The people on the sidewalks and in doorways looked thin, sickly, and dispirited. It slowly dawned on us newcomers that these famished people had been walled inside the district some time ago, several weeks or more. We were looking at ourselves.

Catalina clutched her husband's arm tightly and held me close to her. She and many other women sobbed softly as they filed down the stone streets. I looked behind and saw Yanosh, his wife, and small children. I was glad to see him yet sorry to see him. I wished he'd gotten out of the city and hidden in the forests or found refuge somewhere. Yanosh appeared calm and brave. As I looked about I saw many such displays among the marchers. None among the onlookers.

Gasps and whimpers came from the front. In a few moments we were struck by an overpowering stench. It wasn't garbage or sewage. Those were common enough odors in cities then. This was something else, something that was putrid and sweet at the same time. Off to the left were piles of an uncertain nature, maybe a meter or more high. I soon identified shoes, arms, and then thin gray faces.

"Oh my God, those are dead people!"

Catalina's horrified voice spread fear and nausea through the marchers. The onlookers, I could see, were accustomed to the sight. Some had probably stacked them on the sidewalk themselves. Many of the corpses were in grotesque positions, legs dangling toward the pavement, stiffened arms pleading upward. I saw the corpse of a young girl with a small doll clutched in her hands. Years later I recalled the sad sight and concluded the doll must have been placed there by a grieving parent.

"Dead people. Dead people lying in the streets," I whispered to myself, trying to comprehend what I saw.

"Yes, those are dead people," Joseph murmured. "Just continue walking, Shuly. Head up. Let's go."

That was all I could stand. I looked straight ahead. I'm sure the sight was shocking to Joseph, even though he'd seen many dead in the last war. The corpses that day lay not in trenches and wore no uniforms.

Gendarmes stood on corners and directed people down side streets to their dwellings. There was method in the madness. It became clear that the ghetto was badly overcrowded, despite the decreases in population that we'd seen on the sidewalks. There were newcomers last week, we were coming in now, and more would be arriving soon. The ghetto was about twenty square blocks and there were probably four times as many people in it than in any district its size.

We were happy that Yanosh and his family were assigned the same tenement building we were. They'd be living one floor above us. We had another family living with us. Our apartment was quite small – a one-bedroom apartment one might call it today. There was a twin bed for my folks; the rest of us made do on mildewy mattresses stuffed with straw that filled the room with a rancid odor.

The floor was covered, to some extent, with cracked black tiles. Mold had accumulated between most of them. The walls were bare concrete with dark stains as the only accent on the drab gray. A few ramshackle pieces of furniture were here and there, probably left behind by the impoverished people who'd lived there before us. We later learned that the buildings, indeed the whole district, had been declared unfit to live in. The city deemed the buildings fit for at least some people.

Catalina was distraught. "How can we live like this, Joseph? I can't do it!"

He could provide no answer. "How can they put fellow humans in this squalor? Even in the war we had better billeting."

"A gendarme said it will be only for a few months," said the father of the other family assigned to the room. "My name is Jacob and this is my wife Wilma. These are our four children."

Ever polite, even in these circumstances, Joseph introduced us as he would at a restaurant or school. He looked about the room and shook his head. "I never imagined that it would be this bad. I never imagined anything like this."

Jacob looked at him quietly. "No one did, Joseph, no one did."

"Well, let's get settled," Jacob said spiritedly. The task of organization brought purpose. I think he even smiled. "We'll be here for a few months, and after that we'll be taken to a better place."

People seized upon that idea.

We found boards and nails and made shelving to store our meager belongings. We took the malodorous furniture outside to freshen it as best we could. We made sleeping arrangements for women, men, and children. There were two creaky wooden beds which were allocated to the parents. I slept on the floor.

We gathered what food we had and subsequently scratched up, then stored it in a small pantry shared by everyone in the building. We made a schedule for cooking and cleaning. We also had to regulate the use of the bathroom. We helped each other. We supported each other. We comforted each other.

Sometimes I'd think about my friends in the old neighborhood. They were only a few kilometers away, yet they were in a different world – a world of tidy houses and green parks. In their world, gendarmes held up the law kept them safe. In mine, the gendarmes enforced edicts and intimidated us.

Joseph said that within the next few days the gendarmes would assign us jobs. That was welcome news. I liked the idea of having a job, just like a grownup. After a few weeks, a five-member Jewish Council, or *Judenrat,* was made. That had a calming effect. The *Judenrat* oversaw day-to-day life in the ghetto and tried to solve problems related to food, public sanitation, and administration. I delivered messages for the *Judenrat.* This enabled me to hear discussions and decision making – quite a position for a young lad.

The council comprised a number of Rabbis, doctors, and lawyers – prominent men of the Jewish community of Oradea. Each I believe tried his best to make life more endurable in the ghetto. The same cannot be said of Jewish councils in other ghettoes, I later learned.

There was a dining hall in the ghetto which for many was the only source of food. Soon, a few thousand people ate there on a daily basis. The number of needy newcomers was ever on the rise, and supplies quickly diminished. The old kitchen became too small and a new one had to be set up. Young men were tasked with building a larger kitchen and dining hall in an old laundry. I helped when not running messages. Our pay was a little food.

Within a few weeks food reserves were troublingly low and the *Judenrat* addressed all residents. Everyone was asked to hand over all food beyond what they needed for the next few days. We complied. I put together several jobs which also paid in food. Joseph managed to barter things. We never had to rely on the communal dining hall until late, when the ghetto was being liquidated.

The gendarmerie ordered the construction of a hospital, and a building adjacent to our dwelling was selected for the site. We made simple beds from planks and benches. Bedclothes and sheets were gathered from the population. There were many doctors among us and they pooled their medical equipment. All this we did ourselves. The gendarmes helped not one bit. My family, owing to our proximity, helped a great deal.

I was fortunate to get a janitorial job in the hospital, which of course was never short of patients. Many people arrived in the ghetto seriously ill, and in those living conditions, the number of sick people rose. Some wanted it all to end.

After finishing my janitorial duties I helped sick people eat, wash up, and go to the bathroom. I was what we'd call a practical nurse. The patients grew fond of me as I was attentive and cheerful.

Many patients suffered from stomach problems, pneumonia, and other illnesses related to the conditions. Proper hygiene was difficult to maintain. Water was scarce, both in the hospital and in the ghetto in general. Sometimes the authorities shut off water for hours, sometimes days. The same with electricity. Plumbers had to work hard to open clogged pipes. People got sick, lost hope, and died. People had to relieve themselves in the open, which led to a terrible stench hanging over us.

Amazingly the spirit of life remained with most young children and teens. We simply adapted and didn't complain much. There was enough family strength and community awareness that we felt it our duty to help wherever we could.

One day the authorities levied about two thousand people for labor service. They were ordered to equip themselves with food and clothes to prepare to leave for work the next day. Yanosh was among them. We hoped he was off to a better situation.

I was cleaning the hospital when the news arrived. The commander of the gendarme regiment in Oradea had taken command of the ghetto. At first we didn't think it meant much. What else could be done to us? But the gendarmes issued new decrees and posted them on corners. We could no longer determine when we slept, woke, or dined. Every routine was imposed on us. The ghetto had to be quiet as a graveyard from nighttime till dawn. Anyone caught outside could be shot on sight.

And so an unearthly silence fell upon the ghetto at eight pm. The authorities shut off electricity and darkness fell.

I used to go up to the roof and look around at the lights of Oradea. The air was better up there. In the distance were the sounds of automobiles, trains, and occasional shouts and laughter. Rather than being resentful, I thought it wonderful that there was life out there. I imagined myself again running down the streets to the park with my friends. I closed my eyes and breathed deeply.

THE DREHER

The gendarmes took control of the Dreher-Hagenmacher brewery. We didn't care. We didn't use the place for anything. Nothing had been brewed there for decades. It was an empty building with broken windows.

One day, my friend Isaac arrived at the hospital and told me, "The brewery is being turned into an interrogation center."

"Interrogation center? For what?" I kept sweeping the floor.

"They think we're hiding money."

"There's no money inside this place. It can't mean much."

My reply was dismissive, glib, and wrong.

The Hungarians were obsessed with the idea that some of us had left valuables with friends or neighbors for safekeeping before being marched off, or that we hid valuables with us inside the ghetto. They decided to get the information through torture. The "Dreher," as it came to be known, was transformed from an abandoned plant to a dreaded prison.

Every day, a dozen or so people were ordered to appear there. The gendarmerie sent a messenger to bring them in. We called the messenger for our block "Jonah". Old men and women, young people, and even sick people were taken there. Many died during the ordeal. It was called the Hungarian Inquisition.

It was rumored that the gendarmes had been trained in the ways of torture by the SS. The accounts were horrible and merely hearing them gave me bad dreams. People were stripped of their clothing then beaten with leather belts, whips, or iron rods. Some had their heads smashed against concrete walls. Other were strapped to a chair and given powerful electrical shocks. Parents had to watch as their children went through it.

Loud music came from the old brewery. The gendarmes wanted to hide the screams. There was something like that in Birkenau.

More and more people were called. People were terrified at the prospect of being summoned to the Dreher. Some chose suicide.

My family and the others sat around the rickety wooden table. It was Friday evening and we were about to conduct a Shabbat – a rite that had become important to even secular Jews like us since entering the ghetto.

A white cloth lay across the table. Catalina had washed it as best she could that morning. Each of us sat in front of chipped and cracked stoneware. Two challah loaves, bought that day from the makeshift bakery, emitted a welcome aroma. A silver Kiddush cup held a few ounces of liquid. Catalina was able to get hold of some poultry and the prospect of chicken broth enticed us all. Jacob's family managed to put together a passable salad composed mainly of boiled potatoes.

Catalina lit two candles, and Jacob raised the cup and recited the Kiddush prayer. He blessed the bread and gave everyone a small piece sprinkled with salt.

"Shabbat Shalom!"

"Shabbat Shalom!" came the reply from all in the room.

"Are we hungry?" Catalina asked in a cheerful voice.

It was Joseph's turn for bracing words. "In good times we took the Shabbat for granted. Now, it reminds us that life goes on and that there is always hope."

"I hear that soon we'll all be out of this place," Jacob said hopefully. "We'll be sent to work camps where there will be better food and housing."

He looked tired. Jacob was perhaps fifty but looked older. He'd been a metal worker outside the walls but inside he did any kind of work. Keeping busy was important.

A knock on the door. Everyone stopped.

"Who's there?" Joseph spoke assertively.

"It is me – Jonah. I'm sorry, very sorry. But I was sent to pick up Jacob."

Everyone knew Jonah, or of him. He was the gendarmerie messenger and that night he was sent to bring Jacob to the Dreyer.

"It's the Shabbat, Jonah. Go away and come back on Sunday," Joseph called back through the still closed door.

"You know I can't do that," came a meek reply.

Jacob stood and spoke, his gray beard moving in concert with his words. "I'll go. I'm ready to go. Anyway, I don't know anyone that has money. I'm sure that they'll release me soon enough."

His family was horrified. They looked to us for help but knew we were as powerless as they. I wondered if he could survive. No, I was sure he couldn't.

Joseph went to the door, but didn't open it.

"Jonah, I told you it's the Shabbat. Now please go and come back later."

"I don't want to do this but I'll be punished badly if I don't bring him back with me. I'm very sorry. You know that."

"You could tell them that you couldn't find him. Come back Sunday."

Joseph looked at Jacob, his family, and us. I knew he was doing what he could, but I also knew that he couldn't do a great deal and that there were risks to interfering with the gendarmerie.

After a few moments of painful silence, Jonah spoke. "I'll be back for Jacob on Sunday."

We listened as his footsteps faded in the distance. There was rejoicing, then crying. But Jacob wouldn't have it.

"Let us be jubilant! I've earned another Shabbat. Are we going to enjoy it or are we not?"

His coat was threadbare, his shirt lacked a few buttons, and his toes stuck out from his right shoe. Yet in his eyes there was life and hope for another day.

Jacob spent the rest of his reprieve with his family. They hugged, they sang, they prayed. We knew that in a few hours he would walk down to the Dreher.

Jonah returned early Sunday morning. Tactfully, without actually saying goodbye, we bade farewell to Jacob.

"We'll see you soon, Jacob. Be strong."

Jacob was ready to go. He smiled and gave kisses and hugs to us all. "It's fine. I am already old."

But then sadness came over him.

"Don't let what goes on here remain untold."

I doubt I was the only one who was taken by his words.

We never saw Jacob again.

PERSEVERING

Those of us in our teens tried to find any reason to be happy, and we usually found one or more. Some of us were fortunate to find old friends among the ghetto population. I'd found Isaac, who was my age, Sergei, who was thirteen and had his Bar Mitzvah just a few months earlier, and Haim, who was the oldest at fifteen.

One night we sat outside and talked about our old lives. "I miss eating my mother's cooking," Haim said wistfully. We remained quiet. It wasn't simply out of nostalgia. Haim's mother had been taken to the Dreher recently and come back badly injured. Her wounds became infected and there was nothing the hospital could do but clean the wounds and change the dressings as often as possible. Haim's father told the family to prepare for the worst.

"I miss playing with my friends from our block," Isaac lamented. He was the most outgoing of the group and had the busiest schedule on the outside.

It was my turn and I had to think for a while. What *did* I miss the most? Yes, of course, there were the obvious things such as regular food, clean bedding, and a sense of security. But what would I really enjoy doing right now?

"Football," I said in a hushed tone. I didn't mean to say it out loud.

"What?"

"*Football.* I'd love to play football. I was getting good at it."

"My favorite game!" Isaac stood as though the coach was sending him into the game.

"I never played it, but I'd love to try." Well, Haim was not the most athletic kid in Oradea.

Gears turned in my head.

"Splendid. There are two problems. First, we need a place to play. The ghetto doesn't have an open space for even a small field. Second, we don't have a ball."

What Haim lacked in athleticism, he made up for in resourcefulness.

"Well, we simply can't have a large field. We barely have enough space to live. But who said our field has to be official size? Half or even one quarter of the city's field will do."

"Exactly!" I was the one to stand this time. "We practiced on small fields. We even practiced on corner lots – well, when we were smaller."

"We can play in the yard near the old laundry. We'll clear out the garbage and make space." Haim was in top form.

"We still need a ball." I brought us back down to earth, so we did a little more thinking.

"My cousin Grisha knows a way out of the walls," Isaac announced warily.

"You don't have to speak so low, Isaac. No one can hear you besides us," Haim chided.

Grisha was younger than us, about twelve. He looked for ways to get around edicts more than we did. We thought it both fitting and delightful to cause as much trouble as possible for the gendarmes. As young Jews, it was our duty. We professed willingness to die in the cause, but what did we know of death.

"He knows a way out. I'm sure of it. I've seen him bring food from the outside many times. He sneaks out, pretends to be a local beggar, and gets money. I can ask him to buy us a ball."

Haim gave elated approval. I was more cautious. Risking your life to get money for food was one thing. Food is essential and there was precious little of it in the ghetto. But risking your life to get a plaything, that was quite another. Still, I wanted to play football badly and youthful zeal can overwhelm what little caution a boy has. I came up with justifications. It would make us healthier and cheer up others inside the walls.

Two nights later, after promising Isaac we'd never divulge the secret, he took us to a part of the ghetto perimeter where the barrier was made of dilapidated planks, probably put up by hurried, uninterested laborers several months ago. I looked for a hole in the barrier as best I could. The darkness was only barely broken by a streetlight on the outside. Isaac pointed downward then carefully pulled away a few crates. A hole!

"A tunnel! A passage to the outside world!" I gasped as though seeing the Red Sea about to open. "Did Grisha dig it himself?"

"It isn't really a tunnel, just a small hole under the wall," explained Isaac. "I went with him once. It was very scary because there were gendarmes patrolling just outside. They almost heard us. My cousin is very brave!"

"I don't know about this," Haim mumbled.

"Where did you go?" I marveled at the idea of going off into a forbidden world.

"Nowhere really. I was too scared." Isaac shrugged his shoulders sheepishly. "I crawled back inside immediately. Grisha will be back soon, hopefully with a gift for us – a gift from the people outside the walls of the Oradea Mare ghetto. We'll have to wait, and we'll have to be very quiet."

"How long?"

"How should I know!"

It was summer, yet the night was cool. We sat near the wall and tried to keep warm. Several times we held our breath as we heard the heavy footfalls of gendarmes just across the wall. We imagined ourselves bold soldiers on a secret mission for our nation.

We heard softer footfalls, then scratching noises. Someone or something was negotiating the crawlway. We froze. To our relief and delight, Grisha's dirt-smeared face emerged. He too was frozen in fear for a moment on seeing three dark figures standing above him, even though he was expecting us.

"It's you guys! I brought you treats."

He handed candy and we became the happiest boys in the world.

"That's all I could get. Try as I did, I couldn't get money, only candy. Maybe tomorrow I'll have better luck."

We had a wonderful evening all the same, and there was the promise of things to come the next night or the one after it. It broke the tedium and brought something to look forward to. It was our resistance to the gendarmerie and Nazi-leaning Hungary – the only way we could fight back and assert who we were. We imagined the Reich fearing us.

Grisha snuck out of the ghetto almost every evening. No one outside the ghetto suspected he was Jewish and many people gave the poor ragamuffin a little food or money. He offered to take us along with him but we were too scared, even though we were a year or so older. There were limits to the valor of the resistance movement.

On nights that Grisha didn't go outside, he tagged along with us. We learned that he was an only child. His father had been a schoolteacher but now helped in the dining hall. His mother died at a young age from an illness of some sort. He had a strong, free spirit and loathed gendarmes. He said many times that he would fight them if he weren't so small.

One night we waited for his return. We sat quietly listening to routine sounds of the city streets across the wall. All of a sudden we heard whistles and shouting. We sat still even though fear was surging through each of us. The yelling got louder and we could hear people running on the other side of the wall. We looked to the hole and suddenly saw a football, then Grisha!

"Here, guys. I was a little luckier this night."

We heard commotion just over the wall. Grisha suddenly lurched backward, pulled by someone. A gendarme began to call for reinforcements.

"Get away from here quick," Grisha shouted.

All three of us grabbed an arm, a hand, a shirt and began pulling him inside, but there was now more than one gendarme. One or more were pulling him out, another was kicking him or clubbing him with a rifle and calling him a "dirty Jew". Grisha grimaced and gasped with each blow. Judging by the sounds and the gasps, the blows were getting harder. Suddenly, Grisha fell silent, his body became still. The gendarmes stopped pulling, perhaps thinking their work was done. We pulled him inside.

"Grisha! Grisha!" Isaac called.

The boy stirred, clearly in great pain. He couldn't stand or walk. I suspect now that he had several broken bones. We stooped over him, knowing the gendarmes were blocks away from an entrance and we had a few minutes until they could arrive.

"It hurts so much. But I got you a ball." The brave lad grimaced but held back from crying. He even managed a faint grin.

"Grisha, let's take you home to your father. He'll help you." Isaac started to lift him up.

"No! It hurts too much. Just let me rest here. Stay with me, please. I knew it would happen. The gendarmes spotted me . . . I was too fast. I ran so fast." Another faint grin.

We were helpless to do anything.

"You know, I believe I'm going to die now. I can feel it."

"No, Grisha. Hold on. We'll take you to the hospital. Let's lift him, guys – now."

Again the pain was too much.

"Just let me be, just let me be." A few tears formed.

We all started to cry. He was gravely injured but unable to be moved. Broken bones, internal bleeding. He was going to die right there before us.

Grisha lifted his head. "You guys play. I wish I could play."

We promised to play and held his hands. He feebly extended a hand to each of us, then lay back and whispered, "I'm so tired, so very tired."

Grisha closed his eyes and left us. His trials in the Oradea Mare ghetto were over. We sat near his lifeless body and sobbed quietly. There was no time for lengthy grieving. We carried Grisha's body to his father.

Isaac, Haim, and I continued to meet every night. I'd stowed the ball away in our apartment. There wasn't much to talk about. We were sad, we were angry, we wanted to get back at the gendarmes. We knew, however, that their capacity to get back at us, and at the whole ghetto, was enormous and knew no restraint. I brought the ball out one night.

"You know," Isaac said, "Grisha wanted us to play football."

"Yes, he did," I replied, holding the black and white sphere. "He most certainly did."

"Then we have to play," Isaac concluded.

Haim nodded. "If we play, we have a small victory. We have purpose, we have life."

"And Grisha will have life, with every step," I added. "Tomorrow, we'll meet at the field behind our building. And we'll play with Grisha's ball."

And that's what we did. We played football a few times every week, even in the summer heat and rain. Other kids in the ghetto joined in, and together we had fun and we had youth.

ALEXA

A nurse urgently called to me as I was sweeping the hospital floor. The facility was overcrowded, the staff overworked. Helpers were called in for emergency help from time to time. She hurried me to a room where several people lay on makeshift beds. On a small table were vials of medicine.

"We don't have too many of these left," she said as she plunged a needle into a vial and slowly drew from it. "Please hold her arm tight. She simply doesn't like shots."

The medicine was administered without much of a struggle and the woman lay back calmly. Only then did I notice the nurse was quite lovely – twenty-five or so, with brown hair.

"What's your name, young man?"

"Herman."

"Your age?"

"Fourteen."

She smiled and shook her head.

"Aren't you too young to work in a hospital?"

I shrugged my shoulders. What did I know of what was normal?

"Well, thank you for your help, young man."

She turned to the patients and I watched. She listened to them, spoke to them, got to know them and their infirmities. I was fascinated by her. I was smitten by her.

A few days later, as I changed bedding, she noticed me looking at her.

"Do you have family with you here, Herman?"

I mentioned my folks and Yanosh then asked of her family. The question saddened her.

"I arrived here with my parents. My mother died three weeks ago from liver disease. My father is in another ward. He's in a coma and there's little expectation he'll come out of it."

45

She sat on a wooden chair and collected her thoughts.

"My father was a plumber. He was summoned to a job and I went with him. Two gendarmes saw us and began to beat him. Harder and harder. I called for help but of course no one would interfere with the gendarmes. One of them looked at me and I saw such hatred in his eyes. No plea could have stopped him. The beating stopped and my father has never returned to consciousness except for brief moments."

She cried for a few minutes, then looked about the crowded room with sleeping patients.

"What's the use of a hospital in all this? We're all going to die one way or another. Starvation, disease, beatings. I hear we will be sent to place far worse than this. Some say it's idle rumor, but I'm beginning to believe it.

I hadn't heard the rumor she had. I'd only detected gloom and despair all around. I told her the war would be over soon and we could all return to our homes outside the walls. She laughed joylessly.

"How can we just wait until the end of the war when we have so much hell to go through here? How long until the Russians get here? One year? Two years? Ten? Haven't you seen people die here?"

I told her I had indeed seen people die here. I just thought the day would come when it would all end. Her eyes left mine.

"Well, I have a plan."

After making sure no one was looking, she reached into a pocket and removed a cloth in which there was a small vial.

"This is my escape plan, Herman," she whispered. "A few minutes after I take this, I'll be in a better place."

She saw my discomfort.

"What do I have to lose? What do I have to look forward to? One day I may be taken to the Dreher. What do you think they do to young women in that place? Or one day a gendarme will see me and take me off with him."

She was right. It was all true. I nonetheless urged her to keep her spirits up.

"I don't think I'll survive this, Herman. I don't see a way out. Just this one."

She tapped a finger on the vial.

Knowing she might take her life at any moment made me worry. Many people in the ghetto were opting for that way out. I tried to be close by while on hospital duty. She did her work professionally and kindly, though with a discernible gloom on her face.

We spoke briefly every now and then – about families and schools. She enjoyed running and competed on the track team. Naturally, I brought up my football talents. When she spoke of boyfriends, I must confess to pangs of jealousy, which very much surprised me.

One evening I was cleaning up in a ward where her comatose father lay. She sat on the bedside, her desolation plain.

"He'll never wake up. I'm all alone in the world."

I told her that I was with her and was always willing to help. She smiled and said that someone my age was the one in need of help and comfort. I countered manfully by saying I knew how to get through tough times. It was becoming true.

Sadness returned to her face. In fact, it intensified. She stood near her father's bed and looked outside into the dark, empty streets of the ghetto. I expected her to cry but she was worrisomely calm. I thought of summoning help.

"Your father will get better."

"No, Herman, he won't. And even if he did, what prospects would we have?"

She shook her head quietly, then reached into her pocket. I could see the fluid in the dim light. Should I run to her? Get help from the station down the hall? She opened the vial and paused. I searched for words but a weak hand knocked the vial from her grip.

It fell on the floor and shattered, the contents spread out across the cold concrete.

"No, Alexa! No, I say!"

It was her father's frail but nevertheless stern voice. He'd roused himself from his deep sleep, but was now slumping back.

"Papa! You're with me! Are you hungry, Papa?"

"No."

A doctor arrived and looked at the man and welcomed him back to the world, but he motioned for the doctor to leave.

"Alexa, my child . . . never . . . never even contemplate such a thing."

Alexa wept on her father's chest.

"You are helping people here . . . and you must continue. Your place is here. Your purpose is here, until your time comes. Promise me."

"I promise, Papa."

"Louder."

"I promise to see this through, Papa."

That night, when I returned home, I climbed to the top floor and looked at the city outside the walls. A boy pondered the purpose in life and more importantly, the importance of keeping one's word.

Alexa's father slipped back into a coma and passed away gently not long thereafter. I was in the room when she hugged him and he took his last breath.

Alexa was deported from the ghetto before I was. I didn't expect to see her again.

SOLOMON

Two men brought a battered old man into the hospital and we made room for him in a ward. He was barely conscious and signs of beatings were all over his face and torso. A pair of doctors came to see to him and learned from the men that the injured man had just come from the Dreher.

"What's your name?" one of the doctors repeatedly asked.

The poor old guy was unresponsive. The other doctor whispered, "Brain damage."

Neither doctor was surprised by the wounds or the diagnosis. Nor was the young boy with broom and mop. The doctors lamented that they had no way to help the man. The implication clear, they gave brief instructions to a nurse and left. There were many others to see.

I leaned the mop against the wall and stood over the man. Dried blood had caked inside his ears and down his neck. A good face, a kind man, though time and fists had taken a toll.

"Aaron? Is that you, Aaron?"

His eyes opened slowly. They were reddened and gazed off into a distance.

"My name is Herman. You are in the hospital. I work here."

"Aaron? What are you doing here?"

"I –"

"It *is* you – my favorite grandson! I haven't seen you in so long. I was afraid I'd never see you again, yet here you are."

A faint smile relieved some of the pain on his face and in my heart. I'd seen this delirium before in the hospital, and I'd seen caring people handle the situation.

The nurse returned to wash his wounds.

"Are you related to the man?"

"No, I'm not. He thinks I'm his grandson, though."

"Oh, I see. We'll hope for the best, but these injuries are very serious. Very serious."

The nurse placed a moist cloth to the man's forehead and asked his name repeatedly. Getting no response, she left to tend to others in the ward.

"Aaron? Aaron? Where are we?"

"In the hospital."

"Hospital? But why? Why?"

"You were at the Dreher."

"The Dreher? What is that? Tell me, please."

"It's a very bad place. You were injured there. What is your name?"

"Oh, Aaron, you *know* my name! I am Grandpa Solomon. Don't you recognize me?"

It was good to see the trace of a smile.

"Of course, Grandpa Solomon. Of course, I recognize you."

"I missed you, Aaron. I missed you for so long. Where have you been? Where have you been for so long?"

"I was playing outside with friends."

"Playing with your friends. I'm glad. You are a good boy."

I finished my duties in that ward and was about to leave when the nurse returned. When I told her of my conversation, she wanted to know what part of the ghetto he lived in, presumably to send word. So I asked him.

"I don't know, I don't know."

The nurse thanked me, encouraged me to talk more with him, and went on to her next patient. Solomon's eyes were open, the light of life was dim. He tried to speak but could not.

"I'm here, Grandpa Solomon."

"Aaron? Is that you, Aaron?"

"Yes, it's me. I'm here."

"Thank God you are here, Aaron. I want to see you. Where are you? Come closer."

He extended a hand and I took it.

"Ah, there you are. Thank you for being here, Aaron. I don't see well anymore. I am old. I've forgotten how old I am!" He laughed softly.

"Yes, that's funny, Grandpa Solomon."

I didn't go home that night. The nurse brought me a little food and I stayed with my new grandfather. I fell asleep in a chair, despite the sounds of pain and anguish from other patients. Hours passed.

"Aaron? Aaron?"

"Yes, Grandpa. I am here."

His voice was steadier. I became hopeful.

"Do you remember Grandma, Aaron? We were married forty years. We all loved her cooking."

"Yes, we did. A wonderful cook."

"She died not long ago, on our anniversary."

"Ohh…. I didn't know."

"Children are not supposed to know these things. Rebecca and I had many years together. You know, every couple has good years and bad years. We ended with a good year."

"A good year then. I'm glad for that."

"She became sick from an infection. I don't know medicine, Aaron. She faded every day. Like a candle, Aaron, like a candle near the end. I remember the Dreher now. They beat me, Aaron. All over my body."

He tried to turn to me but the pain was too much.

"I want to tell you something, Aaron. They asked me where my money was. I was going to tell them but couldn't speak. I never told them about the money in a neighbor's house. They beat me so hard. I'm glad I didn't tell them. They don't deserve it. Oh Aaron, look what they do to us!"

"I know, Grandpa, I know."

He closed his eyes and fell asleep. I did the same.

"Aaron? Are you here?"

There was alarm in his voice.

"I'm here. I'm right here."

He reached for my hand and relaxed.

"I'm glad of that, Aaron. I don't want to die alone. I'm going to die soon. Did the doctor tell you when?"

I didn't want to be anything but honest with Solomon.

"The doctor said it wouldn't be long."

"Not long, not long. I'm not afraid. I'm not afraid to die. I'll be joining Rebecca. Life hasn't been very sweet without her. Aaron, I want to tell you something."

"I'm here."

"I want you to have my money when this is over. You're young. Use the money to raise a family. Help others. Give to the poor. Be good. You were always a good boy, Aaron. I trust you to do good."

"Yes, Grandpa Solomon, I will."

He motioned for me to lean down then whispered the location of the cache of money.

His hand loosened as morning broke. Solomon died. I sat for a while in the ward, grieving for the man. I notified the morning nurse then walked home. I'm not sure I comprehended the location he revealed to me, but if I did I forgot it by morning.

ANTON

A gendarme on horseback called for me to stop one morning. "You! Come with me."

Thoughts of being taken to the Dreher came swiftly to mind. Had he seen me that night at the wall? Had someone informed on me?

He was a young man, maybe in his early twenties. His uniform was clean and freshly pressed. He lit a cigarette and smiled at me. Sensing no malevolence, my fear waned a bit and I followed him. We exited a checkpoint and walked down the streets of Oradea until coming to the gendarmerie stables.

"What's your name, boy?"

"Herman."

"My name is Anton."

He unexpectedly reached to shake my hand. I almost pulled back out of instinct. Grisha was not far from mind. Nonetheless, I shook Anton's hand. He probably gave a last name too but I don't call it.

"Do you have family here, Herman?"

"I have parents and a brother. My brother's with a labor detail now."

"You are fortunate not to have sisters. I have two at home and they drive me crazy at times." He laughed in a very casual manner. "I was assigned to find someone to help with the horses. They need to be cared for on a daily basis. Have you any experience in this sort of work, Herman?"

"No."

I immediately regretted my answer.

"Oh, in that case I'm not sure you're right for the job."

"I'll do excellent work! I promise to learn quickly and see that every horse is in the best of shape for the morning."

He noted my eagerness. How could he not? He looked at my dirty tattered shirt, my worn shoes, and my meagre frame.

"So you think you can manage the job then?"

"I'm sure of it!"

I saw an opportunity to get out of the ghetto, at least for a while, and learn what was going in the world. I would even learn things about the gendarmerie. I'd already learned something.

"Good. Then come with me and I'll show you where the grooming materials and food are."

There were about ten horses. Beautiful animals. Some chestnut brown, some shiny black. All were strong and spirited. My job was to feed, wash, and brush them in the evening, so that they would be ready for mounted patrols in and around the ghetto.

He looked at me. It might have been the first time he looked at someone from the ghetto as a human being.

"Are you hungry, young man?"

I nodded.

"Come with me then."

He took me to a cramped untidy room with a desk and piles of papers, and told me to wait. He returned with bread, beef, sauerkraut, and a cup of water. It took a moment for me to be sure this wasn't a cruel trick on a famished boy. Hesitantly, I began to eat, trying not to do so mannerlessly. It had been months since I ate a meal like this. Bread and potatoes were about all we had inside.

"This is from our commissary. Naturally, you're not allowed there, but a good stable hand cannot go unrewarded." He watched me eat, studying me, puzzling over something. "You are Jewish, yes?"

"Yes."

"As it happens, my brother married a Jewish girl. Minna is her name. Very pretty and from a lovely family. I ate at their table many times. Wonderful people. Her father was a shopkeeper and her mother took care of the neighbors' children during the day." He looked out the window toward the walls not a hundred meters away. "When all this started, my brother took his wife and her family across the border into Romania. He didn't want them to end up over there in the ghetto."

I wondered if things were better in Romania. I had relatives there.

"It's not good what's done to you inside those walls. There's nothing I can do. I'm just one man. Finish your meal and do your work well, Herman."

I became a regular sight at the stables, washing and grooming the magnificent beasts. Most people there ignored me or looked disdainfully at a Jewish stable boy. Anton was always agreeable to me. He saw that I'd eat reasonably well and even gave me sweets, cigarettes, and occasionally liquor. I brought them back inside to eager family and friends.

In return, I worked diligently. While stable work isn't always pleasant, it was less onerous and despairing than being a practical nurse at the hospital. I must say that the horses and I developed a certain mutual fondness. Strange and paradoxical, I know. They were the obedient steeds of oppressors. And Anton wore the uniform of the Hungarian national police.

Also strange and paradoxical were my walks to and from work, accompanied by a gendarme or someone from the stables. I walked the streets of Oradea and saw day-to-day life. There were more German troops than a few months ago.

Every night after passing through the checkpoint, oppression and terror came down on me again. The gendarmes were summoning more and more people to the Dreher. Torture victims gave up names of innocent people simply to end the agony. The gendarmes were concentrating on people thought to have had a measure of wealth before entering the ghetto. Poor people had less to fear. Then, however, the gendarmes began to summon people at random. Suicides increased. I was fortunate to get away and work with my equine friends.

One evening, just before work was done, Anton brought me a more generous amount of food than usual. He smiled uneasily.

"Eat, Herman. No rush. I want a smoke before we go."

I had no complaint with that. We sat on a bench just outside the stable, the thick scents of horses, hay, and tobacco intermingled in the summer night. I ate in a more gracious manner than the first time I was given a meal spirited from the commissary.

Anton was pensive. He sat back against the wall and loosened the top button of his tunic.

"You know, Herman, I'm a simple soldier but I have common sense. I see what we're doing here. I know what we do in the Dreher. Have you heard about that place?"

"Yes, I know about it. Some of my friends' family members have been interrogated there." I became silent, but not sensing any ire in Anton, I continued. "Many didn't come back. Others came back badly injured."

He looked up at the sky. "Yes, that's the place. That's the Dreher. A few weeks ago they wanted to assign me there. But I declined!"

He stiffened with pride, than sank down and shook his head.

"I told them I was better suited patrolling the streets, on horseback. It's sickening what they do in there."

He looked out the window to the wide street leading to the ghetto and I suppose we both thought of daily events inside. His face showed sorrow, regret, and vulnerability. I saw human emotions, despite the uniform and the power behind it which was supposed to pervade and inspire him.

"I'm very sorry, Herman."

I was too young and too surprised to know how to reply. Yes, Anton was always agreeable to me, but this was the first time I saw so much humanity in him.

"I hope you survive this. I hope you and your family get through this. Still, there are worse places."

He stamped out his cigarette on the brickwork below and stood – the cue to head back to the ghetto. I entered through the checkpoint and went home. I never mentioned the episode to family or friends.

New rumors spread. The rumors were about a plan to send us to the Far East or to camps to the north. It sounded better than the ghetto. Better quarters, better food, better treatment, and far from the Dreher. The gendarmes told us that we would all stay together and move to camps with better conditions. They mentioned factories, workshops, and farms.

Joseph was heartened. "They need us to work at these camps. We will be valued laborers. We'll be treated much better there."

Later we realized that this was a ruse to avoid panic – and maybe an uprising.

It all happened very fast. One day, when I returned from work, my folks told me that a few blocks had been evacuated. The people, a few hundred perhaps, were given an hour to prepare. The suddenness and mysteriousness naturally caused concern. Why the rush? Why the secrecy? Everyone was asking the same thing in the dining hall and on every street corner.

The *Judenrat* asked the gendarmerie about the evacuations and what lay ahead. They assured that the evacuees were being sent to perform agricultural work somewhere inside Hungary. No more details were offered. No more questions were accepted.

Evacuations continued. For all the privations and horrors of the ghetto, it had the attraction of being known and understood. That was better than the unknown, where our worst fears created dark images. The gendarmerie published lists of the sectors that were next, and shortly later gendarmes closed them off. No one could go in; no one could go out. The inhabitants were told to gather a few belongings and prepare for a journey by train.

After a few weeks the once densely populated Oradea Mare ghetto was almost empty. The dining hall was quiet, save for the occasional sound of a pot clanging to the kitchen floor.

New decrees came. We were forbidden to leave our dwellings except to go to the dining hall or hospital. I was still allowed to go to the stables.

Anton arrived one evening to take me back to the ghetto. As always, he brought food. I began to thank him but he interrupted. He looked anguished.

"Herman, today is your last day here. Orders from the commandant."

He pointed desultorily toward the office. The day I knew would come, had come. I looked around at the saddles, stacks of hay, and gentle horses.

"So it's goodbye then. Thank you for all your help, Anton."

"Listen to me, Herman. You have to listen to me."

I braced for bad news.

"Soon you and your family will be put on a train."

"Yes, I know. We're going to a farm or a factory."

"Forget that nonsense this instant! You have to escape. It doesn't matter when or where. On the way to the train or at any other time – run! It doesn't matter where or when, just go at the first opportunity!"

"I can't do that, Anton, I have to stay with my parents. I can't leave them."

"Run, I say! I know it will be hard, but trust me, you have to get away." He clasped a hand on my shoulder. "You are young. You can do it. I'm telling you, Herman. You must not let them take you to those places."

"What places? Where's the train going?"

"Nowhere good. Just run away. It's for your own good."

His eyes held a horrible secret I knew he could not reveal. He shook my hand, sorrow and finality in every motion.

"I hope the best for you, Herman."

"I hope the same for you, Anton."

He escorted me to the gate. No more words. He turned and walked away briskly then broke into a run.

Anton knew where the trains were going and what went on there, at least in general. He couldn't tell me for fear I would spread the word and he would be blamed for the ensuing panic and resistance. Anton, a man in the detested Hungarian gendarmerie, cared for me and wanted me to survive. I'll always remember his kind heart. In another time, in another place, in another uniform, Anton might have been a great soldier.

I hope he survived.

LAST DAYS IN THE
GHETTO (JUNE 1944)

I didn't tell anyone of Anton's warning. I didn't want to frighten anyone more than they already were. My friend Haim had been evacuated with his family already and the only friend still there was Isaac. We daringly walked through the streets after curfew. They used to be crowded with people and daily goings-on but were now eerily silent, like the rows in an ill-kept graveyard at midnight.

Doors stood open and creaked disconcertingly with the slightest breeze. Pots, dishes, pillows, and toys were strewn here and there. Every block or so we'd come across bags and suitcases stuffed with belongings. There was no sense in picking through them. Isaac and I knew we'd both be gone in a few days, no more than a week.

I helped in the hospital again. Many despairing people went there for comfort. Some pleaded for a way out.

Yanosh returned from his labor detail and his family came to live with us. The husband and wife that lived with them upstairs had taken some sort of poison together. They were old and unable to face another forced removal to who knows where.

Many people dreaded the impending evacuation and hid in deserted buildings, attics, and sewers. Some had long known of holes and tunnels and chose to attempt escape to neighboring villages, though this was discouraged by the *Judenrat*. Others hoped to make their way across the border into Romania. I later learned that a few made good their escapes and that those who had hidden in the ghetto were eventually found and imprisoned by the Hungarian authorities. They were sentenced to hard labor, but they were not sent where we would go, and most survived.

Knowing evacuation was imminent and notice would be short, we removed sheets and tablecloths and wrapped belongings in them. Though early summer, we made sure to pack any warm clothing we still had. We also packed a few items of food. The bundles were placed near the door.

It was our last Friday in the ghetto. Yanosh, his wife, and children were with us. The table was not covered with a white cloth. It had been used to pack clothes. There were candles, plates and bowls, and thin soup. No challah, only old rye.

We dined in silence. The atmosphere was bleak. We were on the brink of the unknown. The prospect of better conditions in a work camp or on a farm faded, though our hearts ran to embrace the idea from time to time.

"Tomorrow we'll make our final preparations," Joseph said somberly. "I want everyone to pack food and clothes in separate bags."

Catalina was dismayed. "Separate bags? But why?"

"Because, my dear, we don't know what lies ahead. We may be separated, at least for a while."

This was unsettling. If there was one sustaining faith, it was that we would face things together. Over the last week or so, Joseph spoke more crisply, more authoritatively, as though he were an officer again and we were soldiers entrusted to him.

We didn't say anything more that night. We finished the meal and went to bed. I couldn't sleep. Many thoughts ran through my mind. Where will we be in a few days? Will we be able to stay together? What will become of us?

The next day, I bundled up underwear, pants, socks, a sweater, and coat. Catalina gave me bread, a few potatoes, and a small apple that had been picked too early. She also gave me a small pot. I wondered what I'd do with it. I came up with no answer but packed it all the same. An old belt held my bundle together.

Catalina cried and hugged me.

"Don't worry," I said. "Everything will be fine soon."

I was a fourteen-year-old boy, consoling her with words I didn't believe.

The evacuation continued. Our block was the only one left. Isaac and his family were taken a day earlier. There'd been no goodbyes.

Our day arrived. I woke up early and walked the silent streets. I knew what would soon happen. I'd seen it often enough over the last weeks. Shouting gendarmes, gruff orders. "You have one hour! One hour!" A line of people, bags and bundles, sadness and fear. Then the march to the train station.

Why did Anton tell me to run? What did he know about our destination? Should I run? No, I couldn't leave my family. I couldn't leave Joseph and Catalina. They may need my help and I may need theirs.

I saw an old shoe, a tattered newspaper, a lonely teddy bear sitting on a broken chair.

Who were the owners?

Where were they now?

THE DEATH EXPRESS

The knocks came, the gendarmes shouted. We gathered our bundles and walked uneasily down the streets toward the train station. The sounds of footsteps and a crying child reverberated off silent building fronts. On one side were neat rows of flowers outside a deserted house. On both sides of us stood gendarmes.

Optimism buoyed to the surface every now and then. I was leaving the ghetto and I'd soon be walking down the streets of Oradea where I'd run and played. A better future was ahead. Anything would be better than the ghetto. Then Anton's words returned.

We slowly funneled through the narrow gates separating the ghetto from the rest of Oradea. Outside, people stood on sidewalks or in windows and watched us. Some had distraught looks. A mother and child stopped what they were doing and stared at us. The mother covered her face. I think she was crying. Others looked sternly, as though justice was being meted out before their eyes. Most had expressionless faces.

At the train station, the gendarmes were supplemented by Germans – the SS. I'd seen some of them in the city center. Old cattle cars sat at the far side of the platform where they didn't interfere with regular traffic. As we were led toward them, some people rushed to be first, as though to get a good seat. An SS guard gave loading instructions to the gendarmes, but they seemed to resent him and did not snap to his orders. The gendarmes, I began to think, were less brutal than these SS troops.

My folks and I were pushed into one car, Yanosh and his family into another. We were packed in, though not as tightly as on subsequent experiences aboard what I came to call the Death Express. We were able to sit on the worn floorboards. A gendarme shouted through the closing doors, "If anyone escapes, you will *all* be severely punished." We were used to barking gendarmes so it didn't mean much.

Would the gendarmes be on the train or were we in the hands of the SS? I found a narrow opening and peered out. I announced that the gendarmes were still out there, and people were relieved. Why did we suddenly feel good about them? Perhaps it was because we had become accustomed to them and understood them, and thought the SS might be worse.

Joseph and Catalina kept saying, "Thank heavens we're staying in Hungary. Yes, thank heavens for that."

Joseph patted my back gently. "The war will be over soon, Shuly. We'll all be back to our normal lives. We can get through this. We're better off away from that filthy ghetto."

Catalina smiled and nodded. It wasn't just us. Most of us on the train felt, at least intermittently and briefly, that getting away from the ghetto was for the good.

The whistle blew. I looked out through the slats and saw gendarmes and SS guards conferring and jotting things down. An SS officer motioned to the conductor and with metallic groans and a sudden jolt, the train began to move out from Oradea. Here we go, I thought. I looked at the buildings, trees, and a dozen passengers standing on the platform. Is this the last time I see Oradea?

Joseph was designated in charge of our car and he oversaw the distribution of water stored in a large military container. Small children had first call. Older people were allowed to spread out on the floor. Complaints were negligible. It was good to be on our way. As we chugged along, people began to talk.

"I heard the gendarmes say we're heading for labor camps near Kassa," a man said as he beamed with confidence. It was Tuvya, a shoemaker, about sixty-five-years old. I took an instant liking to him.

"No! We're bound for Mezotur," said another man named Nachman. "I'm sure of it. I overheard high-ranking gendarmes when I was in the Dreher last month."

We looked upon him with sympathy and respect.

"Yes, I lived through it. I was lucky. They hit me several times with their sticks, and that was it." He shrugged his shoulders. "They must have concluded I had no hidden treasures for them."

Tuvya patted Nachman's back. "I'm glad you made it. My brother was not so fortunate. He was beaten so hard that he died shortly after he got out."

The car fell silent, as most of us knew someone who'd shared the same fate.

The train slowed, clanging and screeching noisily, then came to a stop. Nachman peered out from gaps in the siding and reported that our train was being put on another track. "We're not going to Mezotur now. Shame, I really wanted to go there. I have family there."

I didn't know why he mentioned his family. Even if we went to Mezotur, I sensed we wouldn't be free to move about and look up friends and family. We'd be in a labor camp of some sort and watched over by gendarmes, or by those other fellows.

With the train stopped, the summer heat and close quarters soon affected us. The water ran out and children cried. But there was nothing to do about it.

A gendarme shouted, "We're going to Kassa."

"I know Kassa! I've been there many times on business." Joseph's mention of familiarity brightened spirits. "It's a small town just inside Czechoslovakia. I was there during the war – the previous one, of course. I was an officer."

"I was hoping to go to Mezotur. There are chicken farms there," Tuvya recalled. "Better we remain in Hungary."

"Kassa is in the mountains. It'll be much cooler there," Joseph recalled. "Much cooler. We'll be there soon. You'll see."

People chatted about Kassa, the mountains, and people they knew there. I remained silent. I just wanted to get out of the car and find some water.

The heat worsened and mothers pleaded to anyone outside for water. A gendarme gave us a bucket of water and we all thanked him. The children drank, as did we all, and the car became quiet again save for a few conversations to pass the time. Again, we came to appreciate the gendarmes.

Then the gendarme told us that we were not going to Kassa. Instead, we'd get off six kilometers from Kassa where Jews from Transylvania were being put in a camp under construction. "This is what the SS officers tell me. I'll bring you further news if I receive any."

Joseph spoke. "They want us for labor. It's common during wars when manpower is needed. We'll be working for the army. They'll value our work and treat us well. Hard work is nothing to be afraid of!"

I imagined a small camp with wooden huts for us to sleep in. Green fields all around. My mind was still vacillating between hope and fear.

The train at last moved out and after a few hours, it stopped outside Kassa. I looked out and saw the station platform a hundred meters or so away down a bend. A group of gendarmes conferred. One came to our car.

"One man gets off to fetch water."

Tuvya was our man. He went out and returned with a bucket. Some drank, some washed their faces. Tuvya trotted back for more. I admired the vigor of that elderly man.

The gendarmes conferred at some length with the SS. The gendarme commander showed dismay before barking orders to his detachment. They spread out to the cars and ordered us to turn in all of our valuables. Anyone who withheld anything of value would be executed, by the Germans. People were distraught, partly because they would lose the last of their valuables, but more because they knew they were now in the hands of the SS.

A sack was tossed in and soon filled with money, jewelry, and personal goods. Joseph surrendered several watches he'd kept for bartering in an emergency. Catalina handed in the necklace that she'd been given on her engagement. Other people complied too, as best I could tell. Couples wept as they placed item after item into the sack. A boy of fourteen had no valuables.

The gendarmes collected the sacks then slammed the car doors shut. "Make no effort to flee. Anyone who does will be shot immediately."

It was our farewell to Hungary. It came to me. The gendarmes were never concerned with us. Our desperation made us think there were benign people in charge. But this was simply a delusion we clung to. The gendarmes were servants of the SS. A boy of fourteen could see that. There was only one good one.

Night fell and we all lay on the car's floor, often in unusual positions so as not to discomfort those next to us. I found a place near the back, above which were cracks and openings that allowed me to catch glimpses of the night sky. I slept only fitfully as the train rocked about, slowed, then sped up and sounded its piercing whistle. I looked at the stars and wondered what they knew.

Sunbeams shot through the car, waking me and others. We stood as best we could, stretched our legs, and tried to work out the pains from lying on a hard floor.

"I think we're heading for Germany," Tuvya said as the train rounded a bend.

Joseph looked for the sun.

"I'm not so sure."

"I think we're still heading north," said another man. "In fact I'm almost sure of it."

"Then we are heading for Poland," Joseph said. "But why Poland?"

"Maybe they're take us to Lublin?" suggested one of the women.

I noticed her elegant dress. She spoke with an upper-caste accent that we didn't hear much in our part of Oradea. As light spread, I saw her disheveled hair and grimy face with streaks formed by tears. She had dressed for the occasion of our deportation, and put on makeup as well.

"What else could there be in Poland other than Lublin?" she asked calmly. "I've been to Lublin. Such a *beautiful* city. You'll love it.

All of you." She began to laugh more and more, then uncontrollably. "We're all going to love it there! We're all going to love Lublin!"

People looked at each other sorrowfully. The poor woman had fled into a comforting world of a past visit to a charming town. She was better off there.

Another woman curled on the floor near me and said over and over that she didn't want to live anymore. Some tried to encourage her. Others just there lay listlessly. An older boy, maybe sixteen, offered me a cigarette. I didn't smoke, but I took it all the same. We had no way to light our smokes, but we held on to them.

A young girl reached for my hand. She was about seven. She had long blonde hair and was frightened. I held her small hand and she looked less so.

"My name is Marisha." She spoke quietly and in a friendly manner.

"Where are your parents, Marisha?"

"They both died in the ghetto. I live with another family. They're on the other side of the car."

I was relieved she wasn't with the woman bound for Lublin. What circumstances had brought us together. I held her hand, though unsure how much help I could be. We sat together as the train continued its journey, occasionally turning abruptly and jarring us to one side. We were exhausted, thirsty, and hungry. Day turned to night.

The train slowed and came to a noisy stop. We sat, waiting. We could hear doors opening on the other cattle cars. Moments later, our doors opened. Fresh air at last. I saw hundreds of people standing along the cars in the night. SS guards with snarling dogs at their sides shouted as disoriented people climbed down onto a platform.

There was smoke in the air. Small particles fell from the skies. Not snow in summer. I rubbed some in the palm of my hand.

"Where are we?" asked Tuvya. No one answered.

Three SS soldiers came toward us. An officer announced, "This is the final destination."

People were relieved. The journey was at last over.

The elegant lady exclaimed, "Thank God! We've finally arrived!"

I looked at the SS officer. His affable face put me at ease for a while.

"You're in Auschwitz!"

It was the first of my two arrivals on the Death Express.

THE PLATFORM

"**E**verybody off! Bags remain in the car!"
SS guards shouted fiercely, their dogs snapped and snarled on taut leashes. We left our bundles and climbed down onto a platform lit up by powerful floodlights. People gasped and cried out as rifle butts came down on them. Those who fell were hit more and stepped on by others being pushed forward. Panic and chaos were both created and exploited.

"Men to the left, women to the right!"

We lined up in rows of five. Catalina broke into tears as she was ordered to move away from us. "Joseph! Joseph! Don't leave me!" I heard her cries amid all the shouting and din. I wonder if she'd ever been without him since they wed.

"It will be alright, my dear. We will be back together soon. It's a routine procedure. You'll see. A routine procedure."

She calmed a bit then pressed her face close to mine. "Shuly, listen to me. I've something to tell you. Joseph and I love you very much, more than I can say. But we are not your parents. We are your aunt and uncle. We love you as though you are truly our own. Always know that." She found Yanosh, who'd gotten off another car with his family, and embraced him for the last time.

I was stunned and confused by the revelation, but there was so much noise and confusion that I had no time to think it through. All around me other forced separations were taking place. Female SS guards grabbed Catalina from Yanosh's embrace and directed her into a group of equally frightened people, mostly the elderly and women with small children. Yanosh's wife and children were taken away and put into that group.

Occasional flashes of light found their way across the platform and briefly illuminated Catalina and Yanosh's family standing there. Promises and vows could not be kept.

Joseph held me close as we were pushed to the men's group. "Stay with me, Shuly." I had no intention whatsoever of venturing from him.

A number of emaciated, expressionless men in striped uniforms carried corpses from the cattle cars. There were no such deaths in the car we were on but evidently people had died by the score during the trip. The pile of dead soon exceeded those we saw on the sidewalks as we entered the ghetto. The men and boys eventually took notice and gasped. Only a few were able to find words.

I saw a reddish glow in the distance and someone said it must be a Polish village that the Germans were burning. A revolting stench, quite different from the one in the Oradea ghetto, struck me, though it must have been there all along.

A German addressed us in a stern, intimidating voice.

"You are standing in Auschwitz-Birkenau. You will now go through a brief medical evaluation and after that you will be assigned to blocks. This is a work camp and you are here to work for the Third Reich. For your obedience this night you will be given warm soup and bread."

Then we were introduced to something that we never saw before and that I experienced again many times. A group of doctors and medics, some in white gowns, arrived on the platform. I didn't understand what was going on but Joseph was encouraged. "This is a good sign, gentlemen. They need us for work."

Yanosh was young and strong. Joseph was older but healthy and strong. I'm sure they worried about me, a lad of fourteen who was healthy but not as tall as most of those on the platform. I told myself over and over that I was a fine athlete. Still, I looked around and saw most of those around me were taller and stouter.

The night became cool, despite the crowd. Many shivered, though perhaps more out of fear than from the elements. The SS gathered old men and young boys into a large group. The guards had pleasing smiles on their faces and spoke to them in a benevolent manner. Joseph tried to make sense of the procedure.

"They're sending them to a special area where the young and old are billeted."

"I don't think so," murmured a man.

He was tall, thin, with a dark beard that I thought needed trimming. He was watching the procedure too, and drawing his own conclusions.

"I've heard about this. Those poor people have no special billets waiting for them. They're going to be killed. I know it!"

The man spoke more loudly, his voice quavering, his body trembling. Some looked at him uneasily, thinking he was losing his mind. He would not be the only one.

"Stop this wild talk this instant! You are scaring the young ones," Joseph scolded as loudly as he dared. "It can't be! There are children in that group!"

The old men and boys were led away in the direction of the women, children, and elderly, who were being led away. People cried out to loved ones. A few of them refused to go. Then more and more did the same. The guards began clubbing them with their rifles. The screaming and crying became louder and more despairing. "No! No! Please no! My family! My family!"

A man near me broke away and ran toward loved ones in the other group. A guard shot him in the back and he fell hard on the platform.

A guard spotted an old man among us. He stepped in front of him, almost courteously, and in a friendly manner instructed him to join the other group. We watched as he trod off. I knew nothing yet of the machinery of killing there but felt death all around – in the blank expressions, the eerie friendliness, the cold floodlights, and the stench.

A man right next to me watched the group being led away. He had been on our cattle car – a doctor, we learned on the way. He reached into his coat and removed a small vial. "Goodbye, Sara. We will be together soon." He sent a kiss in her direction and without hesitation, downed the contents of the vial. I looked at him in horror. The couple upstairs in the ghetto had done it. Alexa had pondered it. The doctor saw the consternation on my face and softly, even affectionately, whispered, "Good luck to you, young man. Good luck to you." He collapsed and went into convulsions which came to a stop in less than a minute.

Joseph heard me gasp and felt me shudder, then looked at the man lying on the platform, a few twitches were all that was left of the doctor's life.

"I just saw that man drink poison!"

Joseph was horrified as he realized his expectations of a sane, orderly, military-like encampment were wrong. The poor man had been determined to protect his family and for many years had done just that, even through the Depression and the ghetto. But it was outside his powers in this place.

We were in a place far worse than the Oradea Mare ghetto. This is where we would live, and this is where most of us would die.

THE NEW REALITY

We were marched through the main gate. I would later learn we were leaving Auschwitz II, or Birkenau, and going into Auschwitz I. There was enough light so that I could make out the words written above it in wrought iron – "Arbeit Macht Frei". I thought it augured well.

"Look, it *is* a work camp."

Joseph saw the inscription above the gate, too, but he'd been shorn of optimism.

A dozen or more SS guards set upon us. They beat us and encouraged the dogs to leap and snap at us. We were led to a large brick building illuminated by powerful floodlights. Inside, were guards and prisoners in striped uniforms arrayed at long tables. I held on to the hand of the man I now knew to be my uncle.

At the first station we were told to undress, place our clothing on wire hangers, then place them on one of the hooks on the wall. Our shoes were to remain on the floor.

The second station was for cutting hair – a task performed by inmates. Our heads were shaved and to my alarm all other hair was removed. This, we were told, was for hygienic reasons. My uncle and I moved down to the next station where we were to be tattooed.

"Will it hurt?" I asked.

"Perhaps a little. But you are a brave lad, Shuly. Besides, I will be right here with you."

My turn came. I had no time to think or try to comprehend. An inmate wiped my left wrist with a less than clean alcohol-soaked rag then, with needle and inkwell, he inscribed a number on me. I became a number in a vast system.

My number is B14534.[1]

Next, we were issued uniforms – a shirt, jacket, pants, and cap. All of them light brown with dark stripes. No socks or underwear. Wooden shoes and a thin blanket. At the end of that station I was given a small metal bowl. I didn't know then, but soon learned, that my bowl was crucial to survival. Without it, I would get no food. Sickeningly, it was also a portable toilet.

We were shoved out the back of the building into an open area. Not far away, reddish-orange flames revealed dark columns of chimneys and thick smoke offered to the sky.

A *kapo*, an inmate entrusted by the SS, was assigned to us. He was frail and sickly but nonetheless had authority over us, the precise degree I did not know then. I timidly asked what I think everyone wanted to ask, what was going to happen to us. He initially looked at me sympathetically – a lad hurled into a maelstrom and unlikely to ever know much about life. His face hardened into cynicism. "Do you see the smoke up there? Tomorrow it may be from you." He enjoyed my discomfort.

Uncle Joseph wanted to say something – in objection or in scold – but the kapo went to the other side of the group.

"Don't listen to him, Shuly. He's not telling the truth. We're all going to be working for the Germans. That's what goes on here. Harsh conditions that's all. Hard work and harsh conditions."

I looked at Uncle Joseph, Yanosh, and the other men and felt disorientation swirl inside me. Shorn of our hair and wearing identical uniforms, separated from loved ones and terrorized by men and dogs, dehumanized and unnerved, we no longer looked like who we were yesterday. Nor did we look like individuals. We were indistinguishable parts of an immense, soulless collective. I

---

[1] Research later told me that in order to avoid assigning excessively long numbers to the large numbers of Hungarian Jews arriving in 1944, the SS introduced new sequences in mid-May. This series, prefaced by the letter A, began with "1" and ended at "20,000". Once 20,000 was reached, a new series beginning with "B" and so on. Some 15,000 men received "B" series tattoos. I was among the last of them.

wanted the place to vanish and leave me safe at home in Hungary or Romania.

Instead, SS guards and another kapo marched us to a barracks, or "block", which was back in Birkenau. The one we were assigned to, had been a large stable, perhaps for the Polish army. Rows of rickety wooden bunks which looked like tiers of long shelves went on and on until disappearing into darkness. The odor of feces and mildew struck me at once. My bunk had a rancid, ragged mattress. I ran my hand across it and felt wet fabric and several straws that jabbed through rips and holes. There were soon hundreds of us in that block, leaving the air humid and stifling. Each breath promised disease.

"I can't believe this." My uncle whispered in stunned incredulity. "This barracks is filthy. Human beings shouldn't live like this. We have to do something. We have to notify —"

"They'll kill you," Yanosh said.

People lay down, whispering in bewilderment and horror to one another. I settled into my fetid bunk, Uncle Joseph and Yanosh nearby. Uncle Joseph stared at the rafters and murmured, "We'll not live through this, we'll not live through this."

"Get up! Get up!"

Kapos rousted us from our bunks a few hours later, just as dawn was breaking on the rows of dark blocks. "You will clean up and be out for *appell* (Roll Call) in ten minutes. Bunks will be arranged in a military manner or there will be severe punishment for all. *For all!*"

I remained disoriented, partly out of recent events and revelations, partly out of the rude wakeup. Uncle Joseph helped out. "Watch me, Shuly. I'll teach you how to arrange things in a proper military manner. I learned these things long ago. You must learn them now."

"What's appell?"

"It's roll call, Shuly. Just roll call."

I groggily watched him fold the thin blanket in a manner that seemed needlessly complicated. Then we did my bunk the same way and headed for a small latrine that was by then packed with men and boys. Washing up and the other morning routines had to be done quickly. Kapos, some of them Ukrainians and Poles, mocked us and beat us as we scurried to the field in the cool dawn. We stood in rows and columns, and awaited the first appell. SS guards paced around us menacingly. Classical music played through loudspeakers.

A tall thin man in crisp SS uniform ascended a wooden platform.

"My name is Obersturmführer Koppe. I will direct appell every morning. I am new to the camp. I arrived only a week ago. However, I was trained by the best. I've been assigned this section and I intend to instill strict discipline here. Very strict discipline."

From the second row we could see him very well. He smiled, exposing bright white teeth. So many smiles from the SS personnel. Outside the camp, I would not have thought him capable of any cruelty.

"Because you are new here, today and today only, I shall forgive your tardiness. Also, I'll allow you to have breakfast in the mess hall *after* appell. Typically, you will have breakfast *before* appell."

He paused and looked out at the formation, very much pleased by his magnanimity. We relaxed somewhat. So we would not be punished that morning. An icy sternness suddenly took over Koppe's face.

"But make no mistake. You are here to work for the Third Reich. You are here to work in our factories and other worksites. You will obey camp rules and meet its schedules. Those who do not obey will be severely punished. In order to demonstrate the importance of not being late in the future, I regretfully must punish at least a few of you. Tomorrow morning I expect everyone to be here on time. Kapo! Bring me five prisoners. The rest of you, *watch and learn!*"

He motioned to a kapo with a green triangle on his uniform. I later learned that the green patch was reserved for criminals – murderers, rapists, and the like – who had become trustees. They were the cruelest of the kapos. Some were crueler than the SS.

The kapo pulled five men from our ranks. Something dreadful was about to happen. The Obersturmfuhrer strode down from the platform and approached them. Some were uneasy, others terrified. Koppe turned to the assembly once more.

"All of you, watch and learn! Anyone late to appell from now on will be punished in this manner."

Again, a smile. He turned to the five and assumed a superior, official expression.

"You men, lie down! Faces to the ground. Now!"

They immediately complied. He drew his pistol, held it up for us to see, and began to shoot into the backs of their heads. One by one, the three men were killed. Blood spurted from their skulls for a few moments. A murmur raced through the horrified rows of men. I felt sick.

"No, no. I cannot believe this," Uncle Joseph murmured not far from me. "This isn't happening."

Koppe's pistol jammed after the third shot. He tried to clear it and chamber another round, but couldn't. The last two men lay before him, trembling, praying, awaiting their turns. The officer replaced the magazine with a spare from his holster and chambered a round. He killed the fourth man and as he did, the fifth jumped to his feet and started to run. Koppe fired three shots and the man fell to the ground. The music from the speakers continued.

"Monster!" someone whispered.

Pleased with his marksmanship, the Obersturmfuhrer turned to us. "Now you are to go to the mess hall for breakfast. After that, you'll return for labor assignments. That will be all."

"Have your bowl in hand. No bowl, no food," shouted the kapo as we stood in line at the mess hall. There were a few lines. As we understood later, those who did more valuable labor received somewhat more nutritious food. As my turn arrived, the kapo gave me approximately ten ounces of brown bread, a dab of margarine, and a tasteless, unsweetened coffee or tea of some type.[2]

"I am not eating this garbage!" One man angrily threw his bread on the floor. Another man picked it up with neither hesitation nor embarrassment.

I didn't know that this would be the only substantial meal for the rest of the day, so I was tempted to eat it all. "Eat only half your bread and drink all the coffee," Uncle Joseph told Yanosh and me. "Save the rest of the bread for later." He was developing an understanding of the place.

"I hear this is actually a *death* camp," said a man we didn't know. "We are all destined to die after six months. First they'll use us for work, then . . . then they'll kill us."

"My brother is in another section here. He arrived a few months before me," said another man. "They murder people here by the thousands."

"What was said about the smoke is true then?" I stopped eating. "They burn people here?"

"Yes, they do. First we are worked, then we are killed, then we are burned."

I finished my meal and marched back to the assembly yard with the others.

We were assigned to a labor group, or *kommando,* and taken under guard to the day's worksite. On the way, guards and kapos beat us – mainly for personal entertainment, it seemed. I was hit several times on my back. My uncle tried to intervene and was beaten for it. My back hurt badly and I cried. My uncle told me that this was a sign of weakness to them and it would lead to more beatings.

"Show them your strength, Shuly. That's the key to getting through this. Show them your strength."

---

2   There was little variation in the meals but we sometimes received a thin slice of sausage or a dollop of jam with our bread.

I stopped crying, though more because I no longer could.

We were ordered to lift heavy rocks from one place and take them to another. I'm not sure it served any purpose except to wear us down. The late morning sun was hot but we had no water. Sloughing off brought a beating.

There was a short break for a noon meal. It was *Gemüsen* – vegetables and seeds boiled into a thin tasteless soup. Fortunately, I had some of my bread left.

Most of us survived those first days. As the weeks passed, we lost more and more. Work, malnourishment, beatings, poor sleep. Over and over. I was in a daze but put one foot out in front of the other.

I learned things. Those who arrived at the mess hall earliest got slightly larger portions – more for breakfast, more to stash away for later. Those who received their ladles of soup late, got a few more bits of the potato and sausage that lurked at the bottom of the pot. On Sundays we got pea soup. That helped us know the days of the week and helped keep a sense of time.

Breakfasts got smaller, sometimes the kapos deliberately spilled some of my portion on the ground, and that of others as well. I needed every crumb and drop, and they knew it. Above all, I learned I must not annoy the kapos or SS.

We became emaciated. Skin was taught against our bones, leaving us with a cadaverous appearance. We were being prodded along toward death. Every now and then someone standing for appell crumpled to the ground dead or was shot where he lay moments later.

The poor guys arbitrarily selected for group punishment had to stand all night in the courtyard, shivering, famished, passing out. Uncle Joseph said that, in such conditions, the human spirit has no desire to live anymore. One man said that if he were punished like that, he'd simply sit on the ground and wait for the SS to kill him.

A few Russian POWs passed by our block with a pot of soup. Some guys ran out with their bowls and pleaded for some, and the Russians obliged their fellow inmates. Guards and kapos saw this and held the men's heads in the pot until they died. The soup was then ladled out.

The kapos became crueler every day. Beatings and outright killings were everywhere. A new corpse was an opportunity to get better clothes and shoes. That disgusted me at first.

We had no heat or running water. Hundreds of people used a handful of toilets. Gastro-intestinal diseases were common. Many suffered from bouts of diarrhea during the night which made our sleeping quarters even more revolting. Every morning we took out the corpses of those who'd died during the night.

The block was infested with rats and every mattress was laced with squirming insects. Bed bugs bit me night and sucked blood. Lice were constant nuisances. I slept atop my food bowl and shoes, or clutched them as I slept on my side, otherwise they could be stolen. More people were assigned to my barracks and I had to share my bunk with several people. More than once I woke up to see that one of them had died.

Some inmates in deep despair simply lay down and in a few minutes, gently left this world. Others grabbed hold of the electric fences around the camp and put an end to it. I think they reasoned it was better to go out on their own terms than on those of the Reich. A work detail made the rounds every morning to remove the dead from the wires. Guards would shut off the power in places so that the workers could pry away the hands.

Auschwitz was designed to kill us. We would perform hard labor for a while, but there was no mistaking where we would end up. Almost every week we went through a selection process in which we were judged fit or unfit for labor. The latter were sometimes shot then and there or more commonly led away to one of the gas chambers at the north end of Birkenau.

After six weeks or so, Yanosh and I saw Uncle Joseph weakening by the day. We offered him some of our bread but of course he refused. The three of us used to sit outside our block and enjoy the little privacy available to us.

I must have inquired about my parents back in Romania, though I have no specific recollection of it. I'd been so wrenched away from normal life that the matter of biological parents seemed distant and irrelevant. I was with Uncle Joseph and Yanosh. They had been the family I always knew and I clung to that idea. Whether I was a Davidovich or a Rittman, I had to face a stark present, not look into a lost past.

The stars flickered above us, innocent of any knowledge of what went on under them. Uncle Joseph assessed the situation. "We're not working for the Reich. We're being worked *to death* by it. It's all calculated, planned – over in Auschwitz I or back in Berlin somewhere. There is method here. We need to do something."

There was conviction in his voice, not lamentation.

"What can we do?" I asked.

"We need to make a plan to get out. Otherwise, we'll all die. Sooner or later, we'll all die. There's no other way. You boys are strong and can survive longer than most, but even the young and strong can't live long here. Look what's happening around us. Every day people fall to the ground or are killed."

"And we have to carry them back to the block," Yanosh added, eyes downward.

"We live like rats in old basement walls," Uncle Joseph continued.

"The rats have better odds," Yanosh noted.

The idea of escape was appealing but no one knew how. Too many guards and kapos. And there was the fence. All I could think about most nights was sleep and tomorrow's breakfast. I found my bunk in the dark and climbed up. Sometimes I was fortunate to fall asleep in minutes.

One day we were assigned to sort the belongings of a group of newly arrived persons – things they had to surrender on the platform, things that had belonged to people who were now inmates or dead. This area was called *Kanada*, as it was deemed a place of wealth and opportunity. It was light duty. Occasionally, workers at *Kanada* found items of food in the piles of baggage.

I was given a pair of scissors and instructed to cut open the linings of clothing and luggage, especially expensive-looking ones, and search for hidden valuables. I once found a few photographs. There was a family of four – mother, father, and two daughters. They posed in a tree-lined park, the joy of being together clear on their faces. I wondered if any of them were still alive.

Another time I was assigned to one of the special work details, or what were called, *Sonderkommandos*. These details worked at the gas chambers and crematories. I saw both in operation. There was an anteroom in the gas chamber building, which itself was an ordinary-looking brick building. A group of people were herded into the building where they were to undress and take showers. There was a sign in the anteroom in German – a language most Central Europeans had some knowledge of:

Put shoes into the cubbyholes and tie them together so you will not lose them. After the showers you will receive hot coffee.

The people were pushed into the chamber itself, a dank concrete room with only ventilators above. Small children were hurled in. An SS guard took a few infants by their legs and smashed their skulls against the wall.

Men on the roof dropped Zyklon B canisters down a passageway covered with metal grating. Muffler-less generators atop the building started up and ran on high. The tremendous roar aimed to drown out the cries of the victims below. I was too close. I heard them. Men, women, and children. Horrible sounds, unforgettable sounds, especially the children. They should have been in school or playing in parks. Instead, they were being gassed to death in a dank building in Poland. On and on came. At length, perhaps fifteen minutes, the noise stopped.

Ventilators cleared the gas and workers entered. The SS fired pistol shots into the heads of anyone showing signs of life. Remaining rings and other items were taken. Hair was cut and placed in sacks that were transported to factories. The corpses were placed in piles of ten, then taken to ovens.

One day, there was an event that neared the miraculous. A girl of about ten was being led along with many other women and girls to the gas chamber. They were coming straight from the platform and hadn't had time to learn the camp's secret. I was outside the building awaiting the aftermath. A line of hapless people awaited their final lesson in German politics. It was her fair complexion and blonde hair that I noticed. There was no one close to her. She was alone. Our eyes met. I looked into the soul of a poor girl who had no idea what lay ahead. I fell into those eyes.

I found myself raising my hand and waving, as though we were in a schoolyard or park. She waved back, but instead of feeling joy and hope, I was overpowered by sadness. I cast my eyes downward, ashamed of my tears and the secret.

Then I realized she was alone and needful. It would be selfish not to look at her. I needed to give her a moment of human connection as she continued her walk. However brief that moment was, I owed her that.

She was sad but then suddenly cheered. Tears fell down my cheeks and I made no effort to hide them. It was a moment of complete vulnerability and honesty. She was puzzled but then she understood. I'd let the secret slip. I forced a smile on my face, but she walked on.

The SS shoved the women and girls into the anteroom, but there was confusion and scuffling, and the process stalled. The girl grabbed hold of the doorway. A guard pushed her ahead but she held on. His rifle butt crashed down on her head and back. Blood came from a gash on her forehead. I found myself running to her, an idea only beginning to form.

I grabbed the guard's arm and shouted, "You must come outside and see what's going on! You're needed!"

He recognized me as a boy in the *Sonderkommando* and in a sense, part of the operation.

"Something just over there!" I struggled to come up with something amid the screams and confusion of the anteroom. It came to me. "A prisoner! She's getting away!"

He mulled over his conflicting duties and after a moment, let go of the girl. As the SS guard came with me, I saw the girl run past the other busy guards and away from the building. I didn't know where she went, perhaps to the women's blocks where they'd try to protect her.

"Where is this prisoner? Where?"

"She was right there! I don't know where she went!"

My head exploded into a thousand stars as his machine pistol came down hard on my head. Down I went. His boots pounded into my sides and head. His presence needed back inside, he left me bleeding on the ground. I came to my feet and returned to work. I was in pain, blood trickled from my roaring ear.[3]

Not long thereafter, I helped remove another heap of corpses from the chamber. Knowing I'd helped one girl live another day. It was a small moment of victory.

The days on the *Sonderkommando*, despite my small victory, left a void in my being. The cruelty of fellow human beings and the piles of corpses, horror and agony frozen on the faces of adults and children and babies, made it clear there was no greater being watching over us, and we were not part of the unfolding of an intricate plan. I never wanted to hear another utterance of religion again.

---

[3] When I returned to Romania after the war, a friend told me a story of a similar incident at a gas chamber. The girl was able to escape to a block in the women's camp. She went through the Death March from Auschwitz and was liberated at Bergen-Belsen. Of course, I cannot say it was the girl I saw, but I hope that she survived.

Years later, when I was reading Dante's *Inferno*, I imagined Auschwitz and Birkenau and Dachau as something like the rings of hell, each with parts more horrible than others. Some camps were worse than others and guards had varying degrees of cruelty. The worst ring was complete with fires and chimneys. But unlike the condemned of Dante's poem, we'd done nothing to deserve where we were.

ADOLF EICHMANN

People came and went but I got to know a few of the people in our block, if only for a short while. Our conversations were usually brief. Some were quite memorable. I got to know Eliezer, or Eli, chiefly because of a bold plan he came up with.

Eli was older, perhaps in his forties. There was an exceptional alertness in his eyes. His grey hair was limited to the sides and at times it looked like small wings had cropped up there. It amused me but as a boy I held my view on the matter.

A teacher before all this, he used to absorb all the information he could to put into lectures and discussions. Now, he was ever watchful, not simply for guards and kapos – we all did that. He kept his eye on every detail, in the block and on worksites. And he listened.

Eli was assigned to the officers mess where junior and senior officers ate, socialized, and told stories. Eli listened. He knew which generals were respected and which ones had been sacked. He heard about how the war was going, so we learned that in June the Americans and British had landed in France and were moving east. We didn't have the BBC, but we had Eli.

He heard about the SS hierarchy and probably came to know as much about it as most of the officers dining around him. He knew who was liked, who was disliked, who was up for promotion, and who was going off to a frontline unit. He knew about the systematic nature of the camps. There were work schedules, production schedules, and even train schedules for gathering up Jews across Europe and bringing them to Poland.

The officers chatted away, oblivious to the presence of a deferent inmate who entertained them with old jokes and confessions of ignorance. They laughed at him and saw him as an idiotic Jew. Some even gave him scraps of food as signs of their munificence.

But Eli was taking down their every utterance in his constantly turning mind.

In the evenings Eli gave us reports. Most people were uninterested. What difference did his observations make? Would they help in morning appell or out at a worksite? Most slipped off to their bunks to get every bit of rest they could. Uncle Joseph and I listened. It was a diversion, it was entertainment.

Eli was upset by the passivity of inmates. There should be more resistance, more fighting back. We were lambs to the slaughter. His bold talk did not fit well with his humor or with reality for that matter. Uncle Joseph thought Eli was off his rocker – *meshuganeh*. There were many who were. But Eli held my interest.

"Did you know that Adolf Hitler has never himself visited a single camp?" He asked us one night. "Did you know that?"

Of course, we didn't. How would we know? We didn't listen in on SS table talk.

"Not once. His underlings have, though. They come to make sure everything is proceeding according to plan, especially in light of recent events on the warfronts."

I wasn't sure if he was displaying his wit or leading up to something.

"The officers at the mess discuss Hitler's absence. They speak to friends at other camps, so they know. They think their *Führer* is simply too busy with other things to come to a camp. But it's perfectly obvious why Hitler stays away!"

Judging by the blank expressions around him, he had to enlighten us as to the obvious.

"Hitler knows what's going on here and knows what's in store for those who administer his camp system. He wants no evidence that he knew of this place and those like it."

"What if he *doesn't* know about what's going on here?" someone asked.

"Ha! That cannot be. He knows everything that goes on in his Reich but he doesn't want any evidence pointing to him. He's deluding himself, though. He's in charge, he'll be taken to book. No doubt about it."

My uncle voiced strenuous support for Eli's position. Eli nodded in appreciation.

"I learned something very important this day, my friends. We shall have a very important visitor in a few weeks. Herr Adolf Eichmann is coming to pay us a visit."

"Who is Adolf Eichmann?" some asked.

"This Eichmann fellow is an important figure in the Nazi death system." Eli relished his attention. "I heard much about the man and what he does. He manages the system that brings us here. The trains, the transit points, the schedules are all his work. And one more thing. Did you know that Eichmann is an expert on Judaism?"

"Why would a Nazi have an interest in Judaism?" came an incredulous voice.

"Oh yes, oh yes. Eichmann has studied our religion, history, and customs. He even learned Hebrew. That is why he was given the task to solve the Jewish problem for the Reich. He rounds us up, packs us into trains, then brings us to Auschwitz or one of the other death camps. Yes, there are others. Eichmann's one of the major figures in this."

The cocky look on his face signaled another important piece of information was coming.

"Eichmann is coming for an inspection in a week or so. I will soon learn exactly when. And, my friends, I am going to kill that man."

"What?"

"How?"

"I've formed a plan. I can't let the opportunity slip away."

Eli's announcement elicited looks of admiration and skepticism, sometimes on the same faces in a matter of moments.

"My friends, I'll be the one who'll kill Eichmann. I just need some help. I'll need a distraction."

Eli outlined the plan. Eichmann was scheduled to observe a morning appell and Eli would set upon him with a knife he'd steal from the mess hall in the morning. He wanted some of us to cause a commotion that would distract Eichmann's bodyguard just before he raced at him, blade in hand. When it was objected that anyone who'd caused the distraction would be killed, Eli insisted that once Eichmann lay mortally wounded, all attention would be on Eichmann and the assassin.

"Perhaps, perhaps," Uncle Joseph said. "But perhaps not. The guards will recognize the connection and eventually punish those behind the distraction. Nonetheless, I like the idea of fighting back – like soldiers!"

"This is a risk we have to take if we are to fight back. I am willing to die in this endeavor. It may save the lives of others. I'll know the exact date of Eichmann's arrival shortly."

That night in the bunks, I asked my uncle what he thought of the plan.

"I really don't know, Shuly. Too many things can go wrong. There's too much left to chance. But I like Eli's spirit. Yes, I do like his spirit. Just not his plan." He shook his head and exhaled.

If my uncle had doubts, I had them, too.

The next evening Eli brought pen and paper that he'd taken from the officer's mess. He drew a map of the roll call yard, the stand where Eichmann would be, and where he, Eli, would be upon leaving the mess hall – with a knife.

"I'll stab him repeatedly in the throat, and then I'll be killed. I accept this."

My uncle suggested coming up with a more intricate plan, but Eli was adamant. Eichmann was coming and he had to be killed Eli's way. No alternative. A handful of men announced that they were in. They would cause the commotion and Eli would do the rest. Eli thanked each of them.

Nothing changed in Uncle Joseph's mind.

A few nights later, Eli brought word.

"He'll be here in three days!"

He looked to his fellow conspirators, and their eagerness indicated they were still in. The group went over the plan again.

The night before Eichmann's arrival, Uncle Joseph and I met with the group. We weren't to participate but Uncle Joseph wanted to express his respect for the men and wish them the best.

"Tomorrow we'll make ourselves felt, and we'll bring change," Eli said serenely. "It was a great pleasure knowing you gentlemen."

We all shook hands and retired to our bunks.

That morning Uncle Joseph and I were sent off to work before appell was finished. I looked back as we marched away but saw no commotion or important visitor. All day we were eager to get back to the block and learn how Eli's bold plan had unfolded. That evening, after the mess hall, we looked for one or more of the initiates but couldn't see any of them and were reluctant to be seen making inquiries.

At last we came upon a man who'd met with Eli and the others but who wasn't part of the diversion. His crestfallen appearance told us all but the details.

"It was sad. I stood near the front and could see a notable visitor surrounded by bodyguards and more officers than usual. They all looked sharper than usual and those close to Eichmann fawned over him. I looked for Eli and soon spotted him walking briskly toward Eichmann. There were so many guards around him.

"I looked for the distraction. Men were supposed to argue and fight. I waited and waited. Eli kept on toward Eichmann. Still no distraction. I looked around and saw the men who were to cause the commotion just standing there in the ranks. They just stood there!

"Eli was getting closer. I saw no knife. Maybe he was determined to kill him with his bare hands. He had a look of cold determination. When Eli got within twenty meters of Eichmann, an officer drew his pistol and shot him down. Four or five bullets hit Eli and he fell to the ground.

"Eichmann showed no interest. One officer said, 'A stupid Jew! That's all he was.' The others laughed. I don't think they even suspected what Eli was trying to do. He probably shot him simply because he was out of place. Maybe he killed Eli to impress Eichmann. That's all that became of Eli's plan. A good man, a brave man."

There was less interest in what happened that morning than I would have thought. Uncle Joseph praised Eli as a courageous man and went on to say Eli didn't have sufficient knowledge of military matters to devise a sound plan.

"He certainly had the spirit of a soldier," I said.

"Yes, he did. Unfortunately, no one will know what happened this day," Uncle Joseph noted ruefully.[4]

That night I thought how much I wanted to set eyes on this Adolf Eichmann. I wanted to see if he was as evil as people said. I thought he must look monstrous, more so than the guards and kapos who terrorized us.

After the war I saw photographs of him, and years later I saw him on trial in Israel. I watched the proceedings on television, as did most of the nation. He didn't look evil, though evil he was. It was a case of the "banality of evil" that observers speak of. Banal, but evil.

I also later learned of several attempts to kill Hitler. Why did men like Eichmann and Hitler survive attempts to kill them, even when planned by disciplined, resolute men like Stauffenberg? No, there was no higher design at work. It couldn't have been part of a divine plan. However, I hope that when Eichmann went to the gallows, word somehow reached Eli.

---

[4] According to Yad Vashem, Eichmann came to Auschwitz several times in the spring and summer of 1944.

THE RED CROSS

Not long after a morning assembly, everyone in my block was taken to a section of Auschwitz-Birkenau where we'd never been. The Auschwitz complex sprawled over dozens of square kilometers and no inmate knew all that went on there. We lined up and an officer addressed us.

"You are now assigned to this section and will stay here one day. Consider it a privilege. You'll be sleeping in comfortable bunks and eating good food. You'll be issued new clothes, shoes, and bowls. You will work in a nearby plant where you'll assemble equipment for our brave military. You will remain in one group and have new supervisors. Obey them! Any disobedience will be severely punished."

The prospect of generosity from the SS, even if admittedly temporary, naturally gave rise to suspicions. I thought of the Germans who gave me chocolate in Oradea.

"I don't like this," a man said.

"I hope this doesn't mean it's our last meal," said another bitterly. With that sobering thought, we entered the new block.

We were amazed, though still wary of course. Clean and spacious. Soft mattresses, fresh bedding and even pillows. The air was odor-free. Auschwitz with amenities, one might say. Guys hopped on mattresses, claiming them for their own, even though they were all firm and in sufficient numbers.

Uncle Joseph and Yanosh were behind me. My uncle remained on guard. "This is fishy. They're up to something."

The three of us sat down on mattresses near one another and ran our hands over the clean soft fabric. Yanosh lay down and stretched his arms and legs.

"Don't get too comfortable," Uncle Joseph cautioned. "This isn't what it appears to be. It's a ruse of some sort. A shameful one. I don't understand it yet. But this will not last long."

"Everyone outside! Now!"

We lined up and were marched to a nearby mess hall. I marveled at how clean it was, inside and out. Long tables covered with cloths. Pitchers of coffee and water on every one of them.

An *Aufseherin* asked, almost politely, for volunteers to help serve breakfast. I was puzzled by her gentleness. Requesting volunteers was not the way things were done. She asked once more and a few stepped forward. The rest of us sat down and shortly later, breakfast was served. Dark bread and eggs. The water and coffee pitchers were refilled periodically.

There was little conversation. In part because we were so suspicious, in part because we were busy devouring the ample food.

The Aufseherin spoke once more.

"Now you'll be issued new uniforms."

An hour later and we had fresh clothing and new shoes. Then we were taken to a workshop where for several hours we assembled metal containers with military stampings on them. Warm potato soup and bread arrived near noon. The servings were generous and seconds were given.

We assembled in the yard that evening, and the same officer spoke.

"Tomorrow, we will have visitors from the Red Cross. For those who don't know, the Third Reich is a signatory to the Geneva Convention."

"So that's the game," my uncle whispered.

"They will bring you packages. You will receive them in the dining hall. You are forbidden to talk with the Red Cross people! Those who do not obey this order will be severely punished. The packages are yours to keep. Now you can walk about the yard until ten pm. Dismissed."

It was a strange feeling to walk about freely for a few hours. Yes, of course there were a dozen SS guards watching us, but we took what we could.

"So the guards are putting on a show for the Red Cross," Uncle Joseph said as we walked about. "And we have small parts in it."

"But not speaking parts," Yanosh added.

"Right, son. We'll be back to the old arrangements shortly after the Red Cross cars leave the gate."

"At least we can enjoy decent food and bunks," I added in boyish naivety. I accepted the arrangements as fraudulent and short-term, but I saw them as a welcome break.

"It's a trick of the worst kind, Shuly. Don't get used to it. It will be gone before you know it. I'm thinking of speaking with the Red Cross personnel. We need to get word out."

"They'll *kill* you!" Yanosh warned.

"If I can get the message out, it will be worth it. It's my duty."

He was right, or at least might have been. Nonetheless, I didn't want to see him shot down as soon as he opened his mouth.

"I'll try to talk with them tomorrow," he said in the bunks that night.

As we assembled for appell, cars with Red Cross insignia drove up. A few men got out and conferred with SS officers. The conversions seemed casual. I heard occasional laughter.

Uncle Joseph was angry.

"The ruse is playing out before our very eyes. Those bastards are tricking the Red Cross into thinking this is the real Auschwitz. I know the Geneva Convention. The Germans have to allow the Red Cross to inspect so they built this façade and placed us here for a short time."

I feared for what might happen after the inspection.

SS guards began unloading packages and taking them to the mess hall. The ranking SS officer continued to chat amiably with the delegation, then he pointed to us. We were led to the dining hall where the Aufseherin had prepared our parts in the show.

"After breakfast, the Red Cross delegation will give each of you a package. You'll take it to your block and leave it there. You'll open it only upon returning from work. Now, eat. You have a full day in front of you."

Breakfast was served, dutifully if superficially observed by the delegation and their tour guides. As a nice touch, we were given apples. I partook of more than one and suffered stomach aches later at the plant. We were given packages, each marked with the Red Cross insignia, and taken to the block – all under the eyes of the delegation.

My uncle seethed. He wanted an opportunity to speak with a Red Cross official, but none presented itself. The SS maintained a distance between the delegation and us. The same was true as the delegation looked through our workplace. Judging by their faces, they were satisfied.

That evening, we stood in the yard as the delegation inspected our block. Shortly thereafter, they climbed into their vehicles and drove away.

Back in the block I opened my parcel and was pleased to find a chocolate bar, tea bags, tins of meat, pudding, biscuits, cheese, and condensed milk. There was even a small bar of soap. The inspection was a fraud, but I enjoyed the gifts from Switzerland.

"I suggest that you hide as much of these items as you can," Uncle Joseph said.

An hour later guards entered the block, shouting at us and kicking the boxes about.

"Leave everything here and get outside. Now!"

After roll call we were led back to the old block. Blows fell hard and often along the way. One came down on my face, sending me to the ground where I was repeatedly kicked. Bleeding from the mouth, I stumbled into the block and found my bunk.

The Red Cross inspection was over.

ALONE

As warm weather became less frequent, morning appells (Roll Calls) and selections took higher tolls. Colds and more serious respiratory infections were increasingly common and we had to take corpses out every morning. Work assignments involved putting up new buildings in and around the main camps of Auschwitz and Auschwitz-Birkenau. Think of Auschwitz as a small town with surrounding villages that were all engaged in the German war effort and the Final Solution. The two overlapped.

We were ordinary workers – low in the camp's labor hierarchy. Workers at Monowitz, a chemical plant, and Bobrek, a factory making parts for planes and submarines, had better blocks and more nutritious food. The workers were skilled and valuable. We were unskilled and expendable. New trains of unskilled laborers pulled into the station routinely. We heard the locomotive whistles and the clanging of cattle cars as they came to a halt. Sometimes a new train meant that a block had to be suddenly emptied out.

Work was often episodic. One week we'd work trimming sod and planting it in various parts of the camp. None near the blocks, I assure you. It was probably around SS barracks or administrative centers. I can also assure you that the sod was heavy.

Another time we worked in a beet field. Autumn was at hand and we planted seeds for a crop to come in before the snow fell. Work in the fields had a secret reward. Scratching about the soil we'd often find a reasonably developed beet that had been missed in the harvest. The gleaners found them a welcome supplement to their rations.

One especially weak fellow was charged with pushing a wheelbarrow filled with seeds and topsoil down the rows we'd dug. The poor guy stumbled and the wheelbarrow tipped over. Angered by the slowdown, or just eager to sate his cruel nature, a guard stabbed him over and over with a pitchfork until he lay lifeless. We stared briefly then returned to work. A guard dog licked up the pool of blood on the soil.

Uncle Joseph was in decline. He was malnourished, he'd been beaten and humiliated, he'd been worked to exhaustion day after day, and he'd lost his wife. It was the absence of his beloved Catalina that hurt him most. He tried to look strong for Yanosh and me, but his efforts were no longer unconvincing. He was coughing more and more. Every night we talked outside before the block was shuttered tight.

"My Catalina is gone. I know it," he murmured. "I know it."

"There is no way to know that with certainty. She may be at one of the sub-camps." Yanosh held on to measure of hope for his mother – and for his own family as well. It was possible that Catalina and Yanosh's family were elsewhere. Still, we'd seen them driven into the weak group when we arrived. We'd all asked other inmates we came across at work sites. It was part of prisoner life to learn what they could about friends and family members. Everyone shared what information they had.

"No, I know that she could never survive here. Even if she started as a worker, she could never endure it. I know it. I can feel that she's gone. I can feel it. A husband knows."

He was probably right. She relied on him for her strength. Too much so. She had a very hard time of it in the Oradea ghetto, and here without him? If Yanosh thought his wife and children had shared the same fate, he kept it private. I think he knew.

My words of encouragement were half-hearted and I'm sure they sounded that way. At some point, optimism there was childish.

"Yanosh, I want you to watch over Shuly. I promised his parents."

"You're still here to watch over me, Uncle Joseph. We all help each other."

"Yes, of course I'm still here with you, Shuly. It will not be for long, though."

Yanosh offered more words of encouragement. He struggled to hold in his own emotions. He clasped his father's hand. "You can hold on. We'll help you at work, we'll share our food."

Uncle Joseph coughed lengthily, his throat making a disconcerting rasping sound. I'd heard it before. It almost never cleared up, though it always stopped.

"I'll do my best, boys, but a man knows when his time is coming. Look, this is the way of the world. No need to be sad. I've been blessed to know you. I've enjoyed watching you become fine men. I love you both. I've been truly blessed."

A look of calm came to him.

"And you'll still watch us grow." My words might have been a little stronger.

"Of course, of course. But just in case, I want you two to remain together. Yanosh, you are to watch Shuly. Stay with him. Make sure no one takes his belongings, and help him on details. You two have to see each other through this."

He coughed noisily into a dirty cloth he stuffed into his trousers. There were flecks of blood.

"Yanosh, do you promise me?"

"Yes, of course, we'll stay together – always."

"Shuly, you have to promise me that you'll be strong. You'll keep your strong spirit. You and Yanosh are young and strong. You must survive. It will be our victory."

I did promise, though I was feeling weaker, too.

The next day we continued construction work around the plants operated by IG Farben, a large German chemical firm that made artificial rubber.[5] The site was in the Monowitz camp, which was also known as Auschwitz III, and located five kilometers west of Birkenau.

---

[5]   One of its subsidiaries, I learned after the war, made Zyklon B – the gas used in Birkenau's gas chambers.

A group of SS officers and civilian engineers arrived to inspect the work site. We were told that one of them was the SS head Heinrich Himmler, though I cannot be sure this is true. At the sergeant's command, we stopped working and lowered our heads as the officials motored past.

As the men inspected the site, an old man in our group fell to the ground and called for water. The SS guard who oversaw our detail, a stout, red-faced sergeant, approached him. We knew the sergeant enjoyed his power over us and indeed enjoyed killing one or more of us as he saw fit. He aimed his machine pistol at the man and put several bullets through his head.

The officials looked in our direction briefly but showed no great interest. They continued with their inspection, occasionally looking at blueprints, pointing at particular places, and conferring on matters. It looked like the inspection was going well.

I was peering into another world. There in the entourage were engineers and surveyors. They weren't SS or Wehrmacht or Nazi party officials. They were what I might have thought to be ordinary civilians – men who might build schools and parks and sing hymns on Sundays. They wore ordinary clothing. They had ordinary faces, not famished or cruel ones. I thought they might be horrified by a summary execution, or at least puzzled. They conferred once more and left.

I watched and learned.

One or two more men died of exhaustion that day. We carried their corpses to a large pit just outside the Birkenau fences where piles of dead accumulated, from worksites or the morning dead from the blocks. When there were enough bodies, a mass immolation ensued. The crematories must have been too busy.

The next morning was the coldest yet. We shivered badly during roll call and on the trek to Monowitz. I worked hard, not out of a sense of duty of course, but to ward off the cold. A man laughed not far from me.

"Little man, you make me laugh!"

I knew the voice – it was that of a brutish corporal. He was looking at me, malevolence plain.

"Go on. Keep working, little man. I can use a little entertainment this day."

What was I doing? Working too hard to stay warm? I gradually slowed down to a normal rate.

"No! No! Faster! I enjoy seeing a little man work so enthusiastically. We need more like you!"

I resumed the previous pace, all the while thinking how much he liked to torment victims before beating or killing them. Suddenly a powerful blow come down on my back, sending me to the ground. I cried out, but only for a moment. Worse I feared was coming.

"Leave him alone!" An unfamiliar voice challenged the corporal – bravely but unwisely, I thought. A man in his thirties stood in front of the guard, shovel in hand and ire in his eyes. Though we were on the same kommando, it was the first time I heard him speak. "You can't treat us like animals!"

I lay on the ground and watched a familiar scene play out. Some men saw death coming sooner or later and opted to accept it now, on their terms, with at least a measure of dignity. Some grabbed hold of the electric fence, some stood up to guards. The result was the same.

The corporal wasn't angry. He simply drew his P-38 pistol and killed the man. "Yes, I can," he noted calmly. In his estimation, a rule was violated and he handled the matter promptly and professionally.

I was afraid he'd shoot me too, as I'd begun the incident, at least as someone like him would reckon things. I returned immediately to work, hoping his bloodlust had been sated for the day. But I felt his presence right behind me. I heard him light a match and smelled cigarette smoke.

"I didn't forget you, boy."

This was it. He was going to kill me. I turned slowly and saw his face. I was relieved that his pistol was holstered for the moment.

"Leave the boy alone!"

That voice I knew. It was my uncle's. He looked to me and nodded. Yanosh was a little farther away, anxiety etched on his face. Uncle Joseph's eyes forbade me to do anything. "Stay still and live," he seemed to say. He dashed toward the sergeant like a soldier in the heat of battle. The sergeant began to draw his pistol but my uncle was upon him and seized it from his hands.

"You are in violation of international laws. You're not a soldier. *I* am a soldier and I will die like one."

Uncle Joseph fired and the guard looked awkwardly at the hole in his tunic. Another shot, and he fell to the ground. Kapos called out for more SS but they were well on their way already, rifles and machine pistols at the ready.

Pistol at his side, Joseph was strangely calm and content. "I'm weary. I shall be with Catalina." Several shots slammed into him and he crumpled to the ground. More shots left no doubt.

"Back to work! All of you, back to work!" the soldier shouted, brandishing their weapons.

I cannot speak for all the men on the kommando that day. Most are probably dead, if not from the SS then from the intervening years. But in addition to my grief, I was proud of Uncle Joseph.

As dusk came to Monowitz, Yanosh and I carried him back to the block in Birkenau. We gently placed him where we'd less gently placed many others who were unknown to us, but loved by others somewhere in Europe. We might have cried, or we might have been too tired and confused. But Yanosh spoke a few words.

"He was a fine soldier – honored and revered. He died a soldier this day."

My turn.

"I want to die that way too, killing a guard then accepting the end like a man."

"We have to live through this," Yanosh whispered almost prayerfully amid the pile of dead. "We promised."

Yes, that promise took precedence over my indifference to living and will for vengeance. Still, I wanted to kill a guard one day.

There was nothing more we could do. We gave Joseph a final embrace and went back to the block. In a few hours, a kommando would take the dead to a pit outside the fence where they'd be set alight in a few days.

The young man I shared a bunk with was used to seeing me with my uncle. He comprehended. I woke up and realized once again that I'd lost my uncle and guardian. No more help in the morning, no more assurances, no more guidance. I could hear him say the war would be over soon and we'd be back in Oradea.

Yanosh and I continued to talk outside at night about family and home and normal life. We even made plans about what we'd do after the war. A week later, at morning appell, our block was divided into three groups. One group was to go to Monowitz to work in the Farben plant. The second was designated for Neustadt and Bobrek. The third was to remain in Birkenau for general labor. Yanosh was sent to Monowitz. I remained at Birkenau.

One morning there was a call for musicians to play in the camp orchestra. Strange as it sounds, Auschwitz had a group of musicians who performed in various places. One such place was the platform in Birkenau where trains arrived, though I don't recall a performance the night we arrived. In any event, when the call for musicians came I raised my arm and was marched over to Auschwitz. Playing a violin is less taxing than carrying sod or digging ditches. Also, it was known that such workers drew larger rations and had better blocks.

The conductor was a middle-aged German man who'd been sent to Auschwitz for being a communist. Yes, not everyone was there because of religion. He handed me an inexpensive violin and told me to play. Well, it had been many years since sports took precedence over music, but I put instrument to chin and the audition began.

After less than a minute the maestro's assessment was clear. When the orchestra assembled at the gate in the morning he told me to move my bow across the strings but to try to make as little noise as possible. So, we played. Lines of workers trudged by as they headed for the day's labor. Late in the day we'd reassemble in the same place and play as the lines of workers trudged back inside the gate.

The SS probably thought we raised spirits and increased productivity. I strongly doubt we did either. Maybe a German received a medal for his ingenious contribution to the war effort. I received a respite from hard labor. And indeed the rations and blocks were better in Auschwitz than across the tracks in Birkenau.

There was an SS officer at the gate one day. His uniform was sharper than most and his gait suggested great confidence and authority. He would watch the workers pass by and occasionally give bits of bread to some of them. He favored me with a small portion once.

The conductor couldn't keep a talentless boy on for long, but he tried to place me in block that worked in a munitions plant. I was given instructions on plant procedure but judged too frail. Back to Birkenau.

ESCAPE

Weaker and alone, I passed out every day or so. Fellow prisoners quickly helped me up. Mornings got colder, appells more arduous. More of us died one way or another. One morning, I stood in the assembly yard along with several hundred others, awaiting orders. It was cold, rain soaked my uniform, and wind gusts increased the misery. The wait was longer than usual. Most of the SS were elsewhere, probably indoors, and the kapos were running appell – rather incompetently.

The man in front of me fell to the ground and didn't move. He might have died standing up. It wasn't unknown. Over the next half hour, several more keeled over. My teeth chattered. My body shook and felt numb. I struggled not to keep standing.

The kapo calling roll stepped into the faltering rows and columns and came to me, a lone boy standing, if barely, among many prisoners lying on the ground or struggling to get up. He stood right in front of me and grinned. His gnarled teeth were inches from my face.

"Aren't you the lucky one? One of the last left still standing in your row."

His eyes conveyed power and disdain. After months in the ghetto and camp, I'd seen much hatred but I did him no harm and neither had anyone there that morning. Useless to inquire about the hatred then, but that's what was going through my mind.

He looked at the roster then without warning, hit me on the face so hard that I fell to the ground. As I tried to stand, he kicked me repeatedly in the face and ribs. I fell back down and lay there. No more kicks came. He thought there was one more dead that morning.

I knew what was in store. I'd be collected with the dead or near-dead and taken to the incineration pit. It had its attractions that morning. I'd had enough. I was ready to die. But ideas raced through my mind, and they hinged on getting dumped in that pit. But I passed out and lay back in acceptance of whatever was in store.

I looked up at a dark sky, then around me. I was in a heap of foul, stiff corpses. The stillness was unearthly. It was over. Death had come. Then I found that I could move my hands and those ideas came back to mind.

The kapos and SS would be gone by now, nonetheless I stayed where I was and stared at the stars in the inky sky. I looked around furtively and decided to take my leave. Another body moved a few meters away. It was a guy my age he was as startled to see me as I was to see him. We stared at each other – too scared or too smart to make a sound.

We looked about in the moonlight and saw the fence and a guard tower. We knew that was south. To the north we saw trees and began to make for them. Strength and youth returned, if only barely.

We crossed the field, stumbling occasionally in our wooden shoes, and ran toward the stout trees of the forest. We'd been taught in our childhoods that forests were dangerous places where careless children were devoured by wolves, but the forest that night was shelter and deliverance. Nothing could be as dangerous as what lay behind the fence. The scent of pine was a wondrous departure from the vile stenches of rotting corpses, fetid blocks, and chimney smoke.

I thought at times that night I could have run back to Hungary, though I fell occasionally and had to rest every half hour or so. My companion, almost as out of breath as I, signaled to halt. We sat on a fallen tree and caught our breath.

"I'm Herman."

"I'm Shmuli."

We shook hands then listened hard, familiarizing ourselves with the sounds of rustling branches and night creatures so that we might better recognize a sign of danger such as a German patrol.

"How old are you, Herman?"

"Fourteen. You?"

"Sixteen."

"Did you arrive with your family?" I asked hesitantly, even though it was a common question inside the camp.

"Parents, two sisters. And you?"

"Uncle, aunt, and cousin."

No one wanted to ask the obvious. It was Shmuli that broke the silence.

"They're all dead. I know it."

"My uncle died not long ago. I don't really know how long ago. My aunt was sent straight to her death at the platform. My cousin was sent to Monowitz."

"There's some good news at least. I hear Monowitz workers are treated pretty well."

I nodded in agreement and held out hope for Yanosh. I didn't know what to say about Shmuli's loss. Saying you were sorry had become trivial. A simple nod sufficed. It conveyed more than you'd think.

"My uncle insisted I find a way to survive. He said people like me had to let people know what was going here – there, I mean." I pointed behind us.

"He's right. We have to let people know. Someone will come to help."

"Do you think the Germans will come after us?" I asked.

"We were corpses, not workers. They won't notice two missing corpses. So many of them back there."

"We need to get far away from here, though."

"I heard guards talk about partisans in the woods. We have to find them. But we need to be careful. There might be patrols."

Shmuli was knowledgeable and that comforted me. I was tired and hungry. He read my mind.

"Let's try to sleep here until dawn. Then we'll look for food and clothes. These inmate rags will give us away in a moment."

We slept in close proximity, as we did in the blocks. I lay awake for an hour with one thought – I was away from Auschwitz.

I woke up in a panic. I was late for appell and – but the morning grays above the pines greeted me, not the dark rafters of a block. I had to piece together where I was and how I got there.

It was cold, though only autumn. Shmuli was balled into a fetal position. He soon woke up.

"How long have you been awake?" he asked groggily.

"Ten minutes."

"Let's get going."

"Let's go."

Deeper into the forest we found berries of some sort which clung to their twigs and lay on the ground. There were risks in eating them but they looked more appetizing than the leaves. We ate a handful each. No more.

We came across a rippling creek and drank from it. Clean water. We headed upstream where we found deeper water. Two foul-smelling boys hopped into the cold water and became cleaner than they'd been since they were packed into cattle cars.

"Where are we going?" I asked. Judging by the sun, it was late morning.

"Well, we have to find partisans. They'll help us and we'll join them." Shmuli spoke with brave noble purpose. "The Germans killed my family. I want to get back at them."

"They killed my aunt and uncle."

"And your parents?"

My parents were abstractions. I knew them only as faraway relatives from early boyhood.

"They're in Romania, in a town called Focşani. I don't know what's become of them. Maybe they're in a ghetto. Maybe they're somewhere in Auschwitz."

"I heard people on my kommando say that the Germans haven't done nearly as much in Romania as elsewhere. They'd ask about people from Bucharest and no one knew of any."

"Maybe there are camps in Romania and everywhere else."

"That could be, Herman. But if so, that's why we must become partisans."

So we were to become soldiers. Off we marched, in search of an army. Finding none that day, we covered ourselves with leaves and branches and went to sleep.

Soft clanging sounds in the distance awoke us. We stealthily walked a hundred meters and peered into a clearing – a meadow with cows, a few wearing bells around their thick necks. The peacefulness and beauty of that scene transfixed me.

Seeing no one about, we decided to treat ourselves to milk – a basic part of youth denied us for many months. Unable to find a bucket, Shmuli demonstrated the fine art of drinking directly from the udder. I thought it dangerous. Even a city boy like me knew that cows were prone to kicking, perhaps all the more so if someone besides a calf should try for a drink down there. I watched warily as he put his mouth near the udders and tugged away until milk squirted out. Hunger overcame worry and I lay under the cow. Shmuli and the cow did the rest. It was the best nourishment I'd had since arriving in Poland.

A man's voice interrupted our repast. He was probably speaking Polish. We turned in panic. It was a farmer, about forty, stout of build and non-threatening in demeanor. He could still inform on us and reap a reward, or at least avoid a harsh punishment. We were ready to make a break for the trees. Then he spoke in German, more or less a lingua franca of Central Europe.

"You boys certainly know cows. I'm Emil. And who are you two?"

"I'm Shmuli and this is Herman."

"You boys look like you've had some hard days. Are you hungry?"

We nodded.

"Come inside then. I'm up since four o'clock this morning."

We followed him a half kilometer to a cabin surrounded by chickens and goats. Chimney smoke promised warmth. We sat in chairs before a neat table as Emil fried potatoes and eggs, which he then served with bread and goat cheese. He sat at the head of the table and watched us eat. He said he lived alone. His wife had died five years earlier and his son, devastated, died not long after that.

"Where did you escape from? Don't worry, I'll not hand you over to the Germans. We Poles have hated them for centuries."

"Auschwitz," Shmuli replied.

"Those bastards are putting kids in a work camp? You're children! You should be in school!"

Shmuli and I looked at each other. He spoke first.

"Auschwitz is a *death* camp."

"The Germans murder people there. Thousands and thousands," I added. "They send trains filled with people from cities across Europe and then they work them to death or kill them with poison gas."

"Who told you these things? I'm not one to defend Germans but they would never do such things."

We recounted our experiences at the platform, in the selection yard, on work details. We described the blocks and our food. We told of the deaths of loved ones and guys next to us. A man was learning from boys that the world was darker than he'd believed possible. He'd probably heard much the same from villagers close to the camp, but refused to believe them.

"You stay here with me. The war won't last much longer. The Russians have entered Poland. They'll be here before long. I doubt they'll be gentle with the Germans."

He gave us work clothes and a clean place to sleep. There were occasional patrols in the village and rural roads, and if one were to near Emil's cabin, we were to make for the woods.

Mornings we would rise at dawn. No shouting, no beatings, no selection. Work on the farm was comparatively easy. Shmuli and I returned Emil's kindness and courage with a good day's work. We became healthier and stronger. The world was a decent place again.

CHORES AND MUSIC

We milked the cows, washed them, and tended to the pigs. The hogs were immense, at least to a city boy. Emil told us that hogs were highly intelligent animals and though I was naturally skeptical, I soon saw unmistakable signs of intelligence, cleverness, and even humor. The hogs reminded me of the gendarmerie horses.

Emil said he would hide us until the war ended, and after that he'd enroll us in school. Shmuli and I had an uncle. For now, however, we had to be careful. He took us to the cellar and pushed an empty barrel aside revealing a passage to the outside from which we could make a run for the woods.

Our Polish uncle cared for us, for our help on the farm, out of sympathy for two lost boys, and out of loneliness. One day he brought Shmuli a watch from the village market. "Swiss made," Emil noted with pride. It was wartime and people had to sell miscellaneous things to get by. He brought me a violin. I was swept by memories of lessons in Oradea and the German maestro in Auschwitz.

Emil's face betrayed expectation. A glance to Shmuli indicated the same. So I played. Not well, but my audience was appreciative all the same. A melody or two came back to me. Dinner from then on was followed by a recital.

Emil returned from the market one afternoon in an especially buoyant mood. There had been a young girl there that day, about my age, who played guitar and sang, much to the enjoyment of the people young and old. A few coins were tossed her way. Emil suggested I play with her and bring home a coin or two. I protested that I was a poor violinist but the following weekend, it was off to the village market, violin in hand.

Stands selling all sorts of things were set up at one end of the village commons. Being mid-autumn, there was little in the way of fresh food but people brought jars of fruits and vegetables and cheeses to sell and trade. Women knitted articles of clothing and offered to darn worn attire.

I heard chords from a well-tuned guitar and the mellifluous voice of a young girl. A few steps and I saw her. She was sitting on an upside-down bucket, guitar on knee. Blonde of hair, wearing a dress likely reserved for Sundays and other special days. A pink cloth was spread out before her and people tossed in small coins.

"You see? She plays very well," Emil said.

Shmuli saw my eyes and said, "More than music has reached his heart."

It was true. It was plain to all. She caught my gaze and to my delight, she smiled. She smiled to me! Then her lips moved and through my daze I realized she'd asked my name. Her voice was as lovely in spoken word as it was in song. She needed to repeat the simple question to this awkward lad. I told her my name.

"My name is Emily. I see you have a violin. Do you play?"

"Yes, of course he plays," Emil answered for me. "Herman, play for your new friend."

I somehow managed to nod and she asked me to stand next to her. A dozen or so villagers gathered around. I placed violin to chin, making sure my left wrist remained covered. "Go ahead," she urged.

Properly encouraged, I began. All from memory. My ability to read music was gone by then. I concluded the melody a bar or two early and the audience applauded, much to my surprise.

"You play so well, Herman! Please, let's play together for a while!"

I shyly agreed. Emil said he'd be looking around the stalls and to enjoy myself. She and I played. At first we'd alternate but soon enough she followed along with a melody I'd play. An hour later, the pink cloth held a dozen or so coins – a princely sum to the two young performers.

We took a break and she offered me bread and cheese that her mother had made. The bliss was broken when she asked where I was from. I was prepared to run for the cellar, sprint to the woods, but not for a simple question from a pretty girl. I told her we were from a village near the border with Czechoslovakia. I wondered if my accent betrayed that I was from much farther south than that.

"And where do you come from, Emily?"

"I live in Václavovice. We had a farm but after my father died a few years ago, my mother and I raise chickens on a smaller place. It's lovely, though. Mother's a few stalls away, selling chickens. My father gave me this guitar when I was little. I make a little money, as you can see. Mother and I get by. It's hard because of the war, but we get by."

It didn't matter what she said. I was enchanted by her voice. Yes, the same could be said of her eyes and hair and everything about her. It seems not every ounce of youth had been taken from me. I probably blathered a few things, careful not to reveal how I'd come to southern Poland.

Time raced by. Emil returned to pick me up. To my delight she asked if I could visit her and her mother in Václavovice the following Saturday. Emil nodded. On the way home, Shmuli asked how old she was and if I liked her. I replied she was fifteen and she meant a lot to me already. He and Emil cautioned me about what I might tell her.

Saturday arrived, at last, and we made the hour-long trek by horse cart to Václavovice and Emily's home. We had a light meal – not many people in Europe had large or even adequate meals in those days – then we played music. After a short concert, Emily and I walked outside on the farm, her mother along with us, of course.

"So, where did you say you came from?"

"Oh, I'm originally from Oradea but we moved to a village in Poland."

"What village?" her mother asked.

"Oh, it's near a town called Oświęcim."

"I'm sure it's as lovely as our village."

"Václavovice is much lovelier."

Her mother continued to ask about my family and my uncle's occupation. I answered them obligingly, though not in great detail.

"Herman, let's take a walk."

Emily took my hand and we walked toward the forest where a brook wound its way to a creek then to a river. She invited me to sample it and I knelt and did just that. Cold, clear, rich in minerals.

"What are you hiding, Herman?"

The question startled me.

"I just know you're hiding something. I can see it in your eyes. They dart away at times."

I was frozen. I considered making a run for it.

"Your mouth lies but your eyes tell the truth. Is it your family? Was your family not kind to you? Is that why you and your brother came here?"

"No, my family was very kind to me. My uncle gave up much for me."

She held my hand and I felt trust and honesty.

"Shmuli and I escaped from a Nazi camp called Auschwitz." I spoke quietly and looked straight into her eyes.

"Auschwitz? Where is that? I don't know it."

"It's German for Oświęcim. That's all I know. It's a death camp, a camp for killing Jews."

"Jews!" She gasped the word. "So you are Jews then. The Germans came to our village and told us about them. They are taking them from all the towns and villages."

"Yes, and then they kill them at Auschwitz."

I told her of the Oradea Mare ghetto, the cattle car journey, and in general terms, what went on at Auschwitz. I spoke honestly as though getting word out would help.

"I'm so sorry, Herman. I didn't know. I always saw the Nazis as stupid. Now I understand that they're evil. Why doesn't anyone do anything?"

"Please keep this our secret. No one can know. If the Germans find out, they will kill Shmuli, Emil, and me."

She gave me her word.

Toward evening Emil and I headed back to his farm. She was the first girl I fell in love with. I never told her that but I think she knew. A lovestruck boy gazed into her eyes and held her hand and told the truth. Yes, she knew it.

One day at the marketplace, as Emily and I played to a small gathering, two German soldiers walked down the rows of stalls. I made sure my shirt cuff covered my tattoo. They continued to come closer until they stood before us. Emily launched into another melody swiftly. The Germans seemed to be enjoying the show. Then one of them spoke to me.

"You are new here. Where did you come from?"

"I arrived only recently to live with my uncle."

"What's your name, boy?"

"Herman."

"Your last name?"

As planned, I gave them Emil's last name – Babic.

"And where do you live, Herman?"

"Near Ostrava."

"Where's your uncle?"

"Right there." I pointed to Emil and Shmuli, hoping my hand wasn't trembling much.

"How goes the music business today, my boy?"

Mercifully, Emil came over to help out. Shmuli was with him. We looked at each other cautiously.

"Are these your children?"

"Alas no. They are my wonderful nephews from Lublin, where my sister lives. They are here because it's quieter. Wonderful boys, no?"

The Germans seemed satisfied and sauntered away.

On the way home, Emil decided it was best that we not go to the marketplace anymore. There'd be other Germans who'd ask questions and might not be as easy to put off as the pair that day. Seeing my disappointment, Emil promised to take me to Emily's in a few days. That night I played my violin more yearningly than ever. I was scared and music calmed me.

Saturday with Emily. It still sounds so pleasant. We talked of growing up in Poland and Hungary, in a small village and in a large city. Sometimes I spoke of Auschwitz, mostly I didn't. I preferred to talk about football and the gendarmerie stables. Better for young hearts to talk of pleasant things.

One day, as we walked not far from her home, Emily kissed me – on the lips. It was unexpected, it was baffling, it was amazing. I had no idea how to respond. She was amused by my startled response. I must have blushed.

"Are you embarrassed?"

"No."

I must confess I wasn't telling the truth just then. She gave me another kiss and I was able to savor it. We stood there, two young lovers.

"It will be over soon," Emily said. "My mother says that the war will be over soon and you won't have to hide anymore."

As we walked back toward her house, there were two horses tied out front. Emily directed me to hide in a silage bin. I climbed in and kept still. After a few minutes I heard the voices of German men. Soldiers. Possibly the ones in the marketplace. I peered out between slats. They thanked Emily's mother, mounted up, and rode off down the dirt road.

Her mother said that they'd asked about the boy her daughter was with in the market that day. They seemed to still have suspicions and were likely to convey them to superiors. She knew about me, promised never to let the Germans know, but thought it best I never come back.

There would be no more meetings with Emily. We hugged each other and said goodbye. As Emil and I rode off, I looked back and waved.

Shmuli and I stayed around the cabin, our eyes ever on the watch for a German patrol and mindful of the shortest way to the cellar or woods. Every evening we packed a little food in the event we had to make a run for it.

We helped out on the patch of land but even that had risks. Emil told us over and over that the Russians were driving deeper into Poland. We listened for the thunder of artillery and the buzz of aircraft, but if we heard anything it was likely our hopes getting the best of us.

A sense of dread nonetheless befell Shmuli and me, and we talked in resignation that our dread would, though some unknown agency, bring great harm down on all of us.

One evening we heard cars roaring down the dirt road – more swiftly than we'd heard other motor vehicles come by. Emil peered through the window.

"Black cars! Gestapo! Down to the cellar! Now!"

My dread was becoming event. We embraced Emil. I saw he recognized his hour had come.

"You are my sons and I'm proud of you. I love you both very much. Now go!"

We scurried to the cellar opening and clambered down into the dark, mindful of where the opening was. Above us, we could hear knocks at the door then voices. A man introduced himself as a German officer and asked about two boys. Emil said they were nephews from Lublin who were away just then. The officer said that he'd checked with his sister and she had no children. He curtly added that hiding Jews was a grievous offense. Emil began to berate the Germans for killing innocent people. He shouted about cattle cars and the death camp not far away. Gunshots sounded.

Shmuli and I made our way to the forest. We walked along trails through the woods for hours, headed for Emily's village where I thought we might get information or a little help. We crawled into foliage and waited for dawn.

I could see the village and along its edge, Emily's house. I was fearful of bringing harm to her yet I desperately wanted to see her again, if only from a distance. Young hearts, foolish hearts.

Her house was still. Chickens ran about the yard, pecking for seeds on the cold ground. The door was ajar. How could I not investigate? I stealthily looked into the kitchen. More of my dread had played out into event. Emily's mother was sprawled awkwardly on the floor, numerous bullet wounds plain. Just past her – the body of my Emily in the same pitiful state.

I felt rage inside me. If I had a machine gun I would have taken on the German army. But sorrow and nausea reduced me to a sobbing boy.

I wrote a short note and left it on the table. "I love you, Emily."

We walked for days, searching for the much-rumored partisans. I was beginning to think the rumors were only that. There were villages here and there but we dared not go in them. Exhausted and increasingly incoherent, we fell asleep. We were soon awakened by footsteps and voices – Germans. Shmuli got up and ran but was cut down by submachine-gun fire. I lay there in fear.

I was taken to a holding station where I was beaten and asked for information on partisans. There was nothing to tell. I was taken to a train station and packed into a cattle car of the Death Express.

The following day, I looked out the cattle car slats and judged we were heading west. Hours later, a familiar routine played out. We were herded out of the cars and made to stand in formations. Despite my reckoning of heading west, I thought they'd seen me back to Auschwitz.

Then I heard an SS officer announce, "You are now in Dachau."

DACHAU

The SS officer's words and demeanor were familiar, though of course not in a comforting way. There were confused and worried faces, signs of hope from those who thought a work camp was better than a ghetto, men in one line, women and children in another, distraught faces, and agonized separations.

I was too weak to think clearly and I'm glad for it. Otherwise, I'd have fallen into profound despair and the spiral downward. I solemnly went through the procedure. No one seemed to care that my left wrist had already been tattooed. I saw two or three other people going through the process with similar markings.

Then it was into a block with a blanket, shoes, and bowl. It was even more crowded than the one at Birkenau. Two, sometimes three people shared the same bunk. The stench of feces and urine was everywhere. I walked down the dark aisle searching for a place to lie down. There were either too many people already or gruff refusals from bigger guys. I was near the back when I heard a youthful voice.

"There's room here."

I saw a boy's head. Dark hair and filthy face but kind eyes and a trace of a pleasant demeanor.

"Thank you." I murmured as I climbed up on the bunk. The straw mattress was damp and smelly.

"Sorry. I peed in my sleep two nights ago. My name's Leon Hirsch."

I liked him immediately.

"Herman Rittman. Don't worry about the mattress. Actually, this one's in good shape compared to what was back in Auschwitz."

"You were in Auschwitz?"

Other people heard and turned to look at me.

"How did you end up here?"

"That's a long story, Leon."

"We're not going anywhere! But first let me tell you of your present home."

His wit amused me right away. Leon had arrived from Munich with family. His mother was placed in a group of other women and sent to a sub-camp near Dachau. His father, after a few months, was sent east by train. Leon still had spirit. Spirit and wit. I benefited from both. He explained that Dachau was a labor camp with several plants that produced arms. The camp held political prisoners, criminals, homosexuals, and members of religious sects. He urged staying away from the criminals as they were a separate caste with their own ways. I knew the sort from the Auschwitz kapos with green triangles.

Leon and I worked the same kommando in a munitions factory. I polished artillery shells. Other times we worked at the Messerschmitt factory where we made aircraft parts. This was not the most arduous work at Dachau. Others worked outside at hard labor. Evidently, I'd moved up the ladder. Every two weeks or so there was a selection process and those who failed were sent east.

Leon and I became friends. But I must confess that neither one of us became too close. That was the case with most friendships there, especially after many months. There was the knowledge that a friendship could end suddenly and violently, and the emotional cost would be devastating or even catastrophic. Everyone knew it or soon learned it.

Leon kept hidden away a booklet that held his father's poems and thoughts – a diary of sorts. One of the last entries was:

I'm leaving on a train
I don't know when
There's no need to pack
There's no coming back.

One night, before lights out, we heard shouting and gunfire not far from our block. We hunkered down in our bunks, hoping it would pass soon and not come inside. More shouting, then countless staccato bursts of automatic weapons.

"There will be bodies to deal with in the morning," someone down the aisle whispered. He turned over with a long sigh and went back to sleep.

A boy of about seven snuck into our block, terror on his face.

Leon motioned for the boy to come with us. His face had been hit hard by something more than fists. Rifle butts perhaps.

"Climb up with us."

He eagerly complied.

"But stay quiet."

The violence continued nearby, then at lights out, everything fell silent.

"What's your name?"

"Andrei" he replied. The little light that came in showed the face of a boy in shock. "They killed my family – parents, brother, and sister. I don't know what happened. I just ran. I couldn't stop running in the dark until I reached this place."

"You are a brave boy, Andrei," Leon said. "You can stay with us. We'll take you to work tomorrow."

"We've all lost family here," I said.

He lay down and cried with fellow orphans.

In the morning we had to think quickly. We couldn't just take him to appell then to the factory. He was too small for our kommando. The only thing to do was hide him in the block and bring him portions of our meals.

We were pleased to see him return to life – talk, laugh, and play. He'd find a piece of wood and it would become a car to push around the floor while making motor sounds. We brought him some of our meals but somedays there wasn't any because a kapo would punish Leon and me for a transgression or just because he wanted to. Andrei was disappointed but he accepted it. He'd even pretend he was eating, much to our amusement. He became a kid brother. It was a strange feeling to have someone depending on us.

We wanted to smuggle him out of the camp. He wasn't on anyone's roster; he wouldn't come up as missing in morning formation. We looked for gaps in the fence or holes underneath it. The camps were rarely as solidly laid out as often thought. We knew that from the Oradea ghetto and even Auschwitz. Look as we did, we found nothing.

In the evenings before lights out, Andrei would stand with us outside. It was safe, or reasonably so. We'd stoop to minimize the height difference. No kapo or guard would see anything amiss. It was just a handful of prisoners talking among themselves before being locked in for the night.

Andrei asked, "Why? Why has this happened to us?"

We were older and I suppose that made him think we'd thought the matter out and arrived at an answer. Everyone in that camp, Auschwitz, and all the other camps, had asked the same question, probably every night as they looked above. We never found an answer. Not for Andrei or anyone else. His loved ones had been murdered before his eyes. There was nothing more to say.

Others in our block accepted Andrei's presence, risky though it was. They even brought him morsels of food from the mess hall. We were all in the same plight. Andrei's youthfulness appealed to us. He was a glimpse at our pasts.

Winter was coming. Southern Germany was no warmer than Hungary as best as I could tell. We kept each other from the cold as we slept, but when alone during the day, Andrei was terribly cold and in a few days he became ill. The fever and chills worsened. We applied a cool rag to his forehead. It didn't help. He was losing weight. Leon was taking ill, too.

Yanek, a doctor in our block, took a look at him, as he did for all the infirm in our block and adjacent ones. He had only an experienced hand to gauge Andrei's temperature, and his reading was not welcome news – about 40 degrees Celsius.

"Everyday I see this. Everyday." Yanek walked away.

Leon and I helped Andrei outside and placed him in a trace of fresh snow, then scraped up more for his head and torso. A few minutes of this and we brought him back inside. The fever and shivering eased.

Andrei murmured remorsefully of having been unfair to siblings. I said I was sure they were small incidents and they all knew how much he loved them. When he asked me if I thought his family members were in heaven, I had to pause.

"I'm sure they are, Andrei."

He looked to me and smiled. "It's good to have an older brother, Herman."

I woke up and saw the light of the new day. Andrei's fever was back, maybe worse. Furthermore, he was nearly unresponsive. Yanek came over and gave another brief look. He shook his head. "Brain damage, possibly. I've seen it here many times. Too many times. Very sad, very sad. Perhaps it's for the best."

One by one, pale emaciated men walked by. Some looking on sympathetically but only briefly. Most just walked by.

An older man approached us. Long gray beard, educated, more life in his eyes than the rest.

"I'm Rabbi Mendy. Is the boy your brother?"

"His family is all dead. But I'm his brother all the same," Leon said.

"I understand."

"Can you help him?"

"No, I cannot. But someone greater than us can. Let us say a prayer for –"

"Andrei."

"Let us say a prayer for Andrei this morning."

We joined hands and the Rabbi began to pray in a strong voice – this in a block where people whispered fearfully. Then Rabbi Mendy touched Andrei's forehead and whispered silently.

"It is not in our hands."

He quietly left. Leon and I hid Andrei and went off for appell.

My mind stayed with Andrei as I worked at the parts factory. After trudging back to the blocks, I immediately went to check in on Andrei. I couldn't find him and feared the worst. A kapo? A guard? Did someone inform on us? Then I saw his face groggily appear from beneath a dirty blanket.

He was feeling better and an appetite had returned. We happily gave him bread and a little dab of jam that we were given that evening.

The doctor came by and gave Andrei a look.

"No fever as best as I can tell. Well, a miracle in Dachau. A miracle, but for what."

A parade of emaciated men passed by. The skin of the faces was taut across their skulls, making them look half-dead, which most were. On and on they came. A few showed a glimmer of humanity as they looked at the block's miracle boy. The doctor saw the glimmers too and I might have seen the same thing come across his face.

"Maybe there's some hope. Maybe some of us will see this thing through. Who knows."

I didn't find religion that night. But I was amazed and encouraged. I hoped some of us would survive.

There was a guard named Fritsch. He was memorable for his cruelty, standing out among the ranks of SS guards at Dachau. Beatings and killings were part of his daily work. One day as we marched in the October chill, he called us to a halt and walked through our ranks as we shivered. His face was red from the elements, his eyes flared as he contemplated what was to come.

"You, step out!" He was clearly speaking to me. I complied.

"You, step out." He shouted to another man.

On it went until there were fifteen of us. I'd seen this before. He was going to shoot us. I had the calm of someone who knew death was at hand. My sole concern was Andrei. Who would take care of him? Leon's health was failing.

Fritsch pointed to a lateral plank that was left on an old fence.

"You! Step forward and stand there."

The first step didn't come.

"Step forward, I say!"

Slowly I walked to the plank. My head barely touched it.

"Just as I thought. It's a lucky day for you. You have set the height standard for this day. Anyone taller or shorter than the standard does not belong here. You others, form a line. Hurry!"

A boy reached the bar, and his head didn't reach the standard. Fritsch shot him in the head and he crumpled to the ground.

The next man was taller than the bar. Fritsch shot him also.

The next was taller. So was the following man. Only three of us lived through it.

Back in the block, I hugged Andrei and told him I almost lost him that day. He asked for no elaboration. He simply held me. We spoke after lights out.

"Herman, do you think that right now there are children in the world who live happy lives? Their parents put them to sleep, read them a story, and they just fall asleep without worry of someone killing them in the morning?"

"Of course, Andrei, in many places in the world it's like that. And one day it will be like that for us. All this will end and we'll be back to normal lives."

"No, Herman, life will never be the same for us. We've lost our families. We'll be given away to someone. And after all that we've seen here, we're never going to be children again."

"We'll survive this and you'll come with me."

"Thank you, Herman. But I don't think I'll live long enough to see that day."

"You're young and strong. You'll make it. We both will."

"I hope so."

Where was this world of happy, safe children in loving families? Where were these people?

The following day, on the march to the factory, an SS guard pulled a prisoner from the formation and beat him with a club. Another prisoner suddenly shouted to leave the poor man alone. The guard summoned his kapos and they formed a circle around the two inmates and beat them unconscious. We were all punished by standing in the cold for an hour.

We had musicians, artists, teachers, and doctors among us. One musician had a violin and played for us sometimes. I really don't know how he got a violin but nobody cared. We enjoyed the music immensely. I thought about asking him if I could play it for a while, but I didn't.

Two guards stormed into the block, an officer just behind them.
"Get up, all of you! Get up!"
We jumped from our beds. I covered Andrei with my blanket and told him to lie still.
The guards walked noisily down the center of the block and stopped perhaps thirty meters in. The officer spoke.
"We have reason to believe you are hiding a young boy in here. One or more of you are keeping this child. This is forbidden and requires strong measures."
He relished our fear.
"Before we perform a thorough inspection, we'll give you the chance to disclose the child's whereabouts. If you surrender him now, there will be no harm to any of you. I promise you. We are after all fair men."
Painful moments of silence followed.
"Bah! We don't have time to go through this. We have schedules to meet. If you do not surrender the child to us now, we'll have no choice but to begin executions. We shall demonstrate this resolve with you."
A guard grabbed a man who cried out and covered his head with his arms. We should have rushed them, seized their weapons, and shot them. We were hundreds, they were three. Yes, we all

would have been killed but at least we would have had a moment of revenge or justice.

A guard aimed his machine pistol at the cowering inmate on the floor and fired a burst into him. The poor man's body convulsed as each bullet hit, then fell still. Other inmates groaned and screamed until ordered to shut up.

"Where is the boy?"

Silence.

Another prisoner was thrown to the ground and shot to death.

"We will kill everyone here unless we get what we came for."

How did they find out, I wondered. How will this end? The guards went into a frenzy of beatings. Rifle butts flew, more men screamed and died, blood was everywhere.

A voice called out from the rear, "Stop!" And strangely, the guards did just that. I looked over to the bunk but Andrei was gone. I knew whose voice it was. He walked toward the SS.

"Stop killing them! Here I am. I am who you're looking for!"

He approached one of the younger guards, no more than twenty.

"I had a family until you killed them! I'm alone now."

The guards looked around at the mayhem, then at this young voice of reason, so out of place. The younger guard was unnerved. The officer saw discipline slipping away and fired a dozen rounds from his machine pistol into Andrei. He slumped to the floor.

"You killed me . . . goodbye."

Satisfied that their mission was concluded, and more than a little stunned, the SS exited the block and prepared for appell. I thought about the happy children somewhere in the world.

"Come, Herman, let us say the Kadish for Andrei. He is in good hands now."

It was the Rabbi. We cleaned Andrei's face and arranged his tunic. The weak smile I thought I saw as he spoke his last words was there. We said the Kadish. A few men joined us. We carried the small body out and gently placed it among the bodies of those who'd died in the night.

Having lost the younger brother I wanted to protect, I became listless and inattentive. I was urged on by others, especially the Rabbi, but now I too wanted to say goodbye.

Typhus struck and took away dozens of us, a few from my block alone. Camp administration issued masks to the guards. Any inmate who got too close was considered a danger and shot. Somedays we were ordered to bring corpses to appell so that they too could be counted. The Reich kept its books up to date.

There were many gentiles at Dachau. There was a young man named Kurt Traven who was a political prisoner. I saw him beaten by guards at appell and later noticed that he worked at the artillery shell plant where I was – a vast place covering many hectares. I saw him pacing about a nearby block one evening.

"I see you at the plant. You're German, aren't you? Why are you here?"

"I belonged to the White Rose."

He spoke proudly, a rarity. I think being reminded of his past enlivened him. He asked if I'd heard of the White Rose. I shook my head. What would a flower have to do with being sent to Dachau?

"The White Rose was an organization of young people, most of them in college, who tried to build an opposition to Hitler. We were in Munich, not far from here. I'm so sorry for the Jewish people and ashamed of what my country is doing, here and elsewhere. I hope there's justice someday."

The idea of a college was a frail echo in my mind. I might not have heard that word since Yanosh talked of going to one to learn engineering. So, not far from us young people went to classrooms, listened to teachers, and prepared for the future. And some of them opposed Hitler.

"Is the White Rose still in Munich?"

"I don't think so. Some of us were killed, the rest are here or in other camps."

"What did you study in school?"

"Journalism. We need to tell the German people what goes on in their own country. Germany is such a beautiful country with a rich culture and wonderful traditions. It's all being destroyed."

"You are thoughtful – and brave."

"Well, look where it got me! The leadership should be assassinated and only then will this end. Maybe someday. But how along have you been here?"

"A few weeks. I was in Auschwitz before here."

"Is it true what they say about Auschwitz?"

I told him of selections and gas chambers. His mind reeled. What he knew of Nazi barbarity was important and righteous, yet it was dwarfed by what anyone at Auschwitz knew. The cruel ideology he'd seen in Germany had constructed machinery of death in Poland.

"Those people will stand trial one day."

"What kind of punishment will they get? A little boy was just shot to death by an SS guard. What kind of punishment will his killer get? I saw SS guards smash the heads of small babies and gas thousands of people. What kind of punishment fits?"

"We are a great nation, we have morals!"

His voice was elevated, but he wasn't angry. He knew what his people were doing and he feared what would happen to them after the war.

"I'm sure there are many good Germans who want to see justice and reason prevail again. It wasn't just students in Munich. Some officers tried to kill Hitler only last summer. Oh, I have to go back before lights out. These sons of bitches will have to pay for what they're doing. I want both of us to see it."

He headed for his block and I went for mine.

I saw Kurt argue with an SS guard at the munitions plant. He accused the soldier of disgracing Germany. The guard shouted back that political prisoners were worse than Jews. He was on the verge of drawing his pistol when Kurt stabbed him to death with a file used for removing burrs from artillery rounds. Other workers kept up with their work on the noisy shop floor.

He hid the body in a storage area outside where shavings were kept and periodically sent to a smelter. A few weeks later two officers from camp administration assembled us on the shop floor. I knew why and what methods would be used.

One of the officers referred to a missing guard and stated he'd no doubt someone in the plant knew what became of him. He tried to win cooperation by saying the guard might have been injudicious and cruel at times. His demeanor changed suddenly and he stated that if he did not have information on the matter at once, he would have no choice but to kill every one of us.

The threat was not entirely convincing. Productivity would suffer greatly and with the allies coming from east and west, the Reich needed all the artillery rounds it could get. Nonetheless, a violent response was certain.

Kurt whispered to me that he knew what had to be done. He was resigned. I'd seen the look before. He handed me an envelope and asked that I get it to a loved one. I promised to do so, though of course we both knew it was unlikely. He thanked me then walked toward the SS officers.

In strong voice he admitted to killing the guard and hiding the body in a location he'd show them right away. The officers were proud that their methods had worked so quickly, and that the artillery rounds would keep coming off the line.

A civilian manager spoke up. He insisted that Kurt was a good worker but one who had become somewhat unbalanced in recent weeks. He took on a sympathetic look and said that the poor man had confessed to countless crimes to him. The manager had listened, feigned belief, then sent him back to work with a caution.

When Kurt insisted he could show them the body in the scrap shed, the manager laughed and said he went there every other day and there was no body there.

"Poor fellow. He means well but he's gone a little funny in the head. An excellent worker, though. None better."

The manager took them to the shed. There was no body or signs that one had been there. The officers were baffled and went back to the administration building.

The manager later told Kurt that he didn't like cruel guards in his plant. Yes, discipline was important, but cruelty was beyond what was called for. It interfered with production schedules for which he had to answer with higher-ups.

That night I handed the letter back to Kurt.

My health continued to deteriorate. Fever, coughing. There was blood in my hand after an especially nasty coughing bout. The doctor told me there was nothing to be done but to keep my spirits up. He had to see a man who'd been released from medical experiments. He's been subjected to rapid pressurization then depressurization and was in bad shape.

"Brain damage, it would appear. He'll be assigned to pick up the dead for a few weeks. After that, who knows. The allies will be here soon. Maybe."

ANOTHER ESCAPE

I was able to eat a little in the morning and get through work. That evening I sat with Dr Yanek and Leon. Both were in decline.

"Your youth will bring you back, Herman. I'm going to be fifty. Tomorrow, or maybe the next day, or maybe yesterday. I can't sleep well and when it comes, nightmares awaken me and bring me back to this. It's embedded in my soul. I'm damaged goods. I used to be a respectable doctor. Yes, I remember those days but I don't think I'll see them again."

Had I found any words of hope, I couldn't have spoken them convincingly. Leon asked him to think of his family.

"Yes, I used to have a wife and a son. He was a year younger than you. They were sick when we arrived here and immediately sent to the unfit group. I'm not sure that survival is a good thing anymore."

Yanek had given consent to the downward spiral.

Two days later, I believe in mid-November 1944, there was a selection. Typically they were done quickly but this one was more thorough. We were divided into three groups. One group would stay in Dachau, another would be sent to another labor camp, a third was for the weak.

We waited our turns, naked and in the cold. Yanek and I looked at each other every few minutes as the line proceeded. He reached the stand and was told to cough, raise his arms, and bend down. A doctor placed a stethoscope to his chest, then sent him to the group earmarked for another work camp.

I was next. I did the motions well and breathed in and out with the stethoscope to my chest. The doctor asked me to breathe in and out again.

"You've been sick, haven't you?"

"No, not at all. I've done my work well."

133

He was unconvinced, he was uninterested. He motioned for me to stand with the weak group.

"But I feel fit. I can do good work."

I moved my arms about to demonstrate vigor but he pointed once more to the walking dead.

I trudged over and looked around. They were sick, extremely weak, and barely able to form rows. As much as I'd resigned myself to death, facing it that day was another thing. I reflected on my months of blankness and realized that part of me still wanted to live. Memories of boyhood and play came to mind and they seemed to tell me I should have many years ahead of me.

Yanek attracted my attention from the other group. A bewildered look communicated that he didn't think I should be in the death group. I conveyed agreement. He shuffled nearer to my group and I inched toward his.

"Herman, switch places."

I shook my head.

"Take my place here, Herman. I'll take yours. I'm done, remember?"

I shook my head again, though I must say parts of me insisted that I was younger than Yanek and in at least somewhat better health. A matter of poor judgment by an overworked medic was all that kept me from his group, and him from mine.

"Switch places with me, Herman. It's what I want."

My look of sadness must have also conveyed acceptance and appreciation. I hope so. We waited a few moments until the guards looked toward the selection desks then in the blink of an eye, I was destined for labor, he for death. We reached a silent understanding that I would try to live through this and remember him. Yanek smiled.

"Move it!"

The kapos barked angrily and my group headed for the train tracks. Shortly later I heard the shriek of a whistle and in the distance, chugging out of the morning fog, was a locomotive of the Death Express.

The train came to a halt and the cattle cars opened. As we climbed in an SS guard mockingly said, "You're going to another place where work makes you free. This one is in Poland. *Auschwitz!*"

I almost laughed at the ghastly paradox. The presence of so many emaciated people held my dark humor in check. I wondered if the chances for this group were any brighter than Yanek's.

I thought again of Anton's urging last spring in Oradea but knew I'd be shot down in an instant. We were packed in tighter than in my previous experiences on the Eichmann Line. A few people died within hours.

I peeked through an opening and saw the German night, or was it a Polish night then? What became of Kurt and Leon? My mind vacillated between being grateful for life and returning to Auschwitz.

The slats were cracked and weakened, probably from previous travelers. One slat had been hastily nailed into position and with a little effort could be shoved away. I saw forests along the sides of the tracks and a familiar hope came to me. I showed the opening to the men around me but either from resignation or hope of better treatment ahead, they had no interest. One shook his head and said he didn't want to die in a cold forest.

Though not in the best of health, I determined to make a try for it and waited for the train to slow for a curve. I loved again for companions but saw no interest. I squeezed through the slats and fell headlong onto the stony surface along the tracks, and rolled until I came to a stop. Getting up on all fours, I felt for broken bones and cuts. Happily, I found only scratches and sore areas that I knew would become large bruises.

I was free, but I was alone and had no idea where I was. I walked into the forest, covered myself with leaves and branches, and slept.

The following morning I walked deeper into the forest. Which way should I go? Was there a friendly country nearby? Switzerland perhaps? Were there partisans in this forest? I drank from a small stream and decided to follow its banks. Villages are on the banks of streams. So are borders. But so are government outposts.

I came across an old couple in a cabin atop a hill not far from the stream. They were milking goats and saw me before I saw them. They weren't alarmed so they did not recognize the significance of my pajamas, though they surely noticed it wasn't traditional peasant garb. Old and isolated from the cities, especially Berlin, they had no idea who or what I was. They gave me bread and told me which direction Switzerland was. "Toward the mountains," the old man said. They had no clothes to offer.

On I walked until I again covered myself with leaves and fell asleep. I was awakened by voices then a kick in my side. Men in uniforms, but not SS. They might have been border guards. I was beaten, interrogated, then packed onto a train, judging by the sun, I was heading east, toward Poland. I was going back to Auschwitz after all.

THE ANGEL OF DEATH

Beaten, dazed, and sickly, I arrived late at night and was assigned to a temporary barracks. It had been a month and half or so since I ran from the north end of Birkenau. I saw the orderly rows of dark buildings, the tall fences with electrodes protruding from posts, and the busy chimneys of the kremas.

Morning brought a selection and there was little doubt how I would fare. I was ready for it as I stood in line and listened to classical music through the public address system.

"Move along! Move along!"

I walked as best I could and stood in front of the medic. He was young and bored. I wondered if he thought his work contributed to the German nation. To my surprise, he didn't send me to the group marked for death. I was placed in a block with other boys and young men where we went through appells, hurried meals, and marches out to perform labor.

The respite didn't last. After a week or two, those in my block were assembled in the yard and surrounded by a detail of guards and dogs. An officer conferred with a few sergeants and kapos and we were ordered to march out in the direction of the gas chambers at the north of Birkenau. No explanation was given. Either more space was needed or one of us had caused trouble that called for group punishment.

About two hundred and fifty of us young males moved out from the assembly yard, then came to a halt. Hours passed, probably as one of the gas chambers was being cleared. The guards took a break, smoking and chatting. By early afternoon we resumed the march. Some cried, some prayed, most were silent.

My mind was blank. No weeping, no praying. I walked on with the rest but didn't look at anyone. I didn't really know any of them but in a few minutes I would share a horrible experience with them.

The chamber was a hundred meters ahead. Some in the front were entering the anteroom.

Dark humor seized me. I will add that it buoyed me. It was an assertion of who I was in a dismal procedure that was going to kill me. They would take my life, but not my spirit.

There's no place like home.
All roads lead to Auschwitz.
There's no place like home.
All roads lead to Auschwitz.
There's no place like home.
All roads lead to Auschwitz.

On I walked until I reached the anteroom where we were to shed our uniforms. The motion stopped. A guard looked to the rear. An SS captain accompanied by a handful of guards brandishing machine pistols was just outside the doorway. Their uniforms were crisper than those of the goons we normally encountered. The officer's tunic, trousers, and boots were immaculate and conveyed great importance.

We assembled just outside the brick building. The guards and kapos looked deferentially to the captain. He was in charge now. He had dark hair and an almost pleasing demeanor. In another place, you might think him a good man. Here, he was another smiling Nazi. It came to me. This was the man who gave bits of bread to me and others near the gates during my days in the camp orchestra.

"It is a day of good fortune for some of you!" He spoke calmly and almost gently. "I have openings in my section and some of you will come with me."

He walked into the group and began inspecting us. The first two got only quick glances.

"Ach, unfortunately you will not be one of them."

"You I'm afraid are already gone."

He looked at me.

"Stand straight."

I did.

"How old you?"

"Fourteen."

He nudged my arm with a baton to get me to raise it, then tapped my shoulder with it.

"Turn around."

He looked to his SS attendants and said, "He's surprisingly fit. Take him." He then continued the inspection.

One of his guards shoved me out of the death group.

"You are the first one. He saved you! Come with me."

He laughed at a joke I wasn't in on.

The officer selected about fifty of us, all boys and young men, and his guards marched us away toward nearby brick buildings. Some of us had to grab prisoner uniforms from the piles in the anteroom. The other poor guys went to their deaths.

As we neared the building I brazenly asked a guard who the officer was. He smirked in a vulgar manner then jabbed me with the muzzle of his machine pistol, not nearly as hard as I'd expected. That too was puzzling.

"That was Dr Mengele. He was your savior this day."

The name meant nothing to me. The guard looked at me as though enjoying a secret, then whispered, "Dr Mengele saved you but I have a feeling you'll regret he ever laid eyes on you."

He relished the joke all the more.

So, this Mengele fellow just saved my life.

We were taken inside one of the brick buildings. It was unexpectedly warm. A nurse led us to a dining hall which was smaller and neater than anything I'd seen since schooldays in Oradea. We were given plates with generous portions of bread and potatoes, and a cup of milk as well. It was bewildering, it was suspicious. I wondered if the Red Cross was coming.

"Eat! You need to be strong," the nurse said.

She was young and pretty with delicate features, unlike the rather homely *Aufseherinnen* I'd catch glimpses of in the women's camps and elsewhere.

She pointed to the plate again. "Eat! You are severely malnourished. If you don't eat, you'll die."

Four of us were billeted in a small room with beds, not the bunks we were packed into in the blocks. There was something strange. Yes, it was the presence of a powerful antiseptic smell which while not pleasant, was preferable to the stench of the blocks and it covered up the lingering odor on us. The blanket was thin but softer to the touch than regular camp issue.

I lay down and looked up. No thick rafters, a plaster ceiling. I thought I was dreaming. In a moment I was sound asleep.

The same nurse woke us up in the morning.

"Get up! You need to eat breakfast. You'll also be treated for parasites. You'll feel much better."

Her voice was so pleasant. She told us to follow her, and that we did.

"My name is Herman. May I ask yours?"

It just came out. I have no idea how I summoned the impertinence.

"My name is Anna. So strange. No one has ever asked me that."

She was as perplexed as I, but at least she wasn't angry. In fact she giggled.

"Why are you laughing?"

She didn't answer. Another inside joke, perhaps. We were given a plate with eggs, sausage, and bread and butter. She instructed us to eat and without hesitation, we did.

"Small bites, young men. Small bites only."

I concluded my repast with a glass of milk. My impertinence arose once more.

"How long have you worked here?"

"Oh, too long, I should think."

I was intrigued by the thought of someone on the staff troubled by the work. She didn't fit here, and that was good.

"What's going to happen here?"

Anna looked at me even more sadly, then reverted to the role she was tasked to perform over and over in this theater.

"You'll help us with medical experiments. It is for the greater good of all the world. You'll help us make tremendous scientific advances."

It sounded so high-minded, it sounded so ominous.

I was taken to a room with medical equipment, including a rather large syringe which I judged, correctly as it turned out, was for me.

"Is this going to hurt?"

"Oh, Herman."

It did.

"Come, you'll need to take a shower and get hospital uniforms."

I took a shower with real soap and reasonably warm water. I was weighed. Thirty-five kilograms.

"You are very much underweight. But then so are all of you. So are all of you."

I was issued fresh hospital attire. It felt good to be clean again. After tests and paperwork, it was time for lunch. Chicken soup with ample morsels of chicken. Bread and jelly. Two decent meals within a few hours.

"Today you'll meet our chief doctor. He'll talk with you personally and examine you. He's an expert in his field and we're very fortunate to have him here."

The thought of a doctor was appealing. I remembered the doctors in Oradea and in the blocks. They were good souls, well trained and eager to help. I asked his name.

"Dr Josef Mengele."

That name again. The man who took me from the group of doomed young men a few days earlier. She retreated into detached officialdom. I was another patient once more. One of many who came and went.

Before my appointment, I was able to walk around a section of the building. I met a couple, husband and wife, a rarity in the camps as most were immediately separated on the platform. Hanna and Mendel were in their late twenties and cheerful, though they looked sickly, even stricken. They held hands and said it was a blessing that they were able to be together in that section of Auschwitz. I thought they'd gone mad under the strain of the camp or from something done to them in the building. Hanna looked much weaker than her husband.

When Anna returned, I asked her about them and instantly got a look of distance and regret.

"Hanna is sick and Mendel will be sick soon." She paused and seemed embarrassed. "But you know, Herman, this is for the good. It truly is. We will all benefit from this one day."

She saw my continued puzzlement and might have sensed my disappointment in a less than forthright response.

"Hanna has *cancer,* and Mendel will have it soon."

I'd heard of cancer back in Oradea. The word cast a dark shadow in those days. A friend of Uncle Joseph had died of it. People didn't like to say the word aloud, only in whispers.

"How do you know that Mendel will soon have cancer?"

She was taken aback that a young boy would recognize the implication of her words.

"Because, Herman, we *gave* him cancer. They are part of an experiment. Now we are testing a promising medicine on her. Soon her husband will also be quite ill."

"Has this medicine cured anyone?"

"No, not yet. But we learn more everyday."

"So what's going to happen to her?"

"Her cancer has spread throughout her body. Nothing is likely to stop it at this point. The same for Mendel in all likelihood. But Dr Mengele is learning all the same. So is German science. And that is our purpose here."

She believed this. She believed in the building, in its director, maybe even in the entire camp. They were doing things for the good of mankind. It was all part of Hitler's plan.

"She's going to die, isn't she?"

"I'm afraid she is. But it's good that the two are together. This is the end of their lives and although they didn't know that from the start, they know it now."

"So her husband is not far behind her, and he'll die also."

"I think so. Almost certainly."

She took pride in her professional assessment.

"Are they in pain?"

"Yes, but I must say they are the bravest patients we've ever seen here. They hardly ever complain and never ask for pain medication. Dr Mengele doesn't usually prescribe such things anyway. Mendel and Hanna just go on bravely. Being together gives them more time and gives us more time to learn from them. We're very proud of them."

I understood. They knew they were enduring slow painful deaths, but at least they were together, instead of being separated by a fence, worked hard, then murdered without the other knowing it. And their love for each other gave Mengele and the Reich more information.

"What are you going to do to me?"

"Oh, we haven't quite decided yet. But I do know that Dr Mengele will see you this afternoon."

Anna brought me to an examination room and gave me a gown to put on. Minutes later Mengele entered in those confident strides. He sat in front of me and looked right at me in a cheerful almost ebullient manner. No words, though he seemed eager to tell me something.

His grin revealed a gap between his front teeth. He exuded pride and energy. His brown eyes, however, had none of those things. They were emotionless, devoid of any human quality. They reminded me of the eyes of a rotting fish staring blankly from a store window. If eyes are the window to the soul, I was looking into the soul of death. I saw what lay behind every cattle car, block, kapo, guard, gas chamber, and crematory. If I'd encountered those eyes again decades later, in Europe or South America, I'd have recognized them.

"I am Dr Mengele. I understand your name is Herman."

I nodded. Again that smile and those eyes.

"I also understand that you are from Oradea. That's what you told Anna."

"Yes."

"I'm sure it's lovely there. Do you know what our mission is here, Herman?" he asked as he looked over his notes and jotted something down.

"Medical things?"

"Well, yes. Medical *research*, actually. We're conducting important research on many diseases and injuries. We're developing treatments and cures for many of them. They will help our Reich and the entire world. Do you like this idea?"

"Yes."

"Good, Herman, very good."

He jotted down more notes.

"As you know, with every important endeavor, there's a reward. But then, there's also a price."

He again looked into my eyes, ready to gauge my response.

"You and other people here will help us make important discoveries. That's the reward. The price? The price is *you*, Herman. You are the price. Do you understand what I'm saying?"

I shook my head slowly but thought of Hanna and Mendel.

"You will understand in time, Herman. All will be made clear."

He asked me about my family, medical history, education, and even if I ever had a girlfriend. Then he inquired about my family's medical history. He took occasional notes. He offered me a glass of water then gave me a physical – stethoscope, reflexes, blood pressure, and the rest. He seemed satisfied with what he saw.

"Well, Herman, you're in good shape. Frail and underweight, yes, but of course this is often the case in our camps." He almost looked embarrassed for a moment. "Are you going to help us here, Herman? Are you willing to cooperate with us with our work?"

I nodded. Was there an alternative, besides the obvious one?

"Excellent! Do you have any questions for me, Herman?"

I began to shake my head, but then a question came to mind, one that had been forming in my mind for some time. Mengele was surprised. It had probably never happened before. He sat back and waited intently for my question.

"The couple I met in the other room – Hanna and Mendel. They are sick with something. Do you make people sick here?"

How I came to ask that I don't know. More of my impertinence. Lingering exhaustion and unbridled curiosity. He was briefly taken aback.

"Remember that everything has a price, Herman. Everything, especially important things. Yes, we give you and others certain medical problems here. This is the only way we can experiment with new drugs and methods to find a cure. Do you understand now, Herman?"

"Yes, but are these people going to die?"

"Well yes, that's the price I referred to, and we must be willing to pay it."

The smile, the eyes. He wrote down a few more notes and strode out of the room.

Afterwards, I asked Anna what I would be put through. She avoided a meaningful answer. Two or three days passed uneventfully. It had been a week since Mengele took me out of the line of the dead. I was being plied with food to restore my health. After that, there would be the price.

One evening, Anna sat and watched me eat. She wasn't as engaging as usual. When I slowed my consumption, she urged me to finish up. She was biding her time, waiting for the proper moment.

"Tomorrow you'll start."

Her eyes were sorrowful for some reason.

"You've been chosen for a special experiment, one I've personally helped plan for you."

She saw anxiety pulse through me as I realized my vacation was coming to a close.

"Don't be alarmed, Herman. You'll not be placed in one of the more challenging experiments. You'll be testing the effects of confined places on people. That will be your contribution to our work here."

"So, we start tomorrow then. I'm sure it will go well."

Anna nodded.

Over the following weeks, parts of my body – a hand, arm, or leg – were enclosed inside boxes for several days. After that, the containers became larger until I was told to don a mask with a lotion coated inside, and completely enclosed in a metal case – a small coffin, one might say. I was unable to move much and there was no food or water. My only contact with the world was a tiny round aperture above my face which enabled me to breathe and see light.

The confinement went on for a few days. I became anxious, even terrified, and passed out after a day or two in my above-ground coffin. When at length I was let out, Anna was there with food and water. After a few days of recovery, another session began.

As strange as it may sound, I became accustomed to the procedure. I knew when they'd begin and in general terms at least, how long they'd last. I did not experience severe pain, only tremendous anxiety. No vicious kapo or sadistic guard, there was Anna.

Naturally, a reluctance to place myself in a confined area has stayed with me. To this day, stairways are much preferred to elevators. Not as fearsome a price as I expected, nor nearly as fearsome as many paid in Mengele's medical buildings. I have no idea what purpose the confinement experiments served.[6]

Sometime during that period, the year 1945 arrived and I turned fifteen.

---

[6]   An inquiry to Yad Vashem was unable to figure out any purpose.

I usually ate by myself during the time in the medical buildings. Other people were nearby, of course, but I preferred being on my own. Sometimes Anna was nearby. I think she wanted to chat with me at times but had to maintain official distance.

One evening in the mess hall I heard Anna's footfalls coming down the hallway. She was with a boy about my age. Looking at his emaciated frame, I could see that he was no newcomer to Auschwitz. She led him over to where I sat.

"Herman, this is Yitzhak."

He and I looked at each other but did not speak.

"Yitzhak will be in our section for a while. Like you not long ago, he has to gain strength before he can begin."

We shook hands briefly. Anna was moved, though in a sad way. I had some idea of what went on here, but I sensed he knew nothing. Anna had a meal placed before Yitzhak and urged him to eat. Uncomfortable, she left. Yitzhak looked in amazement at the sizable portions before him and the clean well-lit hall we were in. I had the same reaction when I arrived.

"Go on and eat, Yitzhak. It's all yours. But eat slowly, otherwise you'll get stomach aches. I should know. I ate fast my first meal here and had trouble all day."

I knew he wouldn't heed my caution. Inmates were simply too hungry. Once we took a nibble, an urge to devour everything in sight overwhelmed us. And that's what happened right before me. Yitzhak took a bite of bread, then another, then on to the wurst and whatever else was on the plate. He was working on the crumbs and morsels in less than five minutes. As a finishing touch, he licked the plate, as a child might to please the parents. He looked at me almost apologetically.

He was from Oradea and naturally we spoke of schools and friends, though we soon determined that we had none in common. My estimation of him increased when he said he loved football. Thirteen, an only child, he and his parents had been in the Oradea Mare ghetto and were separated on arrival at Auschwitz. By then, he knew what that meant.

Yitzhak asked what I knew he would ask the moment Anna left. "What will they do to me here?"

I wasn't going to mislead him. That would put me on the other side. I told him that it was medical research – very dangerous medical research. Some lived, some didn't. No, most didn't. He nodded. That's all. He knew enough about the camp to know there was no good place in it, only less terrible ones.

After a week of rest and decent meals, Yitzhak's part began, and I didn't see him for a while. I learned he was undergoing the same confinements that I was, at least initially. Shortly thereafter, Anna led him into the mess hall. He was trembling badly. His eyes were red and conveyed sheer terror. I patted his hand to calm him and urged him to eat.

"It was bad, Herman."

That was all he could say. He didn't have to say anything. His anguish and terror were clear. I told him it would get easier, then spoke of places in Oradea.

His second session went better, his third better still. We ate meals together when we could. He talked of a girl named Sara he was especially fond of. It was good for both of us.

"Do you think we'll live through this?" he asked one night.

"I don't really know. I suppose it's possible."

"I want to get out of this place someday. I want to see Sara again. She's a year older than I am but that's no obstacle. She's so lovely and life is beautiful with her. I hope to marry her one day."

It was sweet, it buoyed him. He never mentioned where she was then and I didn't ask. I mentioned hope of playing sports again on green fields. Try as I did to avoid emotional ties, Yitzhak was becoming a friend.

Yitzhak and I went on different schedules and ate at different times. Anna came in to give me word.

"Herman, I want to tell you something. Dr Mengele has selected Yitzhak for other experiments."

"What type of experiments?"

"We'll know more soon. You might see a change in his behavior and I want you to know that."

Anna saw my concern and for a moment I saw hers. But she wanted no more questions and retreated into officialdom.

"Finish your meal and go to your quarters. And please tell your friend of the change in routine."

Ah, so that's what this was about.

Yitzhak and I ate together soon thereafter. We chatted as I bided my time. He provided the opportunity by asking why I was so pensive.

"There's been a change. You're going to be part of new experiments."

"Oh my God! What kind?"

"I don't know, Yitzhak. I only know they'll be different. Maybe they'll be easier."

"Maybe."

I told him that he'd already been through a lot and he'd have to continue being strong. He smiled bravely and told me he would.

A week later Anna led him into the mess hall. He walked slowly and unsteadily. She helped him sit near me then stood back. His eyes were vacant. I started to greet him but saw he was still elsewhere. He stared ahead blankly. I thought he was replaying in his mind what had happened to him during the last few days. Over and over.

"Yitzhak . . . Yitzhak. . . ."

He remained in the past and refused food. I looked to Anna for explanation.

"He's been like this for a few days. Dr Mengele thought you could bring him out of it."

I had no interest in helping Mengele and Reich science, of course, but I wanted to help Yitzhak. I spoke his name several times, sometimes insistently, other times pleadingly. He remained unresponsive. Disappointed, and I believe saddened, Anna continued to watch.

I asked him questions about Oradea and specific places in the city. I asked about Sara, but there was still no connection. After quite some time, I simply asked, "What did they do to you, Yitzhak? What did they do to you?"

His eyes remained vacant but they blinked, as though trying to come back or at least to send a message that part of him was with me. I placed a spoonful of soup to him and he took it in, sipping and swallowing very slowly. I continued this, all the while talking to him, until he'd ingested most of the meal.

Anna, for one reason or another, was pleased. She patted me on the back.

"He eats, but he's not here with us, Anna."

"He's in there somewhere. I hope he feels safe."

Not long thereafter, she again brought Yitzhak to the mess hall. I tried to reach him but was unable to repeat even the meager results from the last time. Oradea . . . Sara. . . . Nothing could get him back. I did manage to get a few spoonfuls of nourishment into his system.

There was no sign of beatings or any other physical injury. His remoteness was quite different from the resignation I'd seen on those in the blocks who'd given up. They trudged along and occasionally spoke. Poor Yitzhak was further away. Mengele's experiments had damaged his brain.

A few days after that, Anna brought him to me once more. No response. I couldn't manage to get him to ingest a single bite, only a small amount of water. Anna said the he was being repeatedly injected with an experimental medicine. I'm not sure she knew just what it was or what it was supposed to do. That might have been only for higher-ups.

The next evening Mengele came into the mess hall to observe. I was unable to get any response from Yitzhak. In a matter-of-fact way he told Anna, "He's of no further use."

I came to see Anna in much less human terms. She was part of this. She worked for Mengele. I avoided looking at her. One evening she came to the mess hall alone.

"Herman? Herman?"

There was a quaver in her voice.

"Herman, Dr Mengele is sending Yitzhak away from the building. Yitzhak's done here."

For some days I'd known he was doomed, but hearing the hour was close sickened me.

"Herman," her voice became official. "Listen to me. It's not in my power to change anything. I'm not the decision maker. I'm a nurse. Yitzhak is leaving here. Listen, Herman, I want to suggest something. Yitzhak will have one more meal here this evening. He will leave in the morning. You can help him. I'll give you a cup of liquid and I want you to help him drink it."

My look of incomprehension must have been obvious.

"This will be a special drink. One with medicine. It's the best thing. Do you understand? He'll simply fall asleep."

I understood. I understood that Yitzhak's dreams of football and Oradea and Sara would end but at least he'd be out of Auschwitz.

"It's the best thing, Herman. I'll get him now."

Anna brought Yitzhak into the now empty mess hall. I tried to reach him, though I knew it was pointless. Efforts to get him to eat failed too. I looked into Yitzhak's eyes, though his gaze went straight through me.

"Yitzhak my friend, I wish I had better news, but there isn't any here tonight. Tomorrow morning Mengele will send you to the gas chamber. I have a drink here that will put you to sleep. It will put you to sleep forever. It's better this way, Yitzhak. You have to help me. You have to drink it."

He blinked. Yitzhak was giving consent.

I lifted the cup to his mouth and he took a few cautious sips. I raised the cup higher until its contents were soon gone.

Anna thanked me and started to take Yitzhak away.

"Can he stay here awhile?"

"Yes, Herman, but not long. It's better that he be in his bed."

I sat there with Yitzhak for some time, my hand resting on his. I said farewell to him, then watched him walk away unsteadily with Anna's help.[7]

Hanna and Mendel's health fluctuated. They told me of their love for music, especially the violin and piano. They were given instruments to play for the after-work entertainment of the medical staff and some patients. One evening I was in attendance. So was Mengele. I was seated far away.

Hanna played the violin, Mendel the piano. It was lovely. It was also a jarring paradox. There in the room were men and women who conducted procedures that inflicted terrible pain and death, but who were now enjoying a delicate piece of classical music, as though in a fashionable Berlin drawing room. Those men and women were having a social hour, as would employees of a government bureau or a manufacturing concern. Laughter and gayety, conversation and flirtation. Mozart for murderers.

The stricken couple began their performance. A violin beneath her chin, Hanna's face conveyed passion but occasional discomfort. She lost her timing and began to play ahead. Mendel tried to catch up but as soon as he found the right place Hanna would jump to another stanza. They'd conclude one piece but the instant a patter of applause began, she'd start another. Her performance became frenzied and then lost any relationship to the score. Mendel stopped

---

[7]   It's uncertain what Mengele had been injecting into Yitzhak. It's possible that there was some research involved but so much of what went on there had no relationship to medicine. Mengele simply enjoyed inflicting pain and illness on people, until they were of no further use. Maybe it was just a poison that Mengele had a fondness for.

completely. She called out his name, dropped the violin to the floor, and slumped into his arms.

"Mendel, hold me! Please hold me!"

"I'm here with you."

"I'm going away, Mendel. Please kiss me."

Hanna was succumbing to the experiments that people in that room had forced on her. The doctors did not rush to her aid. They watched as though it was part of a research lecture or a scene from a familiar play. Perhaps they planned an autopsy in the morning.

One doctor said, "Such a shame. The concert was going so delightfully." Other staff members concurred. And with that, they filed out of the room. Mengele remained, though. He strode up to Mendel as he continued to hold his wife.

"She was a fine musician."

Mengele spoke without a trace of sympathy or any other human emotion.

"I can't live without her," Mendel whimpered.

"Ah, but you won't have to."

There was neither no intended cruelty. It was simply how Mengele related to us. He could be engaging and affable, but our deaths were of no more significance than that of a small insect.

Mendel was incredulous at such heartlessness. His glare conveyed contempt more than any words could. Mengele didn't care about insect noises. He turned and left. That was the last time I saw him.

A few of us, including Anna, carried Hanna's body to the couple's room and gently placed her on the bed. Mendel folded her hands across her front. I stood silently for a moment. Anna offered Mendel a medicine cup. He looked at it briefly, then thanked her.

I said how sorry I was. Another death in one of the dark blocks or a worksite or a shower room would not have affected me. Not much anyway. But here in the surreal medical experiments building, death hurt me.

He drank the medicine then shook my hand. "Take care, Herman my friend. Take care." Mendel then lay down next to Hanna.

I sat in my quarters, replaying events. Anna came to apprise me of the following day's schedule.

"We'll never see them again, will we?"

"Go to sleep, Herman. New things are coming tomorrow. I don't know if they're good or bad but I hope they're good for you. I simply don't know anymore. Sometimes I think that anywhere is better than here, but only time will tell."

Anna stopped as she reached the doorway. Without facing me she said,

"No, Herman, we'll never see them again."

I kept thinking of Hanna and Mendel playing music together. I fell asleep only very late.

Anna woke me up, obviously worried.

"You're being taken away. All of you. I don't know where to. All the staff here is packing up and going to another camp. I must pack as well, so I cannot stay long. Put this bread in your pocket. And you must change back into a striped uniform."

She was near tears.

"Herman, I don't know how to say this." Her voice quavered and tears fell. "I'm very sorry for what's happened to you and others here. I wish I could stop it."

She looked around the room as though a way might come to her. Strangely, I think she cared about me. Maybe I reminded her of a younger brother who was gone in the war, or of another boy who'd come to the building then paid the price. Was it by chance that I was spared from lethal experiments? No. Someone on Joseph Mengele's staff had grown fond of me, and I of her. So strange what life shows us.

"Oh, Herman. Seeing Hanna and Mendel over the last few weeks saddened me. Many times I offered them something to end the pain, and each time they refused. He once said it was against his religion to commit suicide. Last night I told him it was medicine."

It sank in and fit with my suspicions. A moment of decency intermingled with death.

"But he knew."

She hugged me, as though I was the only source of light left.

"I have to take you and the others out to the yard now."

"Are we –?"

"No. You're going to another camp to the west. Take care of yourself, Herman. It won't be long now."

I left the paradoxical safety of Mengele's building and stood in the January cold. Back again in prison issue, I took my place in the long, silent rows and columns with hundreds of others and listened to classical music from the speakers.

That morning, there might have been many thousands of us. I looked for familiar faces, especially Yanosh's, but without success. I thought how horrid this world is, and wondered what lay ahead.

Death March

Mengele's buildings were warm. I must say that. Out in the field, the bitter cold ran through my uniform and pierced me like a thousand razors. My teeth chattered noisily. We stood for hours, far more than I'd ever experienced.

Appells were usually organized. There was work to be done and German efficiency prevailed. There was less order that morning. A few men fell to the ground. I tore off pieces of bread and surreptitiously chewed them. Fuel for the furnace. Finally, an SS officer addressed us.

"We have received urgent orders to move to another camp – a work camp in the Fatherland. There we shall continue to support the war effort and ensure many more victories to come. We shall depart momentarily."

"Lying bastard! You are losing the war."

An odd, emaciated man in his thirties, eyes sunk into his skull like most of us, muttered not far from me. He saw my interest.

"Germany is losing, I tell you. The Russians are drawing closer and closer. They are deep into Poland and will soon be in his precious *Fatherland*. That's why we're being moved."

"How do you know?"

"I have ways of knowing."

He wasn't in a striped uniform. For some reason he wore dark-blue work clothing. The stubble of his beard seemed glued to his face. When he spoke it was clear he'd lost a few teeth. It all contributed to a crazed look. I thought he had broken from reality altogether and had fled into an inner world of fantasy, like that affluent woman in the cattle car who headed for Lublin. Many in the camps happily took the same trip.

He said his name was Benjamin and asked where my block was. I told him that I was in the medical experiments building.

"Oh, dear God!" He looked at my face and shoulders. "You seem well. Most don't come out."

"Yes, I was lucky."

If I'd told him of my protective nurse, he'd have thought I was the crazed one.

"I know about what's coming. The Nazis are moving us to camps inside Germany because they're losing the war and need labor to build a final defense. What great news that is!"

I can't recall seeing more joy in an inmate.

"We have to get through this journey into his precious Fatherland, boy. We must. I'll tell you two things. First, the journey won't be short, and second, they'll give us no food on it."

Long march, no food. I looked around and wondered how many of us would fall along the way, with an SS guard to finish the job with a shot or two. Then I thought they'd want to save every round for the final defense.

"How do they expect to get us into Germany?"

"That's exactly the point, young man. They don't."

I began to think Benjamin was one of the inmates who prided himself on great knowledge – the inside dope, as they say – but who had only heard a rumor or two and elaborated upon them until they'd become a personal dogma.

"It's another one of their ways to kill more of us. Death by long marches in the January cold. I worked with a man that was on one such march and had the good fortune to survive it. It will be a *death march*, my boy."

It made sense. Clearly, the camps were designed to kill us, either through labor, malnutrition, beatings, bullets, or gas. Someone in an office somewhere had plotted a new method. Men who killed small children with poison gas or by smashing their skulls would look upon a death march as one of their less brutal and less memorable endeavors. I felt how much bread I had in my pocket and wondered how far I had to go.

"Mark this day well, boy. This is the day that you started off on a death march. I don't know where we're going but we'll make it. I was an historian in Munich and I'll be one again when this is over. There's so much to write about. There's so much to document. It has to be remembered. I intend to survive this damn war!"

I looked at him more and saw another scarecrow of a man whose flesh wrapped tightly around his skull. How many had I seen fall down, or get sent into the line for the north end of Birkenau, or stumble out to grab the wire? But I started to see his look not as crazed, but as determined. It fascinated me and I decided that when the time came, I'd give him some of my food.

There was a quick selection and a few hundred were spared the travails of the road. Shortly thereafter we marched out of Auschwitz-Birkenau.

It felt good to be out of there. Instead of rows of bleak barracks and administrative buildings and vicious guards, I saw tree-lined lanes, rural villages, and simple farmers. It was almost pleasant, relatively speaking of course. Only at first.

The cold cut though us, so we bunched together and kept up a pace to circulate thin blood through weak bodies. We had to slow considerably after a few hours. Many could not keep up or fell to the ground. SS soldiers, some in military vehicles, some on foot, finished them off. Loud staccato reports could be heard every half hour or so.

Benjamin walked without any difficulty and again I wondered where his power came from. He marched along with a fierce look. "These bastards will not defeat me." I think he was writing lecture notes and chapter outlines in his mind. He looked to me and grinned. "You have to hold on, boy. Hold on. Freedom is almost here." And so we walked on to the west.

I handed him a chunk of bread. He was amazed. "You must have a guardian angel above you, boy." He smiled and hurriedly crammed the bread into his mouth.

The march went into the night, and all through it. In the morning gray, we entered a village. The road signs were still in Polish. A few people were up and out. They stopped and stared at us as though we were ghastly apparitions from the beyond – kilometer after kilometer of grimy wraiths in tattered clothing, trudging along country roads, escorted by beastly guards.

Some of the villagers looked upon us with sorrowful eyes and tried to hand us food and water. But the SS shouted at them to stop, saying we were Jews and deserved no favors.

One woman was splendidly dressed, as though on her way to a religious service or town social. She was stunned and made a point to look at individuals as they filed by. As we reached her, Benjamin smiled and bowed courteously. He even pretended to tip his hat, conveying kind regards for the new day. She understood his dark humor and smiled briefly.

Another day of the death march was coming to a close. I was near collapse. SS guards came by intermittently and I continued to hear shooting. I'd lost feeling in my toes and most of my body. As night fell once more, we were unable to see more than a few feet ahead of us. We simply followed the fellow in front of us and put one foot out in front of the other.

I looked over to Benjamin and told him I couldn't go on anymore. I was done for.

"Yes you can, boy. You have to show them."

I pushed on. I couldn't see well anymore. It wasn't simply the night. My vision was failing. The glimmers of moving objects were badly blurred.

The temptation to fall and just lay on the ground was strong, though I knew my rest would have ended with a swift dispatch into nothingness. I pressed forward with dwindling powers. I daydreamed of a soft, warm, white bed on which I'd sleep an entire weekend. So pleasant, so appealing – so distracting. I tripped and started to fall. A hand reached out from the dark and pulled me up. It was Benjamin, of course. He supported me for a few more moments until I was able to get back into the rhythm. I was too weak to thank him.

Amid the daze I wondered what force in the world gave him such strength. I was unable to think clearly but there was a vast reservoir of energy near me upon which I could draw as needed.

At length we arrived at the city of Wodzislaw, about seventy kilometers from Auschwitz. We were allowed to sit on the ground as the SS performed another quick selection. The machine pistols rang out. The rest of us were packed into cattle cars and sent across the border into Germany. We soon came to a halt at a camp called Gross-Rosen.[8]

---

[8] On January 18th 1945, tens of thousands of inmates began the Death March from Auschwitz and its many sub-camps to Gross-Rosen and other sites. About twenty-five percent perished along the way.

GROSS-ROSEN

Thousands of us arrived late at night and were immediately allocated into the main camp and several sub-camps. We were given something to eat. It was only thin tasteless soup but it gave warmth and energy.

We were assigned to blocks, the same design as at Auschwitz and Dachau. Inside were the familiar wooden bunks and straw mattresses. After the long march and intermittent executions, the blocks were almost a welcome sight. The straw was quite dry and we were not as crammed in as elsewhere. We later learned these blocks were recent additions and other ones were much worse.

The next morning we were assigned to work kommandos. The regimen at Gross-Rosen was very harsh. The extreme cold and twelve-hour workday made for high mortality rates, especially after the march. The hope that anyplace would be better than Auschwitz faded.

Benjamin and I were assigned to a granite quarry. I knocked away loose material from immense slabs. Benjamin split large stones and ground them into construction material. Very difficult work. Very dangerous too. He was nonetheless optimistic. Liberation was at hand. He had no doubt.

"We're almost there. It's February and I hear the winds of freedom blowing more strongly everyday, from east and west."

Beneath his grimy beard I could see a confident smile. He never ceased to impress me.

"I'm an historian! I have to survive to tell of this. It's my duty. Just wait and see. I will write a thick book about everything my eyes have seen and my body and soul have endured. Ah, my book will be amazing!"

Yes, a man drove himself to survive in order to document it all. He amazed me and gave me strength.

The SS became more abusive. They beat us more and cut our rations. Deaths were increasingly common. We thought the increased brutality was the result of steady losses on the fronts and imminent defeat. The rumors of the Red Army closing in were encouraging. The Russians took on heroic hues in our minds and at night we'd listen for artillery.

One of our tasks was heaping granite into large metal bins that were hoisted out of the pit by an immense crane. It creaked and groaned as it slowly lifted cargo high into the air. The guards enjoyed ordering us to stand beneath the bins as they went skyward. If the material dropped for one reason or another, we'd be crushed to death. And of course the rules of the game stipulated that anyone who refused to play along would be shot.

One day, an obese and sickly guard ordered us to place a greater quantity of granite than usual into a bin. The more weight, the greater danger. A half dozen of us were ordered to stand beneath the bin as it began the ascent. The crane groaned and creaked far more loudly than before. We looked skyward as it protested the unfair burden.

The machinery fell silent. The bin slowed to a halt then swayed back and forth. The engine above sputtered back to life then backfired loudly before quitting again. A moment later the bin began to come down in short awkward lurches. A safety mechanism kicked in, but the descent continued.

"Stay right where you are," the guard chortled amid coughing bouts, rifle at the ready.

As I stood there with tons of rock coming down on me, and a guard eager to shoot me, well, I thought a fifteen-year-old boy would become another nameless corpse. I shouted out to no one in particular.

The guard's chortling turned into uncontrolled coughing. He grabbed his chest, and his face reddened and showed signs of alarm. He was struggling for air. No one rushed to his aid, needless to say. We were still afraid to leave our position beneath the bin.

"I'm coming!"

A voice called out from well above us. I looked up into the sunlight and saw a man racing to the crane. He grabbed a lever near the immense gears and pulled with all this might. More growling metal and squeaking cables, but the bin kept moving. To my horror the man placed himself into the gear mechanism and let the cogs slowly pull him in, crushing him but jamming the machinery. The bin came to a halt.

With the guard clearly incapacitated, a few of us clambered up the long walkway to the rim of the pit to see what could be done for the man. It was Benjamin. He was hideously mangled. Blood was coming from his mouth as his lungs and stomach had been pierced by broken ribs. We tried to extricate him but could not.

I looked to him as though asking why.

"I don't know, Herman. I don't know. I'll not be able to write that history." He looked at his grotesquely disfigured body and wryly said, "My day has been ruined. Take care, my boy."

And with that, he and his chapter outlines were gone.

"Out of the way! Out of the way!"

SS guards were racing to the scene.

"What do we have here? What happened?"

Someone gave a brief reply, then the guard looked at Benjamin.

"I knew that Jew. He was a hard worker. He died saving you scum? Not worth it, old fool, not worth it. Back to work. We'll get the crane back in operation soon."

We left Benjamin's remains in the gears and returned to work. Later that day a team of engineers repaired the crane. The SS told me and another boy to toss Benjamin's body in a pile of dead not far from the pit. We'd put corpses there before. Death worked alongside us. We laid him on the ground near a tree and arranged him to appear as though he was sleeping. A final dignity.

I sank into depression, again. I performed my labor, ate with indifference, and spoke to others as little as possible. I'd loved Benjamin, and wanted no more of the sorrows that came with that emotion. I came to think love had no place in Nazi camps, and that it was only a pleasant but fleeting illusion outside them. I thought of Benjamin's reason for existence, of his request, and of my feeble, unspoken promise to remember.

Cold and alone, shivering beneath a thin blanket, I thought back to boyhood in Oradea, the ghetto, and the camps I'd been at over the last eight months. I'd never forget those events. Yes, they should be written down somewhere, someday, someplace – someplace far from Germany and Poland. I thought it might serve as a record and also as a warning. I fell asleep.

It was March 1945 and everywhere there was talk that the Third Reich would soon fall. We were assembled in the main yard where the commandant informed us of another move, another death march. He noted that those unable to make the march would be shot, so we braced ourselves for the effort. I thought back to the march of just a few weeks earlier and locked my mind into the routine of placing one foot in front of the other. A misstep and I might not be able to get back up. I could no longer rely on someone to help me up.

We were issued a ration of bread and a substance resembling butter, then we marched out of Gross-Rosen. Our destination was unknown to us. As I thought, we marched west, away from the Russian army, deeper into Germany. I wondered how far away the Americans and British were.

The march lasted several days, longer than the one from Auschwitz to Wodzislaw in January. The elements, the hunger, and the exhaustion took a predictably heavy toll. SS guards herded us, others raced by in vehicles.

The roadsigns were in German. Simple villagers came out to look at the march of the emaciated, the parade of cadavers. Again I saw sympathy on the faces of onlookers. So it wasn't Germans

I should hate, only Nazis. I marched with that thought, step after step, mile after mile.

Finally, we came to another camp. I was wrong a few months back as I walked to the gas chamber. All roads do not lead to Auschwitz. This one led back to Dachau.

Dachau, again

As we trudged through the gates I recognized buildings and yards and walls. Why was fate pushing me back and forth between Auschwitz and Dachau? I was trapped on an immense broken record. Fortunately, "Twilight of the Gods" was playing and it would soon end.

Dark humor helped. I thought to myself that the Third Reich should have had the consideration to show me one of their many other camps. I laughed at this – not inside to myself, but aloud. Those near me looked over, then went back to the march into Dachau. I appeared to be another case of someone breaking down into private madness.

It was quite the opposite. My dark humor, which has stayed with me to this day, and which I consider an integral part of me, kept me from hopping aboard the Lublin train. I was mastering the situation by asserting Herman Rittman over it, by placing his stamp on it, then putting one foot in front of the other. Dark humor makes you free.

Something was different. The SS guards and officers were not intimidating us. The first hours at a camp usually saw shouting and beating and summary executions. Nothing like that this day. We were placed into a block and left alone. No one inspected us, no one ordered us into the bunks.

I sat on a mildewy wooden shelf and listened to men talk about the new place, the odd laxity, and the end to the war. One spoke quietly and cynically.

"I stopped believing in this end of the war talk long ago. I've heard it for too long and nothing ever comes of it."

He was another living skeleton. Sunken eyes, grimy uniform. Probably mid-twenties. I looked like a younger version of him.

"I'm Herman Rittman."

"Juda Shapher. How long were you in Gross-Rosen?"

"Not long. A few weeks. We were marched there from Auschwitz."

"Ah, and you survived it. Happy?"

I didn't understand the question or even if it was one.

"Were you happy you survived the march? Or would you prefer to have died somewhere along the way?"

"Surviving was good fortune. A friend helped me through. He died in a quarry at Gross-Rosen. An amazing man, an historian. I was lucky to have come across him under any circumstances."

Juda was neither moved nor interested. I better understood his question. He was bitter and cynical.

"You know, based on what I see here now, I believe the war is truly nearing an end – a bad one for Germany and for these guards here."

"Oh, I see. Please be so kind as to explain to me how you arrived at this cheerful conclusion."

Juda was interested only in my naivety.

"I was here a few months ago and the place is very different. The guards were more energetic, enthusiastic, and how to say it –"

"More murderous?"

A man answered for me.

"Yes, they were more murderous back then. They were eager to do their killing because they had faith in the Reich and in victory. Now? They've lost hope. It's *they* who've lost hope. It's on their faces and in the way they no longer enforce rules like lights out. They just took us here and left us."

Juda waved his hand dismissively. The man did the same as he turned away.

"Ah, that's simply because we arrived late and they were tired. Tomorrow they'll butcher us as usual and you'll all feel right at home again."

At least he had dark humor. I spoke up.

"Maybe, maybe not. New people have the word. They say the Russians are coming from the east, and the British and Americans are coming from the west. The Germans are losing. They're on the run."

"And these new people are correct."

A new voice, one of an older man. He said he was called Moritz.

"Yes, the allies are closing in, but that's all the more reason to be alarmed. The Nazis are ordering death marches from all their camps. They want to destroy evidence of what they've been doing over the years. Buildings can be blown up, bodies can be buried or burned. But us? We're witnesses. We can put nooses around their necks!"

"So they want us all dead."

"Exactly, young man. But their plan won't succeed. There are too many of us. Some of us will get through these last weeks and tell the story."

"I wouldn't count on it. They're very efficient at killing large numbers of people in case you haven't noticed. They've mastered the process," Juda countered.

"I'm only saying that we need to follow their orders and keep a low profile for the next few weeks, until we're liberated. It's April – springtime."

"You talk as though we cause trouble wherever we go! We obeyed – always. We kept low – always. And did it help? No! We were beaten and killed. I agree with what you say about killing all the witnesses, but they're too clever, too fiendish. They'll find a way to kill us just before their Reich comes crashing down. It's in their plan. It's in their culture. It's in their Wagner. Mark my words and mark them well. Aah, I'm going to sleep now. My plan, friends, is not to make a plan. We may only live until tomorrow noon."

With that, Juda was off.

"I've seen many like him. Go to sleep, Herman. We have a different plan for the next few weeks – surviving the next few weeks!"

It was time for me to nod off. I reached for my blanket and remembered I hadn't been issued one.

The next morning we were assigned to an armaments factory, not the one that I worked before that made artillery rounds. This was a smaller plant that made machine-gun parts. The parts were made with very low tolerances to make the weapons fire more rapidly. The plant wasn't operating at capacity. Far from it. Things were winding down, maybe because there were supply shortages.

I tried to learn information about Leon and Kurt, my fellow inmate who'd been with the White Rose, but was unable to find out anything.

There was only one civilian engineer and an SS guard, though at times even the guard was absent. We had time to talk about the war and what might happen afterwards. We were mindful of warnings that we could all be massacred. All we could do was stick to the routine.

One morning we were assembled in the yard, as usual. We stood longer than usual, though. At least it was no longer winter.

"Something's wrong," Moritz whispered. "We should have been marched to work by now."

I too felt uneasy.

After a long period of nervous waiting we were ordered to form rows and columns. A hundred or more of us, flanked by more guards than expected, marched away from the assembly yard and then outside the fences. About a hundred meters behind a pair of guards towed a large weapon mounted on two wheels. I'd never seen one before.[9]

We marched to a small hill in a wooded area. Below I could see a swift-moving stream which might take me swiftly away from there, if I could reach it. We were ordered to march down the slope and line up along the bank. Moritz whispered goodbye to me.

The SS officer finished conferring with the sergeants and stood in a manner of a man about to read a verdict.

---

[9] Many years later I determined the weapon might have been a Flugabwehrkanon 38 – a 20mm antiaircraft gun.

"Today, work will be here in the forest. You will cut down trees and bring firewood to the camp. Implements will arrive shortly. Anyone trying to escape will be shot."

The large weapon was wheeled to the top of the rise and an ammunition belt was seated with a loud clank that reached the riverbank. If any of us made a run for it, the shooting would start immediately, beginning with the escapees. Behind me, a pastoral image of a Bavarian stream complete with ducks gently skimming the glassy surface. Before me, an SS detail determined to eliminate witnesses. It was warm and sunny.

Nazi propaganda about the Jews taking over Germany came to mind. I'd asked my uncle how those lies came about and he replied they'd always been part of history. Here I was in another chapter in that history and in the final act of a Nazi opera.

Fifteen years of life and I hadn't had the opportunity to do much. I thought about all the things I could have done – learning a skill related to cars, finding love, and raising a family. I thought what a dreadful world I lived in.

Loud staccato bursts came from the front. The ducks took flight. The wheeled gun was firing at an incredibly rapid rate, each round giving out a deep report that reverberated in my chest. The other SS guards opened up with machine pistols. Those who made a run for it were mowed down instantly. I went to the ground. Most of us, I believe, had accepted our fates and lay on the ground until the bullets struck. Some remained standing.

Moritz lay to my left. He gave me a look of sad farewell and turned to the ground, closing his eyes. His head jolted back violently as a bullet struck his temple. A dead man fell on top of me. The massacre continued. Men screamed and cried. There were thumps as bullets struck and bodies fell.

The big gun fell silent. I heard that metallic clank and the fusillade erupted once more. After a few minutes, the shooting stopped again. SS guards walked down the hill and stepped through the mass of bodies, occasionally finding someone alive, then finishing him off. A thick boot came down near me but moved on.

"We're done here. Back to camp." I squinted and saw the SS wheel that immense gun around and head for Dachau. One of them looked back briefly at his work.

I lay there for at least a half hour, afraid to move. Blood trickled down on me from corpses but I still didn't move. Behind me I heard the ducks once again, paddling in the stream, searching for food.

"This is your signal to get up, Herman," I said to myself. "You have to find the strength to stand up and get away from here."

I refused.

"You have to get up, Herman – now!"

I moved a hand to the front and came upon a motionless torso. A simple effort normally, it expended a considerable amount of my energy. I pushed one leg back then the other, and used the leverage to slowly raise up. There in the bright late morning light were scores of corpses, grotesquely arrayed along the grassy river bank, blood splattered on the striped uniforms and reeds. Flies were gathering.

My pant leg felt heavy and wet. I reached down and felt a sticky fluid. I thought I'd been shot but didn't feel pain. It was someone else's blood. There was a muffled groan near me. An unsteady hand moved. It was Moritz. The bullet had left a dreadful wound on his head, but he was alive all the same. He tentatively felt the blood and the edges of the wound.

"I was shot in the head, I was shot in the head."

I looked closely at the wound and saw jagged pieces of skull and splotches of bloody hair. I knew of no words for that situation. None.

"I'm dead. I was shot in the head. I'm dead."

"No, you're not dead, Moritz." I clasped a hand on his shoulder.

"I'm dead. I was shot in the head. I'm dead."

"Look at me, Moritz, look at me! There are many dead people here and you are not one of them."

I helped him up but he immediately crumpled to his knees.

"I'm not going to make it."

"Yes, you are. Stand up! Many people are shot in the head and live through it."

I don't know where my expertise in head wounds came from that morning, but my words had their intended effect. He stood and looked at me.

"Pain . . . but not too bad. There are worse things."

"See? The wound isn't serious."

"Yes. I think you're right. I feel good enough. Let's get away from here."

So, a fortunate boy and a man with bullet hole in his head walked away from the slaughter and knelt at the edge of the stream to clean our hands and clothing. We heard motion behind us and saw others rise from the dead and stagger to the water. There were about five of us, ranging from youths to a man in his fifties.

"Murderers," said one. "This was cold-blooded murder."

I looked back at the most recent example of the Third Reich's barbarity. I felt that by surveying the scene for a moment I was showing defiance and paying respect, not just fleeing in horror.

After a few moments I suggested we head into the woods. The SS might come back, perhaps with another group selected to cut wood along the river beneath the hill.

We came to an opening and could see rows of plants and animal pens, though not a single person. I entered a barn hoping to find something to eat. The door creaked eerily and I saw two men and a woman. The men were balling hay and the woman was grooming a horse. They stared at us, and we at them. They would help us, I thought, just as Emil the Polish farmer had helped me.

"Jews!" one of the men exclaimed angrily, pointing a finger at us then grabbing a pitchfork.

Rather than compliment the fellow on his keen observation, I ran back toward the woods with the others. They chased us with pitchfork and shovels but relented once we got well into the woods.

We ate berries and rested. Where were we? Which way was Dachau? Were German soldiers nearby? There was no way of knowing anything. It about noon and I couldn't even tell east from west.

Moritz's wound was sickening to look at. His thin hair was matted over the wound. A trail of black, hardened blood had formed down his face and neck. He nonetheless devoured berries and remained alert.

I mentioned my previous forays into the woods and said that it was best to stay in hiding. When one young man said we should look for partisans, I told him to forget those stories. We got up and walked through the forest, looking for more food and a creek.

We came upon a dirt road. A roar of motor vehicles came from the distance. They were getting closer. I motioned for the others to get back into the woods, but I stayed at the edge. Clangs and screeches got nearer. I saw tanks. But whose?

"They're German," someone said from the woods. Three of our band retreated into the forest but Moritz and I stayed put in a crouch.

I didn't think they were German. I'd seen panzers on railroad tracks and on convoys, but these were shaped differently – higher off the ground. A few foot soldiers were ahead of the column and on either side of it. But who were they?

The sun offered a clue. They were coming from the west. The Russians would be coming from the east. The tanks grew nearer. "What if they turn out to be Germans," I asked myself. Then I saw a marking. No swastika, no red star. A white star.

The lead tank lurched to a noisy stop fifty meters in front of us. Two foot soldiers approached us. They lowered their rifles as they saw two filthy, emaciated, bloodstained scarecrows. The commander of the lead tank hopped down and came to us. The three stared at us and conferred briefly. Then one of them said, "Wir sind Amerikaner. Versteh? Amerikaner. GIs."

I'd lived through it. Incredibly, I'd lived through it.

RETRIBUTION

The others came out to cheer and weep. Days ago we were slaves. Hours ago we were mowed down along a stream. Now we were free. More Americans climbed down from their tanks and half-tracks and looked upon the scarecrows in strange filthy garb. A few of us hugged our liberators and sang songs to them. We picked up one GI and held him high above our shoulders. A medic took Moritz to the rear of the column and that was the last I saw of him.

The Americans gave us water and C-rations and even chocolate bars. They were horrified by our condition and couldn't understand what had happened to us. Many were angry. We told a German speaker of the camps and of the one nearby – Dachau. An officer to lead them there but most of us wanted no part it. I agreed to show them the way as best I could and in a few moments a Hungarian boy stood in a half-track that clanged its way down a Bavarian road. No rifle butt or bullet could harm me. It was impossible not to feel powerful and proud and even victorious. And it was impossible not to think that vengeance was at hand. It was on more than one GI face.

I gave the general direction and army maps provided the rest. We were soon a few hundred meters from the fences. There were no crowded assembly yards or guards leading columns of inmates off to work. The camp was motionless. The watchtowers were still manned, though. I wanted the Americans shoot them but I was hardly in command. Above the din of the engines shouts of inmates were heard, then gunfire.

"They're shooting them," a GI said. He ordered me to dismount and get to the rear.

The Americans fired machine-gun bursts into the watchtowers, sending bright tracer streaks across the sky. Chunks of concrete and wood flew off the towers. Hands went up, guards came down.

The GIs entered the camp in combat intervals and were greeted by hundreds of jubilant inmates streaming out of the blocks and lining up along the fences shouting, "Americans! Americans!" The newly freed men cried, laughed, and hugged the GIs, then cried more. The Americans were dumbfounded by thousands more scarecrows. We were not exceptions, we were the rule.

I warned of worse things to come. "Many dead. You must know. Many, many dead."

Patrols spread out across the camp and occasional firefights were heard, usually short ones. The GIs found piles of rotting corpses. It was remarkable, and in a way gratifying, to see their reactions to something that had become a daily routine for us. They'd undoubtedly seen many horrible things as they fought their way across France and Germany, but not this. Many had to cover their faces to keep out the stench as much as possible.

Toward dusk, a few GIs and I entered blocks and found people lying in their bunks, unable to believe that the ordeal was over. Some were near death and I wondered if they'd survive the night.

In an open area between blocks, two GIs were beating an SS guard. One was shouting angrily at the semi-conscious guard. Maybe they'd caught him redhanded in some horrible act, maybe it was simply rough justice. He poured gasoline on the guard and handed me matches.

There was no hesitation. I thought of countless acts of cruelty I'd seen inflicted on friends and relatives – in selections, on worksites, and in gas chambers – and determined that this man would pay for them. He looked at me fearfully though in resignation as I lit a match and tossed it on him. He shrieked wildly and rolled on the ground futilely until a GI put a bullet through his head. The corpse continued to burn in bright yellow and orange flames, sending dark smoke skyward.

I felt neither remorse nor relief, but I wanted no more vengeance. Judging by the sounds across the camp, reprisals went on for quite some time. The dark, unreasoning spirit of revenge was everywhere. GIs handed prisoners rifles and many SS guards were shot or bludgeoned to death. I heard single shots and also long machine-gun bursts, some preceded by pleas.

So strange to roam about freely and to feel comfortable and even safe around soldiers. There were new discoveries – cattle cars filled with corpses. The SS had tried to take prisoners elsewhere but fled, leaving the men inside to die and rot. The Death Express had been stopped.

American news people, both men and women, arrived. They too were sickened. A minister gathered inmates and soldiers around him for a prayer service. I kept a distance.

It was April 29 1945.

More and more medics, nurses, and doctors arrived in the following days. The foot soldiers and tankers had gone on. I hoped they'd live through what was left of the war and go home to their families.

Field mess units prepared meals. An immense oven baked bread for thousands of us. One mess sergeant broke eggs inside GI helmets and made batch after batch of scrambled eggs. Yankee ingenuity, I believe it's called. The medics warned us not to eat too much or we'd damage our insides. Most of us knew that, or soon learned. Some of us knew but ate voraciously anyway.

News people were everywhere taking pictures and conducting interviews. Benjamin would have been the first to give witness. I made no effort to go to them. One reporter, however, saw me looking on and approached me. He inquired, in German, if he could ask me questions. I consented, less reluctantly than I thought when I first saw him.

"What can you tell Americans about Dachau? How long were you here?"

I didn't know where to begin. Oradea? Auschwitz? What did this neatly attired man want to know? Could I explain what had happened over the last few months? I began to talk and went on for a half hour or more. I don't know how much I said, how much

I left out, what the chronology was, or if it made any sense. How could I explain the last year? He was aghast.

"You're a brave young man, Herman. It's amazing you lived through that. Last question. Do you feel that you were just lucky or do you think there was someone above watching over you?"

"You mean like the Lord or something like that?"

"Yes. That's it."

He looked at me, expecting words of moving piety and strong faith for readers back in America.

"After all I've seen, I cannot believe in a greater power looking over me or anyone else in the world. Look around!"

I motioned to the blocks and scarecrows and corpses of Dachau, and I knew there were other places across Germany and Poland and elsewhere too in all likelihood. He was taken aback. It was probably something he'd only expect from an embittered old man upon whom disappointments and failures had accumulated. But there in front of him was a boy of fifteen.

"Another last question then. Do you hate the German people?"

I thought about his question for a while and looked deep inside myself. Do I? Do I hate the Germans? I thought of German villagers who looked at us in dismay during the death march. I thought of Kurt, the White Rose journalist.

"No, I don't. The Germans didn't do this. Some did, not all of them. Every person acted individually in this. There were murderers. Many, many of them killed innocent people. But there are good Germans, good Austrians. I know there are good Poles."

"Remarkable. Thank —"

"But I do hate Nazis." I added abruptly. I felt my face turn into an angry scowl.

He looked at me for a while, perhaps imagining himself in Dachau. I knew he couldn't understand and if he thought he could, he was wrong. He was lucky for not knowing, but decent for trying. We shook hands and went different directions.

The spirit of religion and the faith in a benign deity had perished inside me, replaced by an abiding disdain for such supposedly uplifting creeds. Religion was a system of lies, perhaps well-intended and often beneficial, but lies nonetheless. They were akin to what was told to people on the selection platform, or on the way across the tracks, or as they were marched to the river bank to chop wood. "Put your clothing on the hook . . . hot soup awaits you . . . implements will be here shortly . . . it's all part of God's plan."

Life is cruel and violent. People should recognize it as such, and not hide behind lies and false hopes and faith in an uncaring sky. At least that's how I felt that day.

A FREE MAN

I remained in Dachau for several days, eating GI chow and getting better. Where would I go afterward? There were many of us who of course despised the camps but felt strangely safe there now. Outside, the Reich was in its death throes and still dangerous. Inside, oddly enough, it was safe.

The gates of Dachau, like those of Auschwitz, had the inscription *Arbeit Macht Frei* – Work Makes You Free. I had no idea that for decades to come the words would be so infamous and sickly paradoxical. I had certainly worked in those places but it was the American army that made me free.

My aunt and uncle were dead. Cousin Yanosh? I had no idea where he might be. There was no telling what Hungary and Romania were like in the spring of 1945, however I would try for those places once the Reich was completely gone. After all, my biological parents were somewhere in Eastern Europe. I had to remember that I was a Rittman, not a Davidovich.

After a week or so, we were to go to one or more of the Displaced Persons camps that GI engineers put up, sometimes in places where Nazi party schools had been. No forced march, no packed cattle cars. We were loaded into trucks for a convoy. We went to DP camps in Garmish and Feldafing, both in southern Germany.

No labor details, at least not long, grueling ones. Separate cots instead of crowded bunks. Tents or wooden barracks instead of those dark blocks. Regular and generous meals, medical attention for the many in need. We stayed inside on rainy days or went on short walks. Some of us put on plays and performed music.

I befriended a German-speaking GI who was on administrative duty both in the camp and in surrounding villages. When asked where I would go after the DP camp, I had no firm answer. Gears turned in his head and he told me to hop in his jeep.

He drove into town, parked where he pleased, and walked toward a row of houses. I kept thinking that at any moment SS guards would pop up and grab me. In my mind I was still prey. I did see German soldiers, but they were unarmed and guarded by GIs, who indeed were armed. There wasn't any confidence in those German faces. They were beaten and knew it. Now I knew it too.

The GI rapped on a door. Two German women, a mother about forty-five and daughter of twenty, peered cautiously from the partially opened door. The GI barged in and sternly addressed the women in heavily-accented German.

"This is Herman. He was a prisoner at Dachau, a place I trust you know of."

He didn't wait for a nod or anything. They were anxious and I presume they knew of the camp. I didn't feel very comfortable and wanted to leave, but I stayed and learned.

"Herman needs a bath, good food, and decent clothing. He's a friend of the United States Army and that has great importance in your country and it will for quite some time. I will leave Herman here with you good burghers and when I return in the morning I expect to find him well-bathed, well-fed, and well-dressed. In short, I expect to find a new young man. *Verstehen?*"

I looked at the GI quizzically. There was something left of my manners.

"Look, Herman, these people knew about the camp and didn't do a goddam thing. Well, now they will make some amends."

And with that, he glared at the women and bade us farewell. As he reached the doorway, he turned to me and said, "By the way, young man, you stink!"

I felt very awkward there with strangers, albeit defeated, intimidated ones. I said I would just leave but they insisted I stay – partly out of guilt, partly out of good manners, but mostly out of concern with disappointing the United States Army.

They looked at my still meager frame and asked, "Didn't they feed you anything?"

It was a question better suited for a different time and place. Then it dawned on them, hard. They'd heard rumors, now they saw evidence, even though I'd put on weight since liberation.

Well, they drew a bath for me and gave me clean, middle-class attire that once belonged to the mother's son. They didn't mention where he was but I suspected he was of military age. My first bath since . . . since when? Oradea? The DP camps had showers, and good ones with warm water, but no baths. It was a pleasure, a luxury. A wonderful feeling drew me into a pleasing distant past. The soap was perfumed, and in time so was I. The clothing was rather large on me but I felt great. Civilization was returning.

They prepared a meal that evening. Clearly, however, the GIs had more food than these Germans did. Still, they put on a good table and I sat there with a fork, knife, and spoon. Oh, and a cloth napkin.

Without any prompting from me, they spoke of the day the Jews of their village were taken away. They said they regretted it, but I wasn't sure at what point they came to regret it. How much did they know and how diligently did they avoid knowing by dismissing it all as rumor, hearsay, or wartime propaganda from abroad? I told them what fate likely befell the Jews of their village – cattle cars, forced labor, and death. As human beings they were aghast, as Germans they were ashamed.

"Oh God," the mother murmured. "I'm sure that very bad days are coming for Germany. They're already here. People around the world will hate us for generations to come. I cannot blame them, I cannot blame them. I would hate us too."

The daughter was silent but clearly distraught. Her face was drawn and fretful.

Over the years it has become commonplace to greet German claims of ignorance with skepticism or dismissal. And while I can speak only of two women, I believe they knew bad things had gone on not far from their home. They knew worse things went on in Poland. They were spared the details but made no effort to learn them.

Defeat forced them to realize that the Reich's boasts of superior civilization and invincible might were lies. Defeat also made them receptive to what I'd said of the Reich and to what they'd hear in coming years, especially at Nuremberg.

As morning came, I decided to leave. I left a note thanking them then slipped out the door.

There was more processing at the DP camp and in time I was issued train tickets and passes to get into Soviet-occupied lands. I boarded a train for Munich and then one for Prague. After a few stations, we came to a Red Army checkpoint. Russian soldiers came into the cars and demanded our watches. I surrendered two that I'd taken from an abandoned store near Dachau before law and order had been established.

There was something celebratory about the process. A handful of Russian soldiers in varying states of sobriety walked down the cars and took what they pleased. Amid the euphoria of the war being over, it was part armed robbery, part tribute to the victors. Watchless and alone, I laughed to myself. I was free and a new life lay before me somewhere. I'd get another watch someday.

Prague was a peaceful city on a gently flowing river. I bought a loaf of bread from a bakery that was struggling to get by. A skinny boy with money was most welcome. I stood on a bridge and heard the sounds of people still celebrating the end of the war. Looking out on the city lights of Prague reminded me of doing the same in Oradea.

A girl, no more than twelve, approached me and asked if I was a soldier. I assured her I was not. As she neared, I could tell she hadn't bathed in a while. Hunger was on her face. Her name was Ina. I tore off a piece of bread and watched her devour it. I gave her more.

"Thank you. I'm sorry. I don't usually ask from strangers but I was so hungry."

She still was so I tore off still more. She ate quietly and upon ingesting the last morsel, her curiosity awakened.

"Where are you from? What is your accent?"

"Where am I from…. Well, I arrived today from Munich."

"What did you do there?"

"I was in a nearby prison camp called Dachau."

The name meant nothing to her.

"My parents died during the war and I've been alone since. I used to work in a grocery store but it had to close and I haven't had money in weeks. I haven't eaten for so long, until now. Maybe it shows."

Something dawned on her.

"Are you a Jew?"

I nodded and felt discomfort.

"So am I. My parents died in Terezin."

I'd heard of the place, maybe from Eli. It was in Czechoslovakia and also called Theresienstadt.

"And Dachau was another camp?" she asked.

I nodded once more and said it was a topic for another time – words that served me well for several decades.

Ina offered to show me some of her city and I suggested we both might search for a place to bathe. She smiled, without any embarrassment, and escorted me to a public facility.

We spent a couple days there. The money was holding out. There were gardens and parks and monuments. It was a welcome reacquaintance with peace and life. But I wanted to get back to Hungary and Romania to find out what I could about my family.

I told Ina and she looked downward and murmured, "I wouldn't mind going to Hungary with you."

She wouldn't mind going to Hungary with me. Oh, what clever ways females have.

"Yes, I don't have anyone here anymore."

Sad eyes are another of their ways.

Well, she was a helpless waif in the aftermath of another of Europe's bloodlettings, as was I. So right after breakfast two waifs set out by train for Romania.

ORADEA AND PLOESTI

After so many deaths, so much upheaval, and so much detachment, it was important to reconnect with someone. Ina suited admirably. We took a train to Vienna then another to Oradea, which was in the process of reverting to Romanian rule. It took two days as so many tracks, stations, and switching stations had been damaged. Air raids and retreating armies aren't gentle.

Arrival brought a pleasant surprise. I expected bombed out buildings, piles of rubble, and hopeless faces. However, the city had been fortunate. Damage was slight and limited to a few districts. Shops were open, people went about their day, though with Russian soldiers here and there. More here than there, it seemed.

We headed to my neighborhood, partially retracing the path I took when we marched from the ghetto to the cattle cars. I didn't mention any of that to my companion. It was a day of wonder and discovery.

The house of my uncle and aunt looked little changed. My mind reeled. I almost expected to see school friends coming down the street. I knocked on the door and a man in his fifties answered.

He must have wondered why I was there. At that moment, I did the same. I had no claim on the place. If anyone did, it was Yanosh. A war and a Final Solution had taken place in the last year. A lot of history had passed through the old neighborhood.

"My aunt and uncle lived in this house. I grew up here."

"Mine now. I bought it from the city a year ago. Fully furnished too."

Something came to him.

"Are you Jewish?"

I nodded.

"I see. We heard things. Wait a moment."

He returned with a few items which he handed to me, surprisingly gently. There were several cracked and faded pictures of Joseph, Catalina, and Yanosh. I came upon one with a young boy.

"Aha, that's me – the little one in the picture. And that's my aunt holding me. I'm in my school clothes."

As I showed the pictures to Ina, he looked for other things.

"This was here too."

It was a silver Kiddush cup.

"I was hoping that someone would pick these up one day. Didn't want to throw them away. Memories for someone. Good luck to you both."

The door closed, not rudely by any means, though there was a finality to it.

Ina and I walked around Oradea. I showed her my school, the parks I played in, and the government building where I encountered Germans bearing chocolate gifts. My memories were of a city and way of life that was gone. How many of the people I knew only a year earlier were now dead?

Oradea held nothing, though I wanted to see one more place. Ina wanted no part of it but I insisted and promised the visit would be brief. We walked into the Oradea Mare ghetto.

The streets were empty, as they were in the last days of the liquidation, as they were when our time came. I showed Ina the house we lived in, the hospital where I worked, and the field we played football on.

We stood before the Dreher where the gendarmes tortured people to divulge the locations of hidden valuables. I stared at it for several moments, imagining blows hitting home and cries of pain, but hearing only rattling windows and creaking doors as the wind swept down debris-strewn streets. The Dreher was once again an abandoned brewery.

"Let's go," I said. "There's nothing here anymore."

On the way to the station I saw a familiar form, though one tired and forlorn. As I got nearer I was almost sure I knew him.

"Yanosh?"

When he turned to me I saw sorrow and despair. Joy came, but only slowly and incompletely. Yes, it was Yanosh. We embraced, eventually more fully. We hadn't seen each other since the previous autumn when a selection sent him to Monowitz and kept me in Birkenau.

He'd been back in Oradea for a few weeks and did odd jobs. We stayed in his rented room a few days. He drank in the evenings, far more than he should have. Sleep was fitful. He cried out repeatedly for his lost wife, children, and parents. As much as I cared for him and wanted to help, I needed to move on.

Yanosh had learned the whereabouts of my family through a government agency charged with helping those scattered by the war. My parents were no longer in Focşani, which is where I'd last visited them as a small boy. They'd moved to Ploesti, about 500 kilometers east of Focşani and just north of Bucharest. Ina and I decided to head there. I urged Yanosh to come along but he was determined to stay and head for America one day.

Ploesti was the center of Romania's oil industry and crucial to the German war effort. The Americans bombed it quite heavily, though the city itself was not badly hit. We found the address Yanosh had provided and I rapped on the door, half expecting another gruff stranger with another handful of mementoes.

A young man answered. He studied me for a while then tentatively asked, "Shuly? It's me – your brother Motzu!"

"I knew it," I exclaimed. I didn't recognize him at all, actually.

Two long-separated brothers embraced. I introduced Ina and we went inside the Rittman home. Some of the sparse furniture looked familiar yet alien, as though from a play I'd seen long ago. So much had transpired since I'd had any contact with the Rittmans. I felt both son and stranger.

Two young women looked at me then shouted, "Oh my, oh my!" It was my sisters Rosy and Viorica. My mother came to see what the commotion was about. "Oh my! It can't be, it can't be! Is that you? Is that really you, Shuly?" She wept, her hands trembled as she held me.

"Yes, it's your Shuly, mother."

"We heard such terrible things about Hungary! We tried to get word from Oradea but there was none to be had. I thought I'd never see my littlest one again. Where were you? Why are you so skinny?"

A river of questions followed, most which I managed to avoid. I introduced Ina once again and added that we wouldn't mind a bite to eat. A light meal was immediately served up.

As we ate, my mother inquired again why I was so thin. She asked as though I simply hadn't been eating well while away at boarding school. Then she gasped, "Shuly, were you in one of those Nazi camps?"

A nod.

"Oh my, oh my! What about Joseph and Catalina?"

My saddened face must have answered the question but I felt obliged to come out and say they'd been killed at a place called Auschwitz. Mother and the others wept. I added that I'd earlier seen Yanosh in Oradea, but that his wife and children had shared his parents' fate. I don't think they recognized the name Auschwitz.

My father raced home from his restaurant on receiving word and in the evening we all had dinner. The reunion was pleasant. The family was never so strong and warm as it was that night. Nonetheless, I didn't feel a member of it, in part because I hadn't grown up with them, in part because events had weakened notions of domesticity.

My brothers, I learned, had been recently released from Romanian work camps. The regimen was harsh but they came through it well. There were pogroms and deportations in Romania but on a less fearsome scale than in Hungary. The Rittmans and neighbors had been fortunate in regard to deportations. I marveled that Oradea was so close to the Romanian border, yet the few kilometers made an immense difference to those on the Hungarian side.

They looked at me expectingly, as though I should recount experiences of my travels across Europe. Looking at the genteel surroundings, I said that there were many stories to tell, mostly of an unpleasant nature, and that this was not the time to go over them. A thousand memories passed through me – events that would sicken them and haunt them. They'd never look at me the same. I closed the door on the past. Over the years I've seen little reason to reopen it.

I found odd jobs around Ploesti and tried to pitch in with household expenses. The Rittmans were never a prosperous lot, neither in war nor peace. Ina and I roamed about Ploesti and played football in the park. Quite the young athlete, she was. Two children that had been tossed about by Europe's worst storm had found a haven.

My brother Lucian announced that he felt confined and wanted to move elsewhere. Many of his friends talked of emigrating to America. The idea appealed to Motzu as well. America was a land of wealth and opportunity, Romania was one of poverty and stagnation – and Russian occupation. The parents objected sternly. The family was back together after many years, and it was going to stay that way.

Parents commanded respect in Old Europe. They issued laws, not suggestions. But there was so much change from the war that old ways were less forceful. The idea of moving on stayed with me. Perhaps it was because my principal family was dead, perhaps because I'd done so much moving about in the last year, perhaps because I could never feel at home anywhere.

My brothers held fast to the idea of emigrating until one day they simply determined to go. Motzu decided to leave for Budapest and from there, for America. Lucian would stay at home for now but would soon follow.

I wanted to go too, and discussed it with Ina. When I told her she was welcome to stay in Ploesti with the Rittmans, she was hurt. I was her family. She insisted on being with me and I could not say no to someone who'd come to rely on me.

Motzu, Ina, and I set out for Budapest where there were businesses that arranged emigration to America. The city was in flux. People coming home after the war, people moving on to other places, former soldiers wandering about.

New people came and went and with them were new ideas, among them Zionism. There was a new country to be built by energetic young people – Israel. The word then denoted only an ancient past and a place where a handful of idealists had gone over the last few decades to scratch out hard lives. It was usually called Palestine.

The leaders of a Zionist group in Budapest told us of the ancient land and our people's role in it, from Moses to the Diaspora to visionaries like Theodor Herzl. More practically, they told us of the warm climate, open spaces, freedom, and oranges. For some reason, oranges had a magical attraction to me. Ina and I listened and expressed interest. Motzu was unimpressed but gave in after a few more evenings.

We went through a training course in Budapest where there were scores of young curious people like us. Excitement was everywhere. New friendships were made for the new land. Motzu met a young woman there, Ilana, and was smitten. A few weeks later they married.[10]

One instructor, Haim Yanai, gave longer and more in-depth lectures and encouraged us to emigrate – or "make Aliyah". Most of the world called the land Palestine, but he always called it Israel.

We were given pen and paper and we took notes on the history of the Jewish people and their ancient land on the eastern

---

[10] They remain so to this day and in fact celebrated seventy years of marriage not long ago.

Mediterranean. The lectures covered everything from the time of Abraham to the present. We also learned, there in the middle of Budapest, how to live on a farm with little in the way of tractors or implements. The whole process took about six months and I look back on the time fondly. A new day was dawning and we would be part of it.

ALIYAH

Yanai gathered us in the dining room where a light meal was spread out on tables. He was a handsome, charismatic, athletic fellow who dressed in simple attire, and when he spoke we listened intently, some raptly. It was October of 1946 and the hum of loud heaters could be heard above the sounds of the diners and speaker.

He explained that the British weren't allowing any more European Jews to settle in what they called Mandatory Palestine. Their navy kept our ships from entering port, and their soldiers patrolled the borders. Many of our ships nonetheless got through. The passengers were met by underground settlement networks and began new lives on farms or kibbutzes. Other ships were seized. The passengers were placed in refugee camps on Cyprus or, temporarily, in the Mandate.

Yanai scanned the assembly proudly.

"You're ready. You've been taught about our country's past, present, and future. You even speak a little Hebrew. Now's the time for the big step. Our people are waiting for you. They will help you start a new life. It will not be easy. You'll dig and plant seeds and dig more, you'll toil in cramped factories, you'll guard homes, and you'll even work in dining rooms, preparing food and washing dishes. But the rewards are there for you. It will be *your* country – a country no one can take from you. No one can humiliate you or make you suffer again. You can raise your families freely and with dignity. You will play important roles in creating a new country."

I looked around and saw a sea of bright, eager faces. Most of them were enthralled by Yanai, especially the women. I liked what he was saying, and I indeed wanted to go to the new land, but I must say his breathless oratory and the crowd's acceptance of his every word, amused me.

"In a week we shall travel to a city named Bakar in Yugoslavia. British ships try to interdict our vessels and prevent us from reaching our destination. However, we've formulated a plan to get around them."

The room fell silent save for those heaters.

"Two ships will be leaving Bakar. A large one named *The Jewish Resistance Movement*[11] and a smaller one named *Anastasia*, or as we call it, 'the Saint'. We will deceive the British. The Saint will transfer her people to the larger ship near Greece and then attract the British navy's attention. The British will catch her and her crew and return them to Europe. They will be pleased with their catch, and you will be on your way to safety on the shores of Israel!"

The room became loud with murmurs, questions, and comments. Most felt they were in good hands. Many, however, found the plan rather shallow. Motzu, Ilana, Ina, and I certainly did. Yanai must have thought the British were overworked school monitors and he was a clever student.

He held out his arms to quiet the room.

"It will not be easy. It will not be easy. The larger ship will not have enough room for all of you to travel in comfort. The conditions will be unpleasant but it will be only for a few days. You have to be strong. And remember, this all we have and we *have to* succeed. We *have to* reach the land of Israel, at any cost."

He spoke with greater strength and determination than before. Charm gave way to will. That was Yanai, that was his organization.

---

[11] The ship was also named העברי המרי תנועת – later changed to *Knesset Israel*.

They were determined to bring us to Israel and create the new nation, at any cost. We'd see how clever they were.

On November 5 1946 four thousands of us gathered in the port of Bakar. The atmosphere was optimistic and joyful. The Yugoslavian government was helpful. Having been occupied by the Third Reich, and having suffered immense casualties fighting it, Yugoslavia was willing to help those who'd also suffered at its hands.

Prime Minister Josip Broz, better known as Tito, visited Bakar to see our preparations. It was said he directed the fiercest partisan resistance in all Europe. That impressed me. The local people greeted us and every night brought us baked goods. They spent time with us and exchanged stories in broken German.

Tito sent us a gift. Three hundred German prisoners of war were ordered to help prepare our ships. Many people were angered by their presence but Yanai insisted we show them no malice.

"Our greatness is in not stooping to their level. We are humans and we will treat other people as humans, even if their countrymen did terrible things to us. If we do them harm, we become like them."

His words were stated forcefully and thoughtfully, and we treated the POWs well.

We lived in a hostel that was rented by the Jewish Agency, or Sochnout (סוכנות). We spent a restless week there. At night I could look out and see the ship illuminated by the harbor lights. Men, some of them those German prisoners, were loading crate after crate. One night, word came from Yanai that we would sail in the morning.

It was our last night in Europe. Tomorrow we'd set out for a new land. New language, new customs, new people, new lives. I stared out on the harbor, Ina beside me. She was eager to get away from Europe. We would be in a new land that would be ours. She was echoing Yanai's words, as were many.

I thought of the British, their policy on immigration, and their navy. I knew nothing of Balfour or the Mandate or the Arab countries in the region. And while no one can predict the future, especially in those chaotic years after World War Two, I knew that nothing came easy in this world, and nothing would come easy for a people trying to build a new country anywhere in it.

The next morning, without anything more than nibbles of bread, we marched to the dock. Motzu and Ilana boarded the larger vessel, Ina and I headed for the smaller one – the Saint.[12]

Three men arrived from Israel – the Saint's owner, Yossi Harel ("Amnon"), the captain, Reuven Hirsh Yatir ("Abraham"), and telegrapher Yoash Zidon ("Maty," later a member of the Knesset). All three had the rugged good looks of Israeli pioneers. Every one of us wanted to look like them one day. Americans had movie stars, we had *Sabras*.

As I climbed the Saint's gangplank, a crewman said I was the last one. Ina was not allowed to board, despite my insistence that she was family. "You'll meet again in Israel, young man. The ship is already overcrowded. You'll be reunited in Israel." Ina was being led away by a member of the organization who echoed the promise of reunion. I called out to her with the same hope.

A while later a call came for two people to help load late-arriving cargo. Though the call was for volunteers, a man pointed to another fellow and me and down the gangplank we went to become stevedores for an hour. As we pushed a large crate along toward the freight opening, someone joined us. It was Ina! We stored the crates below and the Saint sailed from port a while later with a young stowaway. It was a misfortune.

As evening came I asked Ina if she would care to join me in the posh dining room where an excellent meal complete with fine wine would be served. Opting not to don evening wear, we walked arm in arm into the cramped, foul-smelling hall and ate rice, potatoes, and a substance that was rumored to be meat. Afterwards we stood

---

[12] We were later told that the ship was to be called *Abba Berditzev*, in honor of a man who served, and died, in the resistance in Czechoslovakia.

on deck and watched the Saint ply the cold, increasingly choppy seas of the Adriatic.

The poor girl became seasick. We'd been warned of that before boarding. Undoubtedly, the less than elegant dining room and cuisine figured in her illness. I fared better. Down below, in the fetid bunk area, she vomited, then lay down, weak and still nauseous. Someone with a measure of medical knowledge said she needed rest and sufficient water to prevent dehydration.

The weather was not on our side. The Adriatic got rough and the ship rolled about disconcertingly. Though hardly a seafaring man, I looked upon the crew with suspicion.

Still unaffected by the seas, I walked about the ship and noticed a great deal of rust on the old vessel. How many voyages had the Saint made already? How many more did she have left? Those questions were for the organization. I headed to my bunk. We'd soon transfer to the larger ship.

A few hours later I was awakened by a loud noise and a powerful jolt. People looked at one another fearfully. We thought our voyage would be safe until we reached the coast of Israel and the British navy. Something had gone wrong not far from port.

If a ship's in trouble, it's better to be on deck than below. Many of us had the same thought and headed up. One man said we'd hit a mine, another was sure we'd been torpedoed. Though it was noisy from the commotion and high seas, I was pretty sure the engines had stopped.

"We're going to sink! We're going to sink!" people cried out.

A crewman insisted the ship was in no danger of going under. *Knesset Israel* would arrive soon and besides, the water wasn't very deep. He was dismissive and far from reassuring. Someone pointed to a rocky island in the distance which I did find reassuring.

After an hour, word came that the engines had broken down and we'd drifted into submerged rocks. The weather worsened, and a few waves crashed over the railings. The Saint began to list to one side and we were put to work bailing water with whatever was handy. A line of men handed bucket after bucket up the dank stairwells to the deck. I can only presume the ship had pumps a work, too. The listing stabilized but we were still leaning to one side rather awkwardly.

A loud metallic sound startled us and the ship lurched to its side even more. The Saint was breaking apart. Some people jumped into the water and made for the island. The loudspeaker system crackled on and the captain gave the order to abandon ship. I raced below to Ina's cabin but found the way blocked by twisted metal, a fallen beam, and rising water.

I called out to her and she pleaded for my help. A passerby and I tried to move the beam for many frantic minutes but a dozen men couldn't have budged it. We looked at each other and silently agreed there was nothing more to be done. That was clear. Dreadful, but clear.

"Shuly! Shuly! Get me out of here!"

I closed my eyes and summoned all my courage.

"Ina, I can't get you out."

"What?"

"I can't get you out of there, Ina. I just can't. We've tried to reach you but we cannot."

"No! No! Please!"

"I'm so sorry, Ina. So sorry."

There was nothing more to say. Ina was doomed. In time, even as the water rose, she accepted the situation.

"Shuly, I want you to know that I understand."

The only sounds were the rushing water and the clamor above. The Saint was sinking fast, water reached my rib cage. The passerby, though eager to get to the deck, showed great compassion, and stood by us.

"Ina, I don't know what to do."

"Shuly, listen. You have to leave now. You have to go. Otherwise, you'll die needlessly. The water is rising fast. Please go, Shuly, I don't want you to die."

I closed my eyes and suggested the man head up to the deck, but he still would not leave.

"Shuly?" Ina's voice trembled. "Can you stay a few more minutes? I don't want to die alone."

"I am here, sweet one. I am here."

"I want you to know that you were my family, Shuly. I love you and your family. You were my family."

"We love you too, Ina, and we always will. I'm holding you now. I'm with you."

"Oh, the water! I don't want to die! I don't want to die! Oh! Oh!"

I could only hear small hands pounding and scratching on the door. The sounds stopped.

The man led me up the stairwell to the deck. We leaped into the choppy water and swam a kilometer or so to the rocky island. In the morning the other survivors and I were picked up by lifeboats and taken to *Knesset Israel*. I was given a place to lie down and I fell asleep, as sad and sickened as ever in my life. Another orphan had been lost.

The morning brought welcome news. I found my brother Motzu and Ilana. Or rather they found me. There were three of us now.

The captain and crew of *Knesset Israel* imposed a strict regimen on the passengers as we idled in Greek waters for several days. I was assigned to a team that did various chores, especially swabbing out the bunk areas where many people had been seasick. As might be imagined, work on the deck was a welcome break.

At breakfast I heard someone speak my name. It was Yanosh. He'd opted for Israel instead of the United States. In time, my brother came by and we held an informal reunion – a common enough sight in the postwar years, and a powerfully moving one as well. Fortune had placed us on the same ship and we were all bound for Israel.

That evening we spoke more on the deck. We had caught up on our pasts, it was time to talk of our future. Europe was old and dying, much of it lay in ruins. Motzu spoke of the warm weather and beautiful land of Israel. It held great promise. Yanosh saw Israel as an intermediary goal. He wanted to see the new land but then go on to America. Motzu's wife Ilana, however, was determined to stay in Israel, and that was that. Israel sounded good to me too.

On November 21 we met as scheduled with a fishing boat near Piraeus which took the Greek crew and our skipper, who was slated to head back to Yugoslavia to organize more ships. Our new skipper was Reuben Yatir, his first officer was Yossi Harel. They announced the new plan to hug the shorelines of Cyprus and Lebanon, evading the British navy, before steaming south for Israel.

Not long thereafter, a small plane circled overhead. The captain spread the word that it was a British reconnaissance aircraft and that it had radioed for our identity and destination. We identified ourselves as *Santa Maria* destined for Alexandria, Egypt. Later that day, a British warship came up behind us. His majesty's navy was on to us.

The warship suggested we seek port on Cyprus where we would receive provisions and medical help, if needed. Our captain, I later learned, had an SOP which the *Haganah* had come up with. We clambered below deck as the crew hoisted the Panamanian flag, a common enough sight on merchant ships in the Mediterranean. It fooled no one.

That night Yossi Harel gathered us.

"We have to prepare for the British. Let's not delude ourselves, we will have to confront them but we have to do it in the right way. When we reach Haifa, we will resist them. We will not shoot or even injure any British serviceman. If you have a firearm, you must drop it on the floor. Otherwise they will shoot you and many others as well. We are going to resist the British quarantine policy – but not violently. We will use sticks and buckets, but no firearms. We will use our moral strength to appeal to the world to grant us passage to our land."

We sailed past Tripoli in northern Lebanon, the British warship still trailing us. Israel was only 150 kilometers away. As we neared Israeli waters, three more British ships came in sight. They announced they'd board us and we prepared to resist. Some of us were directed to stand on deck. I was one of them.

The British sent launches with an inspection team. They said, quite politely, that we were to be sent back to Europe. Our captain countered that an international court had sanctioned our disembarkation on Israel's soil. As he spoke, British sailors were taking up positions around the ship. Scuffles broke out as they tried to physically remove people from *Knesset Israel*. We outnumbered them, of course, so we hurled them overboard and prevented them from climbing back up.

The British ships fired tear gas canisters and smoke drifted below decks, including parts where many children were. Among them were babies who'd been born in Hungary or Yugoslavia. A few were born aboard the ship. Our captain would not risk their lives. He gave the order to give in.

The poet Nathan Alterman wrote about the tear gas from a young girl's perspective.

אֲשֶׁר הַפְּצָצָה הַשְּׁלִישִׁית בְּמִסְפָּר
פָּלְטָה זֶרֶם עָשָׁן בְּתַחְתִּית הַסְּפִינָה
הַיַּלְדָּה הָחִוֶּרֶת הִפְשִׁילָה צַוָּאר
יַעַן שָׂמוּ לְפֶתַע מַחֲנָק לִגְרוֹנָהּ

As the third bomb
Released its choking smoke
A pale little girl held her throat
As all her air was lost.

We were taken to Haifa and housed in an aircraft hangar. The food was fairly good, I'll say that, and the blankets made sleeping on the concrete floor less uncomfortable. I was behind a fence again.

We soon boarded a British ship that took us to a refugee camp on Cyprus – Camp 64. Sad that our visit to Israel was so brief.

Some of us were fortunate to be billeted in shacks rather than in tents. When people complained of the harsh conditions, Yanosh and I would look at each other and enjoy a moment of private humor. British hospitality greatly exceeded that of the late Reich, I assure you.

The British allowed our organization in Israel to send food, a dental team, and even recreational items. Football is a wonderful past time in almost any situation. We formed our own camp government. We were given a taste of life on a kibbutz.

Months passed. Several people I knew managed to escape and with the help of local Jews, make their way to Israel on small boats. But life on Cyprus was largely uneventful. We had dances where young people socialized and talented people performed. A few untalented people also performed. British and Israeli speakers told us about life in Israel and in time, the British allowed several hundred people a month to enter Israel.

The stay was not uneventful for everyone. More babies were born in the camp. Motzu and Ilana had a child there. Many more babies were conceived in Camp 64.

As I watched a group boarding ship for the voyage to Israel, I saw a young woman who looked familiar. She saw me and a look of partial recognition came to her. Distant places and events whirled in my mind and a name came to me.

"Alexa!"

She looked at me for a moment.

"Herman!"

It was Alexa, the nurse at the hospital in the Oradea Mare ghetto whose father had died with her by his side. Her group was going up the gangplank so there was no time for a reunion.

"Good luck to you in Israel, Alexa. I'll be there soon."

"Good luck to *you* in Israel!"

No more words were exchanged. She was on the deck and being led to quarters.

So, Alexa had survived the ghetto, Auschwitz, and whatever other camps she might have been sent to. She had persevered and she had kept the promise to her father. I'm sure we both thought back to that night in the ghetto.

She waved to me one last time before heading below.

Not long thereafter, after seven months on Cyprus, we were told that we would board a ship in the morning and sail to Israel. My brother's family and I awaited the hour. This was it. We were on our way. What began many months ago in Budapest was about to come to fruition. I asked what we'd do when we got there and no one knew, at least not in any detail. A new land was there for us and we'd make something of it. I thought of oranges.

Motzu asked about my pensiveness and I mentioned an obligation.

"I promised – I think it was about a year and half ago – that someday I would write down what I saw in the camps."

"Promised who?"

"More than one person, but most importantly a man named Benjamin. We marched from Auschwitz to Gross-Rosen together. He died in a quarry. It has to be written down someday."

Motzu must have thought it odd that a seventeen-year-old boy would speak of chronicling those days. I certainly did. And while I wanted to put those days aside and live my life, I knew there were so many others that had had no such life. And I determined that one day I'd write about some of them. And here we are.

KFAR GILADI

The next day we sailed and in a few hours docked in Haifa, only 160 kilometers away. My brother and cousin wanted to stay in Haifa but I'd become attracted to a kibbutz called Kfar Giladi. We were saddened at the thought of another separation but Motzu reminded us that Israel was not large and we'd never be very far from each other.

Kfar Giladi is in Galilee, in northern Israel. I'd learned of kibbutzes from the lectures in Budapest and on Cyprus, and the idea appealed to me. People worked together for each other. About forty of us assembled in Haifa and were taken by bus through rolling hills and pine forests until we came to a settlement in the low mountains. A few armed men and women patrolled the perimeter.

We were greeted and assembled in front of a modest administrative building. A lovely young woman named Naomi, attired in khaki shirt and shorts, welcomed us and told us of orchards, poultry coops, and dairy cows. The names of elders and an outline of the rules followed. The introduction lasted an hour.

When she asked for questions, my hand shot up. I hesitated for a moment as all eyes were on me, but soon found my words. "My name is Herman Rittman and I have a question, please. Do you have orange trees here?"

Naomi smiled, quite pleasantly too.

"Aha, many newcomers have heard such good things about our fruits. Of course, we have orange trees. Lemons and grapefruits abound here as well. Our orange trees are few in number, though. We don't sell their fruit in the marketplaces. They're for our enjoyment. Shall we see them now?"

As splendid a suggestion as I'd heard in quite a while. We ambled a few hundred meters to a half-hectare or so of orange trees. We were encouraged to sample the sweet fruits of Kfar Giladi. I held a large one, still on the branch, and felt the cool rind. It was true what they'd said back in Budapest. The oranges of Israel are beautiful. But I didn't want to separate it from its home.

"Go ahead. Pick it," Naomi encouraged. "You'll not ruin anything. A fruit is meant to be enjoyed. We toil, then we enjoy. It's the circle of life, for us and for the children. Welcome. You're one of us now."

I picked the orange and peeled away the rind, revealing bright, juicy segments separated by soft pulp. A Romanian youth became a member of Kfar Giladi and an Israeli.

I looked out at the mountains in the distance, took in the bracing morning air, and savored another orange. It was Saturday morning and we relaxed and enjoyed the day. We had no luxury save for the community itself. Oh, but there was really no such thing as a day off on Kfar Giladi. Cows needed to be fed, sheep and chickens too. They stated their case noisily and persistently.

After chores we'd gather on the grass in front of the dining hall and talk of our work and lives. We came to know each other and to care for each other.

Many days I lay on the grass and reflected on my seventeen years of life. They were different from those of most fellow kibbutz members, though a few had gone through hard experiences back in Europe. Some said so. Others had tattoos or the occasional vacant stare.

The Oradea ghetto and the Nazi camps were vivid memories, yet I didn't think of them as grave burdens. I'm not sure why. Maybe it was the military-like upbringing Uncle Joseph had instilled. Maybe it was the wonder of the new land that made me think the past was just that, and a new life lay ahead to which I should devote my thoughts. Maybe I was just too young.

As part of my dedication to a new life, I took on a new name, a Hebrew name. Heretofore I would be "Zvi", meaning "deer", but I was called by the diminutive form "Zvika". My European name, Herman, was behind me, though I used it much later in my intelligence career.

I apprenticed under a man named Yossi Dotan. He was twenty-seven and like me had come from Hungary. He was lucky enough to have arrived before the war and had lived on the kibbutz for many years. I worked with him in the orchards and also received training on light weapons and basic military tactics.

It was comfortable to speak in my native language but Yossi insisted on Hebrew. I'd already taken some Hebrew back in Budapest, but I wanted to speak like a *Sabra*. After a few months my Hebrew was quite good but I liked to revert to Hungarian just for fun. I do that to this day with old friends.

Yossi was tall, ruggedly handsome, blue-eyed, and bronzed from the sun – the pioneer ideal. The men respected him and the women adored him. He had strong principles but he was not without a fun side. Every Friday night after Shabbat dinner, the young men and women would gather on the lawn behind the dining hall. Yossi made sure we had a few beers to help us relax and enjoy life after a hard week. He'd quaff a few then tell amusing stories and even risqué ones which I will not retell here.

Men and women were equal in everything – a novel social relationship then, and one that is only rarely equaled in most countries today. We worked side-by-side in the fields, orchards, dining hall, dairy, chicken coops, and barns. We washed great mounds of dishes and pealed bushels of potatoes. In the barns there were other great heaps that had to be shoveled out. Yes, some labors were less agreeable than others.

Kfar Giladi sold its produce in friendly villages nearby and in cities down the coast. This brought in steady though not immense revenue. The kibbutz had a few vehicles. If someone needed a car for an hour or two, he or she would register a request and get use of one for travel to a city or a family trip. Each of us received a modest allowance every two weeks for clothing and necessities. Everyone lived in small apartments and could choose to have a roommate or live alone. Each unit had a bed, simple furniture, a small refrigerator, and a radio. Married couples had their own apartments. We all lived and worked in dignity.

One of the most interesting aspects was the way children were raised. Shortly after birth, the newborn was taken to a communal home where all the children lived and learned. Nurses took care of them day and night. Parents visited daily but offspring grew up in a sub-community.

It was very peculiar to me – a departure from everything I'd seen in Romania and Hungary. I have to say, however, that the kids grew up to be excellent community members and citizens.

Some people couldn't adjust to the toil and customs and chose to leave for more conventional lives in the cities. I stayed on with my family on Kfar Giladi.

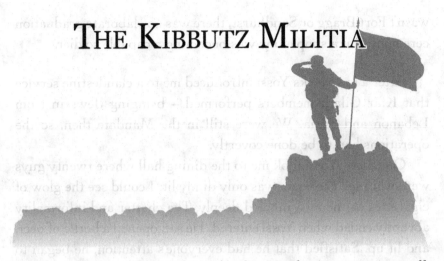

THE KIBBUTZ MILITIA

Yossi began to instruct ten of us boys and young men in small arms, basic martial arts, map-reading, and radio operation. The training wasn't long or sophisticated by the standards of regular armies, but the knowledge proved useful and gave us a sense of importance. We were no longer hapless victims of outside forces. We were confident soldiers.

Young Zvika became a pretty good shot with pistols and rifles. We had Mauser K98s, which were the standard rifles of the German army, and Lee-Enfields from the British army. Both were in abundance in the years after the war, when armies stood down and weapons flowed to various parts of the world, legally or otherwise.

I studied the terrain and paths running from Kfar Giladi into Lebanon and Syria. A glance to the sky revealed which way I was heading. I developed a sense for where a hill would have draws that might offer water. A Druze taught us how to hide our tracks and leave a deceptive trail to throw off the British or whoever else might be looking for us. I could go without food for more than most people thought possible.

Toward the end of training we learned to use and maintain Bren guns and light anti-tank weapons. We even saw a crude mortar that might have been a prototype of the Davidka which would be produced in small factories during the War of Independence. It wasn't Fort Bragg or Sandhurst, there was no elaborate graduation ceremony, but a simple boy was becoming a capable soldier.

After a few weeks Yossi introduced me to a clandestine service that Kfar Giladi members performed – bringing Jews in from Lebanon and Syria. We were still in the Mandate then, so the operations had to be done covertly.

One night Yossi took me to the dining hall where twenty guys were waiting. The room was only dimly lit. I could see the glow of cigarettes as the men inhaled deeply. The chatter and informality abruptly ended when Yossi entered. He sat, opened a bottle of beer, and lit up. Satisfied that he had everyone's attention, he began to speak calmly and clearly.

"Tomorrow we're going to help more of our people come in from Syria. I expect a large group. Maybe a hundred, maybe more. As usual, we'll cross the border just north of Kibbutz Misgav Am, then make our way to the village of Aadaisse. Local people will help us there. We've done this a few times already without incident. I don't have any reason to believe this time will be different.

"Yet as I always stress, we have to be careful. Two threats face us. The villages of Taibe and Markaba are hostile. The villagers hate us and will not hesitate to open fire if they see or hear us. Second, the British. They have intelligence, they have informers. I don't think it's the case on this operation but we have to be ready to beat a path home."

I'd been trained to be a soldier, and I'd faced fear and danger before. Nonetheless, I felt tension.

Armed with rifles and pistols, ten of us set out the next night. We marched silently through orchards and pine forests which gave the night air a refreshing scent. It felt like a pleasant evening walk, at first. Shots rang out and bright tracer rounds pierced the dark sky. I went to the ground. No, Yossi shoved me to the ground.

"Down! Down!" he ordered in an urgent whisper.

Yossi had told us, "When you hear bullets, don't think of anything else. You must immediately hit the ground. Nothing else matters. Your life will depend on it. Stay alive."

Unfortunately, we were in a field with thorny underbrush and my body was stung by a dozen barbs. Sticky blood ran down my arms, legs, and abdomen but the bullets whooshing overhead held my attention. Yossi and others began to return fire. I gathered my wits and joined in. After a few moments, the shooting stopped and once we determined none of us were injured, we moved out again toward Syria.

We met our contacts in the village of Aadaise as planned, though a few minutes late. Yossi talked with them briefly, money was exchanged, and they led us to a darkened building. The interior had a few lanterns that cast yellowish light on the faces of a large number of men, women, and children, about 300 of them. How could we lead so many people across the border? We weren't crossing Sinai with the Pharaoh's army in pursuit, but it seemed an unmanageable task.

"Don't worry", Yossi said upon seeing the concern on our faces. "I've taken large groups across. Well, maybe nothing quite this large!"

Our charges looked at us in fear and hope. Some held children, some held parents and grandparents. A profound sense of duty came. I had to steel myself and help these people get into our land. I owed it to them and to millions of others who'd wanted to escape Europe.

We divided the assembly into manageable groups and assigned two kibbutz members to each. So, we set out into the night once more and headed for Misgav Am where food and water awaited.

Young Zvika led the way for one group and a fellow named Gideon took up the rear. There were a hundred meters or so between each group and we had to keep sight of the group in front and behind. My group bore the hardships very well, with only a few whimpers and cries from children. The people amazed me. And maybe they were amazed by a teenager with a Lee-Enfield in his arms. I must confess to thinking about Moses. Maybe some in my group did too. Maybe not.

Not far from the border, shots rang out behind us. Yossi gave the word over the walkie-talkie that a rear group had come under fire but my group was to keep moving.

I motioned for my group to quicken the pace. A small hand clutched mine. A girl of twenty was looking at me in fear. Despite the darkness, I could see she was exceptionally beautiful. She wore a gown more commonly found among Arab women than counterparts on the kibbutz or in the cities.

"Ana kha-iff," she whispered.

More shots from behind. A skirmish was breaking out with Syrians.

"Ana kha-iff."

I took her hand and we moved forward as fast as we could given the craggy earth beneath us. After a half hour or so we came upon border markers and reported our position over the crackling radio net.

My group was safe. We were inside Palestine and not much later the people of Misgave Am welcomed us into their dining hall. In time, the other groups arrived. Yossi's hand had been grazed by a bullet and a doctor dressed it with a clean bandage.

An elderly man from my group approached me. "The young woman said she was frightened. The bullets." He pointed above and made the sound of a large insect flitting by. "She's from my village in Syria. A wonderful young woman. Very pretty as well."

She looked at me demurely. In the better light she was all the more beautiful.

"My name is Zvi. Everyone calls me Zvika."

"My name is Amalya," she replied with an Arab accent.

She was from a village not far from Damascus. Tensions, she said, were rising between Jews and Arabs. She and her family wanted out. We enjoyed a little time together but events were moving fast. We made for Kibbutz Ayelet HaShahar where the group was given clothing and papers. After that it would be off to Haifa for settlement. Had Amalya and I had more time, who knows?

Kfar Giladi came under fire more frequently. In a few weeks, months at the most, Young Zvika was as skilled as almost anyone on the kibbutz and was teaching boys and young men how to shoot. I also learned more trails in and out of Syria and Lebanon and was Yossi's second-in-command.

One night, when Yossi was off with a group I later learned was the Haganah, I was asked to lead a group of people from Nabatieh to our kibbutz. No hesitation. On the way back I reconnoitered a clearing and came across a man leveling a rifle at me. I fired an Enfield round into his chest and he fell hard. I motioned for my people to hurry across the opening. My constant companion had met up with me once more. That time, though, I was his agent.

I was a soldier in an army that didn't exist and defending a country that hadn't been born. I was seventeen.

HAGANAH

The Jewish population in Palestine was growing. Legally or not, despite the efforts of the British and Arabs to stop them, we kept coming in. Arab attacks stepped up and the British were not inclined to intervene. We needed to defend ourselves and so a secret army that dated back well before World War Two, the Haganah, grew in numbers and strength.

Yossi had belonged to the Haganah for quite some time. After about eight months on the kibbutz, I was asked to join. No hesitation. We of course had been told of the Haganah back in Hungary, about its bravery protecting the *Yishuv, or* Jewish settlements.

There was an inspiring ceremony for those entering the Haganah back then, as there is today for those entering the IDF at the ancient fortress of Masada. Young Zvika's initiation took place late at night on Kibbutz Ayelet HaShahar. I was led by the regional commander, Alon Caduri, to the kibbutz school where a simple desk stood next to a blue and white banner that would become the flag of Israel. The windows had been covered with black curtains, conferring secrecy and mystery.

Alon led me to the desk upon which lay a Bible and a Lee-Enfield. Then one of the commanders called me in front of the flag. I put my hand on a Bible and read an oath:

I hereby declare that I volunteer of my own free will and recognition to enter the Jewish defense organization called the Haganah in Israel.

I swear allegiance for the rest of my life to the Haganah, its constitution, and functions as defined by its high command.

I swear to dedicate unconditionally and unreservedly my life and actions to the Haganah and obey its discipline, and abide by its call to enlist in active service at any time and any place, to obey all orders and fulfill all orders as demanded from me.

I swear to devote all my strength and even sacrifice my life to protect and fight for my people and my country, the freedom of Israel, and the redemption of Zion.

Then I signed statements on heavy stock paper:

These rules were read before the foundations of the defense organization of the Haganah. I am familiar with them and accept them voluntarily and indefinitely.

I pledge to be loyal and dedicated to all matters of the Haganah and its members for all my life. I accept the Haganah discipline and organization and commit to strictly comply with the orders authorized by its commanders.

I swear to keep all information confidential for my entire life and in every situation.

Alon handed me a Lee-Enfield rifle – *my* Lee-Enfield. I held it with steady hand. Although my heart was racing, I was determined to show the men around me that the lad before them was up to it. The rifle was heavy, its muzzle cold. Alon handed me a paper with large print:

> With this weapon, entrusted to me by the Haganah in Israel, I will fight the enemies of my people, for my country, without surrendering, without hesitation, and with dedication.

My fellow soldiers smiled and shook my hand.

"Welcome into the Haganah," Alon said. The words were powerful and meaningful.

I marveled at the Enfield's craftsmanship. The wood and metal were smooth and oiled. It betokened security and responsibility. I'd sworn to give my life to Israel if need be, and I meant it.

The Haganah assigned me to help Yossi smuggle more people into Israel. The influx was on the rise after the UN announced a plan to partition the Mandate into Jewish and Arab countries. We probably brought in about five thousand people in a year.

My kibbutz and others in the area were growing. Most members were talented people who helped the austere outposts become small towns with schools, newspapers, and health systems. Young guys like me were trained for battle and called the "Field Unit", older guys were assigned to the "Guard Unit" to protect the kibbutz itself and convoys leading to and from it. I was placed in charge of ten men, making me the equivalent of a sergeant.

Meanwhile, I knew that the Haganah was smuggling in more weapons, vehicles, and even a few planes. It was only a matter of time until the state of Israel was declared, and that we all knew would bring conflict.

Arab attacks increased both in number and lethality. Many men, women, and children were killed while they worked the fields and drove the roads. British soldiers were supposed to maintain order, but didn't. They looked on as Arabs attacked and rioted. I witnessed British soldiers shooting locks off of Jewish shops so Arabs could loot them. Soon enough, the British were handing over important crossroads to them.

The Arabs were not able to seize control of any Jewish town or kibbutz but they controlled the roads connecting them. Our settlements were scattered from Galilee to Gaza and the Negev. My unit moved from village to village, town to town, helping where we could. With each move we realized how thinly stretched we were. The word came that the Jewish population in Jerusalem was in danger.

World opinion did not favor us. Why support us if the Arabs were going to crush us in a few months? The United States was urging us not to declare independence. Wait, Washington counseled, wait.

Chaim Weizmann met President Truman in the White House. It was an important achievement since Truman supported the idea of a Jewish state. That meant some assistance, but what of the surrounding countries? Haganah commander Yigael Yadin had his doubts.

One night I had the good fortune of attending, along with a hundred or so Haganah troops, a meeting at Kibbutz Deganya where General Yadin spoke. It was a boost for my confidence. The general spoke calmly and sparingly, pausing to puff on his ever-present pipe. The Haganah soldiers listened, rifles by their sides.

"You are doing great work defending our villages and communes. Without your courage many of our people would be dead. I thank you all for this. Nonetheless, the situation is not good. We are brave and dedicated but our numbers are few. The Jewish quarter of Jerusalem is cut off and in dire need of food. The Arabs control the Latrun Way through which our trucks must pass."

I'd learned back in Hungary that throughout history nations and empires fought to control Jerusalem. Besides its religious and political significance, it was located high in the hills which gave it command of the lands all around it. It had military values well. Arab Legion troops held Latrun and Shaar Ha Guy (Guy Gate) and prevented convoys from reaching the beleaguered Jewish quarter.

"We have to seize the approaches to Jerusalem or our people will be in grave danger. They could be massacred. We have to unite scattered defensive units into a modern army, one capable of offensive operations. There is no alternative."

A hum swept over the room. The purpose of the Haganah was defending our people. After all, "Haganah" means "defense". Many associated organized armies with aggression and oppression. An officer rose.

"We were established to defend Jews, not attack Arabs."

"And defending our people is what we shall do, but we need to change how we go about it. Otherwise we will perish before our people can build a state. It's a matter of life and death – unfortunately, *our* death."

To my astonishment, I stood up.

"He's right!"

All eyes turned to me. Young Zvika was new to the outfit and quite young. Most must have thought me impertinent.

"I've been defending our people here for months and seen the Arabs' hatred for us. I've seen such things before. If we want to be safe, we must have an army."

Young Zvika sat down. Opposition to Yadin hadn't been strong or passionately put to the floor. His motion was accepted.

"I'll present my recommendation to Ben-Gurion in the morning."

Heads nodded, hands shook. Yadin approached me and looked at my arm.

"I want you to come with me to Tel Aviv tomorrow, young man. I want you to be there when I present my proposal."

Who would not have consented? Tomorrow I'd stand before David Ben-Gurion, I suppose as a symbol of my people's past and future. I can't imagine why else Yadin wanted me along. I was a soldier, not a strategist. Oh, and the impertinent boy would speak there too.

DAVID BEN-GURION

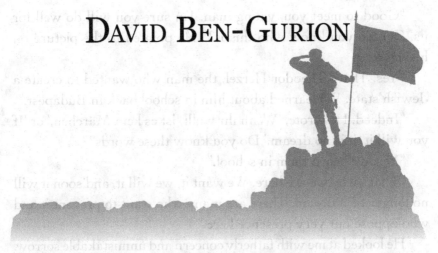

The next day a general, a few junior officers, and a young sergeant drove the hundred kilometers down the coast to Tel Aviv. We all knew of Ben-Gurion. He was the leader of our country and as such, enjoyed mythic status.

We parked near a modest house and announced ourselves to a secretary in the foyer. After few if any preliminaries, we entered a sparsely furnished office with a large desk. A photograph of a man with a long dark beard caught my attention. After a moment, I knew who it was.

"Come in, gentlemen. Be at home. Have a seat. Shall I have coffee brought in? Bread?"

The father of Israel was offering refreshments. The general declined. The young soldier did not, but his words came out as incomprehensible mumbles.

"Coffee?" Ben-Gurion offered again in kindly voice.

"Yes, please," I finally managed to say.

"This is Zvi Rittman. Though young of age, he is stout of heart and has proven himself at Kfar Giladi and elsewhere. We are fortunate to have someone of his abilities."

This was news to me and I tried not to look surprised. Yes, I was young of age, but so was Yadin. He was barely thirty, yet a general. Young men can rise quickly in a new army.

"Good to meet you, young man. I'm sure you will do well for us. Zvi, do you know who this is?" He pointed to the picture on his desk.

"Yes. That's Theodor Herzel, the man who wanted to create a Jewish state. We learned about him in school back in Budapest."

"Indeed. He wrote, 'Wenn ihr wollt, ist es kein Märchen,' or 'If you will it, it is no dream.' Do you know these words?"

"Yes, we heard them in school."

"That's why we are here. We want it, we will it, and soon it will no longer be a dream. There are many who want to prevent it and who oppose our very presence here."

He looked at me with fatherly concern and unmistakable sorrow.

"Zvi, were you in the camps?"

I lifted my arm.

He nodded. "I'm sorry. You must have lost precious family members."

"Yes, I did. So did many others."

"I trust you to protect the people in our land."

"You can rely on me – always."

Yadin, possibly sensing Ben-Gurion's leaning, got down to business, right after lighting his pipe. The officers opened maps that showed various settlements and Haganah positions. Yadin argued for marshaling units for an offensive operation from the coast to Jerusalem. Units and commanders were identified, winding roads and hilly terrain were underscored. Yadin drew circles around Arab positions and arrows where we needed to take action. The presentation was short and well-prepared.

Ben-Gurion nodded, conveying thought rather than agreement.

"But it's not just Jerusalem. The kibbutzes in the north are isolated."

More circles and arrows came from Yadin's pencil. Ben-Gurion looked at the maps but his thoughts seemed to be elsewhere. Yadin added a few comments.

"Jerusalem is sacred. It's central to our people's history and identity. Our people there may have to surrender to the Arab Legion. And after that, who knows what will happen to them."

Ben-Gurion ran a hand over his sparse hair and sighed. His reflection didn't take long.

"You gentlemen are right. If we're to will our dream and not remain a scattered vulnerable people, we have to combine the forces, clear the way to Jerusalem, and defend the land. Other areas will have to hold on. We have more men and weapons coming in. They can be deployed in time."

The young officers were happy. So was a young sergeant. Yadin was surprised. He expected vigorous debate but his pipe bowl never went dark.

Statesman and officers spoke more but the former's time was pressing. We shook hands and returned to the car on the streets of Tel Aviv. I'd met great man, one even greater than Yadin. On the way back I kept thinking how difficult the battle for Jerusalem would be. The general knew it. So did the young sergeant.

THE ROAD TO JERUSALEM

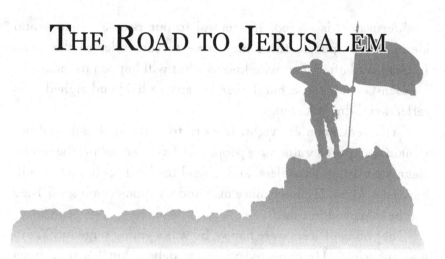

The Haganah seized several locations to help convoys from village to village, kibbutz to kibbutz, city to city. The road to Jerusalem, though, remained subject to attack. A convoy of doctors and nurses was ambushed and dozens were killed. In response, the Haganah assigned Yossi, me, and about a hundred men to escort the next few convoys. We had only a few lightly-armored vehicles and jeeps.

We lost many men on the first mission. We were up against Jordanian troops of the Arab Legion, a force set up by the British in the 1920s. They fired on us from caves, boulders, and woods along the hilly winding roadway. Yossi studied the maps and divided our force into two groups to sweep the hills. It was tough going. The enemy weren't simple villagers with the odd rifle from a bygone era. Many had fought against Rommel in World War Two and knew how to maneuver, use defilade, and fire accurately. Some Haganah troops had also served with the British against Rommel, though not many.

The convoy reached Jerusalem and the operation was hailed a success, but my force took very heavy casualties – about fifty percent killed and wounded. The task was beyond the abilities of so young a man, annealed though he was by ritual. Yigael Yadin came to inspect the battle site, pipe in hand. He immediately recognized me as well as my sorrow and doubt.

"Listen, Zvika, this was your first battle against experienced soldiers. It was Yossi's first too. The same for almost all your troops. For many of them it was their last. The supplies got through, Zvika. It was costly, but we succeeded."

I shook my head.

"If Israel is to come about, there will have to be more. The Arab Legion has many good fighters. It's a test of will, Zvika – ours against theirs."

A general taking time to console a young soldier was quite moving. It still is. That was the Haganah – not a large formal institution with delineated procedures, simply a few thousand young men who knew many of each other personally and had genuine concern for one another, regardless of rank or social station. I uttered a few soldierly words in a voice that probably conveyed determination mixed with resignation.

"There is no other way, Zvika. And we will drive them out. I'm assigning more soldiers to you and Yossi. You'll escort another convoy in a week."

Yadin patted me on the back and went on to encourage others. Yossi sat next to me and lit a cigarette. There was a lot of smoking in those days. I tried to think of a better way to sweep the hillsides. An idea formed in my head and I outlined it to Yossi. It relied on Gadi.

Gadi was about my age and eager to prove himself. He grew up in Haifa and knew Arabic and a thing or two about the Druze people west of Jerusalem. Some were friends. He'd used his language skills for us already to get information and settle minor disputes.

He knew people who had ties with villagers around Latrun and Jerusalem. We asked him to gather information. Were any villages less hostile than others? Were there predictable infiltration routes? Gadi was a bit surprised but said he'd talk with old friends.

We drove to Daliyat El Carmel high on Mt Carmel. The dirt road was narrow and our wheels were only centimeters from a steep precipice. The village did not promise safety. If recognized as a member of the Haganah, I would be shot or hanged or hurled down one of those steep precipices. It had happened before, though perhaps not at Daliyat El Carmel. That's the way it was with war coming and the British leaving. Riots, feuds, and acts of violence broke out everywhere.

We arrived about midnight and went to meet an elderly Druze named Hakeem who resided in a large stone house. A cautious rap on the door was answered by a young servant who bade us in but said his patron was ill. Inside, the dim light revealed a welcoming smile. Unknown aromas filled my nostrils. Fine rugs made me think this Hakeem fellow was prosperous. Later intelligence work better taught me that wealthy men stood atop patronage networks that made for excellent sources of information.

We entered a large room with a spacious bed, low to the floor with a crimson canopy hanging loosely above it. A flickering hearth took off some of the chill and made the room seem alive. Hakeem lay heavy in the bed, his wife and sons nearby.

"Marhaba, Marhaba. They tell me you're not well."

"Don't listen to them! I am well and more than content. People worry needlessly in this house. How are you, my young friend? Good to see you."

Hakeem smiled warmly, maybe even paternally. His face, though drawn, showed kindness and experience. He barked out for refreshments and his wife obligingly scurried to the kitchen. This was no kibbutz.

When I started to decline the offer, Gadi's eyes scolded me. Hakeem recognized the silent exchange.

"Hospitality governs here, young man. It doesn't matter when or why you arrive at my home, I will greet and warm you. Refusal is an insult. You will learn, young man, you will learn."

Hakeem's wife and daughter served us dutifully. Although the hour was late and the environment strange, I dug in. After weeks of going without a decent meal, my enjoyment must have been clear.

Hakeem's serious expression signaled that we should talk of the reason for our visit to Daliyat El Carmel. Gadi noted the need to supply Jerusalem, the resolute defenses, and our high casualties.

The old man asked if I'd been there. When I said I had, he shook his head. "So young, so young."

"Zvi and I must find a way to reach Jerusalem without so many casualties – on both sides. We need information on the strength and positions of the Arab Legion."

He remained silent for a few moments but didn't seem put off by the request. He was an Arab but not a Muslim and perhaps opposed to the prospect of their rule.

"I'll see what information can be found. People talk, I listen. Sometimes there is a cost, sometimes not."

Invited to stay the night, and apprised of Druze custom, Gadi and I were given beds and blankets. It was the most comfortable place I'd rested my head in weeks. Nonetheless, I stayed awake long after Gadi drifted off. It was due to either the tea that Hakeem's wife had made or images of the fight for Latrun flashing through my mind.

The drapes allowed very little light into the room and we slept well into the morning. No matter. We had to wait. By late-afternoon, Hakeem was back. We gathered in a dining area with his sons and key retainers.

"The villagers along the road are at one with the Arab Legion. They want nothing to do with a Jewish state anywhere near them."

We wondered if our trip was coming to naught. But Hakeem spread blank paper across a table and began to sketch the roads and hills west of Jerusalem.

"Here are likely positions and the trails leading back to the Arab Legion's encampment. I hope this crude map will be helpful."

We thought it would. Our troops could infiltrate the area well before the next convoy, eliminate the handful of sentries, and hit the Arab soldiers as they tried to take up positions. We would ambush the ambushers.

Hakeem promised to send updated intelligence if any reached his ears. We gave him, albeit warily, a secondary radio frequency. As we left, I thought we'd gotten the edge over the Arab Legion, at least for a while.

Hakeem's intelligence was indeed useful. We reconnoitered the positions and trails one night and marked them more precisely on our maps. A few days later we gave signs of an impending convoy to Jerusalem. There wasn't one. We infiltrated the Latrun passage the previous night and struck the Arabs as they prepared to reinforce positions above the roadway. We gave more than we took and the convoy passed through more easily than expected. For a while our convoys made it through Latrun with only light opposition.

Shortly later I attended a conference where General Yadin gave an overview of the situation. In many respects we had the upper hand. Our villages and kibbutzes were safer, as were the roads connecting them.

On the other hand, the British were about to leave Palestine. The armies of surrounding Arab states and local allies would try to strangle our young state in the cradle. We were few in number and our supplies were unreliable, though the British departure would make smuggling in young men and weapons easier.

The men at the conference talked about whether or not Ben-Gurion and the others in the political leadership would declare independence. Whatever the decision, things would not be easy. That's how it was in Europe, that's how it would be in the Middle East.

INDEPENDENCE AND ITS PRICE

The political leadership was set to vote on Friday, May 14 1948, just before the Shabbat came for the observant. A crowd gathered outside the Tel Aviv Museum to hear the outcome. They were not disappointed. Six votes favored independence, four wanted to delay the matter. There it was. Israel was born. Jews around the world celebrated.

Yossi, the others, and I were in Latrun, about fifty kilometers west of Jerusalem, when word came over a civilian radio. Independence – the word had a wondrous incandescence. Those of us in the Haganah wanted a Jewish state but it meant foreign armies would attack with greater vigor and many of us would die. We celebrated, of course, but then returned to preparing our positions, cleaning our weapons, and waiting. The vote wasn't well received by the other side and its response would not be to demand a recount.

My troops were positioned near Latrun. We'd fought in the area before and were assigned it for the battles to come. To my surprise, I was considered more able than Yossi now and placed in command. The men were roughly my age, most a little older, a few a little younger. Many of us had fought together before and trusted each other. The newer guys were committed and disciplined.

I was responsible for their lives. I was eating, smoking, and joking with them now but tomorrow I'd order them to move out.

Some would be struck by bullets or shrapnel. Some would die. Most agonizing was the knowledge that in the confusion of battle I would make mistakes.

I'd seen death before, in Hungary, Poland, Germany, and Galilee. It had become a constant companion in the last four years. I must have worn the burden on my face for all to see. General Yadin had noticed it a few days earlier. Now my captain, Nir Segev, saw it too. He sat by my side and knew what was tormenting me.

"Zvika, we are a young army defending a new nation. Our leaders are all young – the statesmen, the generals, and our officers and men. It's all been discussed, and at every level. We see intelligence and determination in you. I have no doubt that you are a leader."

"But these young men."

"Some will die. Yes, we all know that. But without able men like you and Yossi, many more will fall. Think more of those who didn't die because of your judgment. You are the difference between low casualties and high ones. And that's critical to us right now."

I imagined the same conversation had taken place before battles since my people had come to this land four thousand years ago. Joshua and David probably had moments of doubt. I was not going to become a judge or king, but I'd lead my men to the best of my abilities.

They were tense and silent, looking down the barrels of their Enfields and Bren guns, lubricating bullets and magazines for reliable chambering. Some looked at each other anxiously and smiled awkwardly on making eye contact. Who among them, they wondered, would be dead in coming days or hours?

I gathered them.

"I can see concern and fear on a few faces. If you do not see those things on my face, I have done a remarkable job of hiding them. Fear can paralyze us but it can also spur us on to do our duty and keep each other alive. We will work together, we will cover each other, and we will secure the road to the men, women, and children in Jerusalem. We must not let them down and we must not let each other down."

The words of so young a man will not be written down in history books, but I wanted my men to know I was one of them and cared for them. Shortly thereafter, I had the startling thought that young Arab men were having the same anxious moments a kilometer away.

A few hours later, on the morning of May 15 1948, a large force from the Arab Legion struck us as we moved toward Latrun. The war had started with great fury. There were a few damaged vehicles from previous engagements and we used them as defilade from the fire raining down on us. I determined where the machine gun positions were and knew we had to silence them. I didn't order a squad to do it. I looked at a young man named Israel and said, "Let's go".

He was a frail quiet youth, roughly my age. I'd seen his fortitude over the weeks and was glad he was nearby. We scurried up the slope taking advantage of every rock and bush. For all we knew there were enemy soldiers behind each one, but fortune was with us.

As we neared the crest I saw bright tracer rounds cut through the morning grays leading back to an Arab machine-gun position not more than forty meters from us. I told Israel that I'd sneak behind them and that he was to cover my back. I drew my pistol, a heavy British Webley, and found my way to the position. It was easier than might be imagined as the machine gun's loud staccato covered the sound of my steps. I saw two soldiers busily firing below, then aimed the Webley and silenced them.

I motioned for Israel to come up and for a moment we looked at the two dead Arabs. There was no time for more than a momentary reflection there on approaches to Jerusalem any more than there was a certain night along the Syrian border. Automatic-weapons fire still rattled nearby.

As we neared a second position, the gun was silent and the position empty. Something was wrong. We'd been tricked. Several shots were fired and Israel fell. I saw two Arabs firing their rifles and shot them down. I felt a searing pain in my thigh as a bullet fragment hit me, probably after striking a rock.

Israel had been shot in the stomach but was able to walk, albeit gingerly. The emplacements silenced and our troops clambering up the hillside, I helped Israel down to a vehicle that would take him and others to an aid station a kilometer away. The road was reasonably safe and a convoy proceeded. We stayed behind and secured the hills. The convoy, we learned, took hostile fire farther down the road but reached Jerusalem.

The battle for Latrun wasn't over. The area was reinforced by Arab Legion troops shortly thereafter. Both sides valued Jerusalem and sent more and more troops into the struggle for it. Fighting was continuous for several weeks.

A later convoy was halted. Its guard detachment was overwhelmed and a massacre followed. Ben-Gurion and the generals planned another operation to secure access to Jerusalem. My unit took part.

In April 1948 Shimon Avidan, an officer with the rank of colonel, gathered us in the dining room of Kibbutz Hulda. We spoke with friends from other units before the meeting began.

I'd heard of Avidan. Most of us had. He was born and raised in Germany and in the 1930s he audaciously infiltrated the Nazi party. When his identity was discovered, he wisely fled to France and later served in the International Brigade during the Spanish Civil War. He made his way to Palestine and joined the Hashomer, the defense force that became the Haganah. He served in an elite unit known as the Palmach which fought alongside the British against Rommel's Afrika Korps.

A legend was about to address us. Avidan motioned for silence in the room and the roar of conversations came to a halt.

"The road to our people in Jerusalem remains precarious, despite our best efforts. The city holds great historical significance but it also has future importance for our new country. It will be a center linking the past to the present, and to the future as well.

"We are deploying 1500 troops to clear the way in what will be called Operation Nachshon. You know the enemy. Losses will be high. We'll take over the Arab villages between Kibbutz Hulda and Kiryat Anavim. The villages are not thought to be openly hostile but they are almost certainly sympathetic to the Arab Legion. Our infantry and armor will take them one by one. We will destroy them the same way."

My unit joined that of Joseph Tavenkin and we were assigned to secure the area between Shaar Ha Guy and Kiryat Anavim. It was hilly and densely forested – tough terrain for attacking forces.

We left Kibbutz Hulda at midnight and blocked off the side roads to the highway. Another unit took control of Arab Hulda and Muchasin. These villages were taken without great bloodshed. From there, both units spread into other villages and these too came into our hands relatively easily.

Haganah forces were joined by rival military organizations, the Irgun and Lehi. Their ranks had increased greatly with the declaration of independence. Many of their troops had seen the results of Arab attacks on Jewish civilians and wanted revenge. Most of us had seen the same things but maintained discipline. About 150 Irgun and Lehi troops attacked an Arab village called Deir Yassin. They suffered heavy casualties and afterward slaughtered a number of civilians. They took other villages with the same results. Unfortunately, it would not be the last shameful act that Israeli forces would be responsible for.

No rest. We were immediately assigned to other regions where there'd been heavy casualties. We participated in Operation Ben Noon 1, which made another breakthrough to Jerusalem. Our intelligence in its infancy, we didn't have adequate information about the enemy in front of us. The Arab Legion, we only later learned, was able to bolster its numbers by recruiting local volunteers. It turned out that in one engagement we were outnumbered three-to-one and faced heavy mortar and artillery fire. Casualties were high, especially as we retreated across an open area. Fortunately, our armored vehicles gave us covering fire. My unit was almost put out of action. In retrospect, it was clear the operation suffered from poor intelligence and planning.

Operation Ben Noon 2 fared no better. Again we encountered heavy fire. Frankly, we were not trained for combat on this type of terrain. Our armored vehicles collided with each other and fell over the sides of narrow roads. The disorder led to needless casualties. We had to retreat there too. I was angry with our political and military leaders. They were so determined to control Jerusalem that they didn't plan well, and we paid the price.

I came to realize, only many years later, that none of us had any real knowledge of military matters. We were determined amateurs who had to become professionals outside of academies and training grounds. We were forced to learn the craft of war not by reading Clausewitz in a tidy classroom, but by fighting in the unforgiving crags of Palestine.

Though it's in keeping with a form of narrative to boast of optimism in dark hours, I must confess to dispiritedness and pessimism in those hills. Our enemy was more numerous and better trained. Failures outweighed successes.

Tired of reckless orders and excessive casualties, many soldiers melted away from bivouacs. They didn't desert, at least not in the sense of quitting military service and going home. They drifted to Palmach units which had better leadership and equipment. Although I felt we were poorly treated by our leaders, both civilian and military, I stayed put and followed orders, as Young Zvika had sworn he would.

Many times we requested air support but were told that what few planes we had were busy against Egyptian troops. "Manage until we can get you help." And of course "managing" meant seeing my unit ground down, day after day. I recall the desperate faces of Haim Laskov and Zvi Horowitz as they pleaded for permission to retreat so as not to take further casualties.

Operation Yoram was our third attempt to take Latrun. It was also the one that hit me the hardest. One of my closest friends was a lad named Goren. He was about a year older than I and had come from Czechoslovakia. He'd lost his parents and sister at the Sobibor death camp, about 150 kilometers west of Warsaw. In Israel, even amid the war, he was cheerful and trusting in fortune. He buoyed spirits in hard times, including my own. Guys like him are essential to unit morale and cohesion.

"Our cause is right and therefore we'll win. In the long run, good always triumphs." He'd say that in his confident, optimistic, and good-natured voice, even after all the casualties of recent weeks. Even after Sobibor.

Operation Yoram had us attacking the wrong target and again we underestimated the enemy. They held the high ground and knew well how to use. So many casualties. As we pulled back I heard Goren cry out and clutch his thigh. I tied a tourniquet and helped him to the rear. Progress was slow. Mortar rounds whistled and bullets whispered the whole time.

"Zvika," he said, "go ahead."

"I don't leave men behind, Goren. Let's keep going."

His blood soaked my tunic, but we finally made it over a small rise where the rest of the unit was arrayed in a defensive position. I called for a medic and assured him he'd be fine. A dull thump came from his chest and another bullet whooshed overhead. An Arab soldier was firing from behind a tree a hundred meters away. A machine-gun crew opened up and the Arab fell to the ground.

A dark crimson stain was spreading across Goren's shirt, life was draining from his eyes. A medic arrived and tried his best, but the chest wound was too serious. He died. I sat silently beside my companion until a truck arrived to carry him away with the others.

Not much later I was sent to work on road construction. We'd all but given up securing the main road from the coast to Jerusalem, so we set out to build an alternative. It was called the "Burma Road", a nod to the supply route the Americans had built during the Second World War to supply Chinese armies. Work went on day and night.

The army was like an extended family with many cousins and uncles and one-off connections. I was fortunate to encounter David Marcus, the former American officer who was then serving with us. He'd been given the rank of *Aluf*, or general. He strode among us one evening and assured us that the road would be finished and our cause would prevail. "Rome wasn't built in a day but if it was, we should hire their construction firms!" he quipped in halting Hebrew.

One evening the *Aluf* sat down with a young soldier and asked where he was from. I told him of Romania and Hungary. That led to the natural question.

Disgust filled his face. "I saw Dachau, after the war. I saw what went on there. I played a role in bringing some of those bastards to justice. They went to the gallows!"

I thought of unspeakably cruel guards and kapos and felt a sense of satisfaction that justice had played out – better justice than what I saw meted out after Dachau was liberated.

"So how did an American get involved in a war in the Middle East?" I asked the senior general as I would an older relative.

"Ben-Gurion asked me to find experienced officers to help build the army. I couldn't find many willing to come, so, Zvika, I came myself. You have to be a little meshuganah to come over too. You know, I had to come here under a false name. We didn't want the British to know an American lawyer was here. That would really upset them!"

"Do you miss the United States?"

"Well, I'd welcome the opportunity to have a good hamburger."

When I said how courageous it was for him to come here, he instantly replied.

"No, Zvika, you're the brave one. You survived the camps and made your way here. I'm just trying to do what's right. I took part in the war in Europe – a major event by any standards. Yet I still wondered about my purpose in life. The prosecutions were one step, but I've found my purpose here. This is my place. I'll live here, I'll die here."

He did die here, though sadly not in the fullness of years. A few days later, when challenged by a sentry, Marcus gave the correct password but his limited Hebrew wasn't understood and the sentry shot and killed him. Marcus's body was sent back to America for interment at West Point, his alma mater. Moshe Dayan accompanied the remains. There are many roads and sites here named for General Marcus.

We were sent north to face a different enemy, Syria. Operation Brosh tried to seize a Syrian bridge at Mishmar HaYarden. I learned the background from older hands in the division – that is, guys who'd been in it for a few months. In June 1948 the Syrian army crossed the Jordan River over the Bnot Yaakov Bridge. According to the 1947 partition plan, the area was to be part of the Jewish state, but the Syrians took it and tried to drive west. That would isolate the Etzba HaGalil region from the rest of Israel. We stopped them at the Yarda ruins which lay atop a hill.

The battle took place in July and was quite bloody. We had no air support and only a few armored vehicles, yet we had to take on fixed Syrian positions. Initially, we fared well, taking the Galabina and Durigat ruins without too much effort. A few mornings later came a fierce counterattack from two or three thousand infantry backed by tanks and aircraft. Despite our defenses and determination, we had to retreat.

My platoon dug in at the village of Dardara. We still lacked armor and aircraft but had the support of the Jewish villagers. They supplied us and bolstered our numbers while the young and old hunkered down in homes.

Our most sophisticated weapon was a single mortar, probably a Davidka. A young woman of perhaps eighteen, Abigail by name, helped prepare the position with stones and earth. She had the weathered, determined face of the early settlers. As she positioned the tube, she insisted that she could handle the weapon. When we chuckled and suggested that it might not be so easy, she glared at us and said she knew full well how to handle a mortar.

Almost on cue, rifle and machine-gun fire came from a few hundred meters out. Abigail looked at the tracers, judged the distance and wind, and positioned the tube. One guy dropped the rounds and she watched for the impact then adjusted fire. The Syrian fire was silenced. She looked at us with a decided "told you so" look. Tough those settler women were.

A ground assault would surely come. We positioned ourselves in the trenches that we and the villagers had dug, and in a few minutes, mortar fire rained down and troops advanced toward us. Fortunately, we had sown a few dozen mines in the fields to our front and they took a toll.

Abigail and one of our men directed the mortar on the Syrians and we took careful aim with our Enfields. We didn't have a large amount of .303 ammunition and there was no certainty when the next trucks would arrive. In an hour, the Syrians relented. The village was safe. We looked upon Abigail and the other settlers with new respect. We were all tougher than we thought.

The next morning, we deployed to Ayelet HaShachar – a kibbutz with orchards, a dairy, and apiaries that produced rich honey which made for a treat. Ayelet HaShachar, like many kibbutzes, was under intermittent attack. We had about forty men with a few light machine-guns and the one mortar. No Abigail this time, though.

On July 16, Syrian aircraft attacked. They did considerable damage to buildings but no one was killed or badly hurt. We had the good fortune of shooting down one of the planes. It was a North American T-6 Texan (Harvard), which was an American training aircraft that somehow found its way to Syria.[13]

We moved to the Yarda ruins. A day or so later, after a few brief skirmishes, a ceasefire was signed. It held fairly well. Despite

---

[13] The Syrians later requested the return of the crew's bodies. This was unusual. It led us to believe that one or more of them had been from prominent families. After a temporary truce was agreed to, a Syrian detail crossed over and picked up the two bodies.

all the bullets fired and soldiers killed, the lines had changed very little. However, the Jewish settlements were safe.

We participated in battles to secure the Galil Elion (Upper Galilee) area. After that we deployed south into the Negev where Jewish villages were endangered by Egyptian troops. We drove into Sinai and reached El Arish, about thirty kilometers west of Gaza. This put the Egyptian troops in jeopardy. Protests from Britain and the United States ensued and regional commander Yigal Allon ordered us east to the frontier. Though skirmishes continued, they were fewer and less intense.

In March 1949 I took part in Operation Ovda which secured Eilat and the Arava desert. Later that year we signed ceasefire agreements with Lebanon, Jordan, Syria, and Egypt. The War of Independence had come to a close. Israel was born and its borders reasonably secure. We'd suffered some six thousand casualties, almost half of them civilians.

I was transferred to the Haifa area and assigned to the Carmeli Division. The Haganah became the Israel Defense Forces, which defend the nation to this day. I learned about explosives, sowing and clearing minefields, mortars, anti-tank weapons, and bridge-building. Somehow I was keenly attracted to explosives and mines. Work in that field was plentiful. The enemy had placed minefields in many places and they had to be cleared.

After the wars I was able to indulge in personal life. While doing some routine banking, I met a lovely young woman and made a point to meet her outside work. We shared many interests, including a fondness for football. More dates followed and we soon married, even though we pulled for different football teams.

THE SINAI WAR (1956)

There was no peace between Israel and the hostile countries around it, only a ceasefire. With ill-defined borders, skirmishes were inevitable. Acts of terror, too.

Israel wasn't the strong, prosperous country it is today, so there was constant fear that surrounding states would launch coordinated attacks that would overwhelm us. Egypt was a special concern. It had a large population and was avidly buying weapons from communist countries. Its president, Gamal Abdel Nasser, spoke very belligerently toward us. Indeed, it was a foundation of his populist support.

In August 1955, Egyptian-backed guerrillas known as *fedayeen* began slipping across the frontier to attack our villages and sabotage whatever targets they came across. They killed many civilians.

In July 1956 the British relinquished control of the Suez Canal, as per agreement, and handed it to Egypt. Shortly thereafter, Nasser took over the company that managed and drew revenue from the Canal. Further, he closed down the channel that led to Eilat, the Israeli port in the south.

Ben-Gurion was reluctant to go to war for many reasons. The IDF was still young. Its weaponry was limited and unsophisticated, though France and Britain were helping. War might bring trouble at the UN which had far more Arab and communist countries than those friendly toward us. Tensions and attacks persisted.

Israel, in conjunction with Britain and France, decided to go to war. We did so in the hope that defeat would undermine Nasser and bring him down, leaving the country in turmoil. Operation Kadesh in Sinai was successful, although it brought disagreement within our army high command and opposition from the United States. President Eisenhower all but ordered Britain, France, and Israel to pull back. We were able to secure the right of safe passage to and from Eilat.

My role was in a branch of the military known in the US as combat engineers. We destroyed Egyptian rail lines, landing strips, and other sites of military value. This reduced dangers from the south for a while.

The IDF also demonstrated formidable military capabilities with airborne troops, mechanized infantry, and fighter aircraft. Israel was becoming a regional power. That was clear, or at least it should have been. It was made perfectly clear in 1967.

NEW ASSIGNMENTS

Danger of another war subsided for the time being and Israelis returned to work and family. Over the next several years the economy grew. Factories popped up everywhere. Many were on kibbutzes which made the transition from growing fruits and vegetables to manufacturing electronics and pharmaceuticals. Villages became towns, towns became cities, especially along the Mediterranean coast.

My wife and I lived in Haifa, as it was close to the Carmeli Division's headquarters. My brother Motzu opened a car repair shop there and it was good to see family. In 1962 my first child, a son, was born in Rothschild hospital in Haifa. I was responsible for a new life and loved it. In time, two more children arrived. The military was highly demanding and a manageable mean between army and family was difficult to find.

I studied civil engineering, a field with civilian and military applications, though I steered more to the latter as might be expected. My purview included bridges and fortifications – building them and destroying them. A time to build, a time to destroy. My expertise was used against Black September and its like in later decades.

The IDF sent me to European training centers to learn from other armies. Upon return from one such course, I was privileged to enter officers training school, after which I was a career army officer.

The game of football had been dear to me since boyhood in Oradea. As often as possible I scrimmaged with fellow soldiers, family, and neighbors. I was pleased when one day my commanding officer, a wonderful colonel named Yagodnik, encouraged me to form an IDF league. Units put together teams and a championship series came about. It might be humbly added that the engineering team won the championship on two occasions. I continued to coach even after retiring from the IDF after the 1973 Yom Kippur War.

It was easy to be lulled into thinking Israel was safe, but there were always border skirmishes and arms sales to enemies. The Middle East is like a dormant volcano that occasionally rumbles and steams. Periodically, and often unexpectedly, dormancy ends.

I arrived at the base after a long night. Happily, it wasn't due to war. My young son Danny had come down with the flu. Two hours of sleep. That was it. I spoke briefly with two fellow engineers, including Colonel Yagodnik. He ran the unit in a paternalistic way, though he was eminently capable of sentencing a young soldier who'd violated a minor regulation to a few days of peeling potatoes or digging ditches.

Most mornings Colonel Yagodnik and I discussed what was in the papers, *Yedioth Ahronoth* and *Maariv*. I much preferred the former. Our Arab neighbors were planning to divert the Jordan River much to their advantage and much to our disadvantage. There was also talk of the newly-created Palestinian Liberation Organization which we'd hear a great deal from in coming years.

Outside the building, fresh recruits marched here and there. They were young people, boys and some girls, some the same age Young Zvika was on taking the Haganah oath. It would ever be thus in our land. I looked at them wistfully.

Colonel Yagodnik too was looking out at the youngsters and when my attention returned to the room, so did his. He had something on his mind besides the morning news. He'd received a message from another unit, one outside the IDF.

A civilian about my age called me into Yagodnik's empty office. He was with an intelligence outfit called Shin Bet. He ran down my service record from the Haganah to the present, then asked where I'd lived in Europe and what languages I knew. I replied that I'd grown up in Romania and Hungary and was reasonably at home in Romanian, Hungarian, and German. He likely knew all this before he arrived.

"We would like you to work with us on certain occasions. Your language skills and knowledge of Eastern Europe would be helpful."

Well, a secretive intelligence organization was recruiting me. In the 1960s one couldn't think of intelligence work without conjuring up images of James Bond. The novels had been popular for years and the films were drawing crowds at Haifa theaters.

"Perhaps you were expecting someone from Shin Bet to be dashing, debonair, and more handsome than I am."

The man was clairvoyant.

"Actually, we diligently avoid that image and try to look very ordinary so as to blend into surroundings. We look average, say, like bookkeepers, salesmen, teachers. People say I look like a grocer from Tel Aviv."

He did.

I demurred by saying my skills were in engineering, not espionage. I chose not to opine that my looks were at least somewhat above average. He listened carefully and allowed me to finish each sentence, all the while sizing me up.

"Zvi, we've learned from your records and superiors that you're resourceful and fearless. You know how to get things done in unfamiliar situations. You have ability in the abstract. From time to time, we'd like to use your skills on missions of short duration. Afterwards, you can return to duties here with the Carmeli Division. And though we cannot pay you in a manner to support an exotic lifestyle, there will be hazardous-duty pay."

My interest must have been evident. He went on to say that operations had to remain confidential. Fellow soldiers, friends, neighbors, and even family could know nothing of what I did.

Well, dangerous situations had followed me most of my life. Working in the intelligence field would bring more of them than a young father should want, but I'd be protecting my country. I agreed to serve Shin Bet and abide by its rules, even though there'd be no Aston Martin.

Over the next few months, I spent a couple of weeks at a Shin Bet training center whose location shall go unspecified. I learned about radio systems, special weapons, safe house procedures, and key personnel I'd work with. I also learned what dread things might befall me and how to hold up as much as possible.

Shin Bet was pleased with what they saw. Nonetheless, I wasn't parachuted behind enemy lines or sent to romance a femme fatale. I was sent back to my engineering unit and told to check in periodically with "Zeev".

Months past. I settled back into the army routine. I began to think that Shin Bet had scores or even hundreds of people like me in a reserve pool. I began to doubt Zeev would ever have any need for me, resourceful and debonair though I was.

One day Zeev sent word for me to be at a certain location where I'd be picked up and apprised of an operation.

EARLY OPS

The briefing made it sound straightforward, even dull. A colleague named Yair and I, posing as civil engineers from Czechoslovakia and issued appropriate papers, were to travel to Prague then Paris, check into a specified hotel, and await further instructions.

Yair was a man about my age who'd already been on several operations. He was relaxed which helped make me the same. On the flight we discussed engineering matters, and as we deplaned I felt very much the part of a conventioneer. The hotel was quite good, though perhaps a star down from the Michelin Guide's top rating. We dined at a restaurant that might have ranked higher. The next day we visited the Louvres. We were enjoying the town.

A package was waiting for us when we returned to the hotel. Yair brought it to his room, but before opening it he scanned the room with a pen-like instrument. There were no magnetic fields signaling the presence of listening devices. I was in awe.

Our assignment was to bug the room of a Russian engineer. His room was next to mine. Yair explained the procedure. We'd enter the room and attach listening devices to the phone and table lamp. Down the hall we went. Yair took out a metal wire from his jacket and jiggled it inside the lock. In a moment we were in. We closed the blinds, did our work, and were in my room ten minutes later.

"How did you know the Russian wouldn't be there?"

"Because, Zvi, we knew his flight hadn't arrived yet. It's not due for half an hour."

Hours later, we heard footfalls and the opening of the door next to us. Yair took out what looked like a transistor radio, plugged in an earphone, and listened intently. I heard the muffled sounds of a phone call. Soon a visitor came to the room and there were more muffled voices. Yair scribbled down notes. Apparently, neither Russian had a pen-like device that detected magnetic fields.

The next morning we enjoyed a delightful breakfast and headed for the flight back home, by way of Prague. Training had cautioned me not to think every operation would be extraordinary. That excursion to France did nothing to contradict it.

The next mission involved Soviet influence in the region, especially in Syria. The USSR was ever seeking to expand its power in the world and the Middle East was high on its list of places of opportunity. Syria was attractive as it would create trouble for western countries backing Israel. Soviet weaponry exported to Syria constituted a danger to us.

In May 1966 we were assigned to pick up detailed information on an impending agreement between Moscow and Damascus. This would take me to Berlin. We surreptitiously exchanged envelopes with an agent at a news kiosk. Our envelope contained a goodly number of Deutschmarks, the other party's held information on Russian military hardware.

Missions in Europe became more frequent. I traveled to France, Germany, Czechoslovakia, and Bulgaria. In these cases I was again called upon to exchange coin of the realm for sensitive material and take it back home. Shin Bet was pleased. I was given a higher rating and allowed access to more sensitive information.

Phone calls at four am only rarely bring good news. Colonel Yagodnik called me at that hour one morning and told me to come in to HQ. The base had unusual activity. Troops marched and trucks rolled in greater numbers. Headlights revealed grim, uneasy faces. Engineering troops were warming up trucks and tanks equipped for bridge building.

"You've only just arrived? We've been waiting for you for hours!" A colleague smiled and handed me a cup of coffee. I'd probably need more before the day was through. In the office were fellow officers Amos Vilnaei and Ron Zohar. Colonel Yagodnik began to speak as soon as we were seated.

"Today, Soviet intelligence sent Egypt and Syria a report stating we've deployed several brigades to the Syrian border and intend to attack soon. The report is false but we have to take action. First, we're inviting a Soviet diplomat to inspect the Northern Command area and see for himself that there've been no extraordinary troop deployments. Second, false report or not, we have to be ready for war."

The four of us exchanged thoughts about the Soviets' intentions then focused on matters related to our engineer battalion. Naturally, I'd packed a "war bag" with enough things to see me through a few days on base.

Over the following days we analyzed practical details of mobilizing the unit's men and materiel, with contingencies for deploying north or south. Nasser was taking the Russian intelligence report seriously and moving troops into Sinai. Alexei Kosygin flew to Egypt and publicly expressed his country's support. Nasser again closed access to Eilat.

War seemed in the offing. I was ordered to report to Shin Bet.

LEBANON

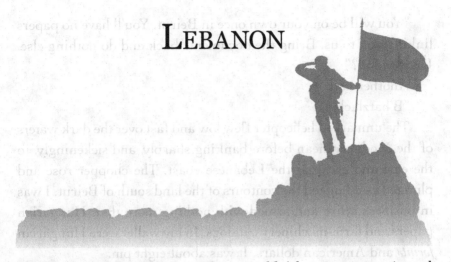

The mission was in Beirut. There wouldn't be a more experienced partner with me, nor would there be any partner. Just me. With the international situation as it was, Shin Bet was stretched thin. I wasn't a kid in the Haganah anymore. I was thirty-seven with almost twenty years of military service under my web belt. Still, going alone into a foreign and somewhat hostile country was daunting.

"You are to leave tonight and return in twenty-four hours. A helicopter will take you to a location outside Beirut where you'll be met. The contact will take you by car to Beirut where you'll meet Hussam. He's an agent of ours with extensive experience and contacts, some inside the Arab League. He will have timely material for us."

He handed me a thin envelope.

"You are now Herman Kardos, an Hungarian citizen in Beirut on business. To be more precise, the agricultural-machinery business. Hussam has a firm that manufactures such equipment. We subsidize it. In the envelope you will find a list of safe places. Memorize them then burn the list. Do not try to send them messages. You'll have to get there in person."

I nodded.

"You will be on your own once in Beirut. You'll have no papers linking you to us. Bring the documents back and do nothing else. Understood?"

Another nod.

"B'hatzlacha."

The unmarked helicopter flew low and fast over the dark waters of the Mediterranean before banking sharply, and sickeningly, to the east and crossing the Lebanese coast. The chopper rose and plunged as it hugged the contours of the land south of Beirut. I was in business attire and armed with nothing more than Hungarian papers and farm-machinery catalogs. In my wallet were Hungarian *forints* and American dollars. It was about eight pm.

The helicopter yawed and slowed before touching down on a dirt road. An Hungarian businessman hopped out into Lebanon, nodded to his Israeli crew as they lifted off, and got down on one knee. As my eyes adjusted to the dark, I saw neat rows of trees. It was silent save for the occasional chirping of insects. Twenty minutes passed.

Headlights came my way. A vehicle bounced about as it negotiated the rough road. As it came to about fifty meters of me, the lights dimmed and the engine rattled to a stop. A man stepped from the vehicle.

"Herman Kardos?" He spoke my name in low voice and a thick Arab accent.

"I'm here."

I walked toward him and he motioned for me to enter the car – a Peugeot 404 of recent vintage. The smell of stale cigarettes was almost overwhelming. Neither of us spoke, which in my limited experience was the norm in such situations.

In an hour, we reached Beirut. There were only a few cars every now and then on the cluttered streets lit only by an occasional streetlight. We drove through Beirut and came to more open spaces and eventually to a farmhouse surrounded by a formidable iron gate. A guard scrutinized us then open the gate.

The driver and I walked toward the partially-lit farmhouse. Inside was a spacious living room with a half dozen candles offering flickering light to the mosaic wall tiles. A man in a red and white *kafia* entered and sat on the sofa. He was a man in his fifties with weather-worn features and sunken eyes. He looked confident and guileless.

"I am Hussam."

"I am Herman Kardos." He didn't believe me for a minute. "Do I detect a British accent?"

"Indeed you do. I was a student at Cambridge University for more years than I care to remember. But Herman, we must show each other courtesy and trust. I have given you my real name and taken you into my home. Please be so kind as to tell me your true name."

"Zvi."

"Welcome, Zvi."

"My name really is Herman. I changed it to Zvi when I arrived from Europe twenty years ago."

"Ah, so you are one who found his way here from that time. Well, we have two hours before you have to meet you transportation. Shall we enjoy conversation and a meal?"

I was a bit peckish just then.

In an adjacent room was a table with an array of light fare which we enjoyed with a carafe of wine. Oddly, he spoke at length of his children, his passion for horses, and his hope for peace. The hour ended with a few puffs from a *nargila*. Arab informants, as best as I could tell, put out a good spread.

He handed me a package of documents and cryptically said, "Operation Assad. That word means 'lion' in my tongue."

My Arabic was limited then but I did know that word. It was the surname of a prominent Syrian politician. And so with the word on Operation Assad in my hands, I was driven to a different desolate place where the same helicopter swooped in to spirit me back to Tel Aviv.

In a cramped Shin Bet room known as "the pit", intelligence people and I pored over the documents. Egypt was crossing into Sinai in larger numbers and Iraq was making threatening statements about correcting the error of allowing a Jewish state in the Arab world.

The Soviet Union was behind them. It had become increasingly irksome toward us. MiGs were flying photo reconnaissance missions over our positions, possibly with Russian pilots. One recently swooped over the Negev desert and photographed the secret Dimona nuclear site. If its Arab allies were successful against us, Moscow would have a great deal of prestige in the region.

THE SIX-DAY WAR

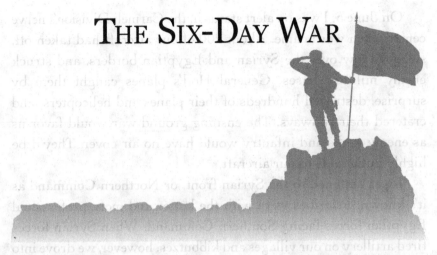

June 2 1967, we were preparing for the worst. Moshe Dayan came to the IDF nerve center, also called the pit, and noted the superior numbers and in some respects the superior equipment of Syria and Egypt. This led to discussions at the highest political and military levels of the need for a preemptive strike. Hit them first and destroy as much of their equipment as possible. The correlation of forces would then favor us.

Dayan called for a critical review of targets. We looked at those where engineering expertise might shed light – airfields, staging areas, bridges, and the like. We were to show no signs of imminent moves. In fact, thousands of reservists who'd been recently called up were sent home. Who would start a war with so many troops at home? But Israel is a small country and reservists can get back to their units on short notice. Not so of the larger countries around us.

Dayan was a man of great charisma and vision. His honored place in Israel's history is secure. Yet something about him made me uneasy. Others too. Deception was more than just a foreign policy tool for him. It was part of his nature and he used it well, in and out of uniform, with enemies and friends. It's how he made it to the top.

Dayan publicly stated that war was not imminent and that negotiations were easing the crisis. A few days later he ordered the IDF to strike.

On June 5, I was on alert status in the Carmeli Division's nerve center when word came. About 200 of our aircraft had taken off, swooped low over the Syrian and Egyptian borders, and struck enemy military bases. General Hod's planes caught them by surprise, destroyed hundreds of their planes and helicopters, and cratered their runways. The ensuing ground war would favor us as enemy tanks and infantry would have no air cover. They'd be highly vulnerable to our aircraft.

I was assigned to the Syrian front, or Northern Command as it's known. Priorities were with the larger and more professional Egyptian forces facing Southern Command. When Syrian forces fired artillery on our villages and kibbutzes, however, we drove into Syria to establish a protective area.

In a few days, the Egyptian army neared defeat. IDF reinforcements came north and the offensive into Syria progressed more quickly. I was at the battle for the Bnot Yaakov Bridge and we later reached Mount Hermon. (Over the years I've returned to Mount Hermon on more pleasant visits.)

Troops from Central Command went into action against Jordan once it unwisely entered the war. All of Jerusalem and the West Bank of the Jordan River came into our hands. Guns fell silent on all three fronts in a matter of days – six of them.

I wasn't raised in a religious household by any means. My experiences in World War Two did nothing to instill faith. Nonetheless, I was moved when our paratroopers took control of Jerusalem. My emotion stemmed from the schooling I'd received in Budapest shortly before making *aliyah* in 1947. Jerusalem was something my people had yearned for since the Romans defeated us nineteen-hundred years earlier. Centuries passed. Hopes flickered but remained lit.

The period after the Six-Day War brought great confidence in army and society. I was less celebratory. I'd seen many deaths and I knew the war, however glorious it then seemed, would bring problems. The Arab countries would want revenge someday.

INS EILAT

A friend named Or, a few years older than I, was a fellow Holocaust survivor. He was at a death camp called Sobibor in east-central Poland. He and I met at the Cyprus refugee camp and became fast friends. Over the years he and I attended many football matches, even though, like my wife, he pulled for a rival team. Or served in a rival branch of the IDF, the navy.

He'd recently been selected to serve on INS *Eilat*, a British destroyer sold to Israel in 1955. He loved the navy, the sea, and his ship. He enjoyed recounting the ship's proud history ever since it was commissioned in the Royal Navy during World War Two. It had escorted many a convoy, including some to Russian ports on the Arctic, and engaged in duels with Hitler's U-boats. The ship was an amazing part of history and naturally I was delighted when my friend invited me to come aboard for a cruise.

I walked up the gangplank on October 20 1967 while it was moored at Ashdod. Or, attired in dress whites and exuding pride, met me on deck. The crew of about 200, including a few recent graduates of navy schools, went about their duties as Or gave me the grand tour. I ran my hand along the railing and watertight doors and traveled back to a time when Nazi wolfpacks plied the seas. My friend noticed my boyish fascination. How could he not.

We went down to the boiler room where details of the propulsion system were given.

251

"This lady can reach forty knots, maybe a little more if we really need to scoot."

We cast off lines and sailed west in the direction of Egypt. Our mission, it was explained, was to signal Egypt that we were ever-present. There were dangers so soon after the war and the crew was trained to reach battle stations in short order.

Meals were served in a cramped dining hall but the food was surprisingly good, though not up to the standards of my officers club. Naturally, I did not voice my opinion. By nightfall we neared Port Said at the opening to the Suez Canal, the eastern side of which we occupied. The seas were calm and a bright near-full moon shone above.

The following evening, I heard the crew rushing about. Any landlubber could tell this was more urgent than a drill. A bright flash and thunderous explosion came from the port side. The ship rocked violently as though a giant hammer had struck it. There was a good deal of smoke and despite the ringing in my ears, I heard sirens and voices on the loudspeaker system. Another powerful blast came minutes later.

Sailors raced about with damage-control materials. Lookouts scanned the horizon. The ship began to list to the port. Or informed me that we'd been hit by Styx missiles fired from Egyptian vessels in Port Said. The communication system was out and we were dead in the water. He sent me below decks to lend a hand wherever I could. Sections of the hull were bent inward grotesquely. Efforts to stem the inrushing water didn't look promising.

About two hours later another blast sounded, though the ship didn't shudder this time. A crewman said another missile had detonated not far from us. We returned to work but not much later still another blast came. This one undoubtedly struck us. Another Styx had struck the stern this time. Its warhead failed to explode but its fuel burst into flames and was setting off the ship's ammunition.

The order came to cease damage control and try to reach crewmen trapped in the mangled stern. The effort was hopeless and soon the order came to abandon ship. Only then did I realize the gravity. The proud *Eilat* was going down.

Or's face was ashen as he informed us that most of the lifeboats had been destroyed. We placed the wounded on the remaining ones then donned lifejackets and leapt into the sea. The Mediterranean was warm compared to the Adriatic when the Saint went down in 1946.

We swam away from the ship and stayed in groups. The stricken vessel was listing badly and more secondary explosions shook it violently. It wouldn't stay above water for long. In less than an hour Eilat wearied, raised its stern, and slipped beneath the waves with eerie groans and whooshes. In a moment the seas were calm and silent. The only sound was the soft voice of a sailor as he prayed the *Shema Yisrael*. Many joined him.

The ship's fuel spread across the water and reached the clusters of orphans. Word was passed to keep the fuel away from our eyes and mouths as best we could. Long hours later, our planes circled overhead and dropped inflatable rafts. As many as possible climbed aboard, but a few of us stayed in the water until a Super Perlon helicopter picked us up and sped to Rumani beach. After preliminary attention there, we were taken to El Arish for further care. The next day I was taken to a hospital in Tel Aviv and discharged not long thereafter. My friend Or had lung damage from the oil and smoke but was back on duty in a few weeks.

We sent divers to the wreck to recover as many bodies as possible. The decision was later made to destroy the hulk to deprive the Egyptians of an intelligence coup and tourist site. An explosives expert, I was detailed to the navy for the task. Charges were placed in various parts of the hull in order to render it into unrecognizable junk spread across the seabed. I was not present when the charges were detonated.

The attack caused great public anger. *Eilat* was not in Egyptian waters when the missiles hit. Israelis wanted to strike back, so we destroyed refineries near the city of Suez.

Over the next few months we got a better understanding of the attack. We were overconfident and unprepared. There was much of that after the Six-Day War and it didn't end when *Eilat* went down, as will be made clear later. The navy retrofitted ships with better detection equipment and practiced damage control more diligently.

The attack had not, as many suspected, been instigated by Moscow. Soviet personnel had apprised the Egyptians that our patrol boats would be ideal targets for their missiles one day, and were on hand when the missiles were fired. Egypt, on its own, moved naval vessels into position and ordered the people of Port Said to stay off the streets.

Nasser informed the Soviet embassy of the attack only after the missiles had struck. The ambassador wasn't pleased. He cautioned Nasser that further events like this could bring another war for which Egypt was ill-prepared. Nonetheless, the ambassador took part in a celebration of what to the Egyptian public was a great victory. That's politics.

I'll always have a fondness for INS *Eilat*. I kept a picture of the graceful ship on my desk. In the short time I spent aboard it I came to love it, especially as it cut majestically across the Mediterranean. The skipper of *Eilat* suspected that our intelligence had known or at least suspected that his ship would be attacked, but failed to warn him. The debate goes.

THE BAR-LEV LINE

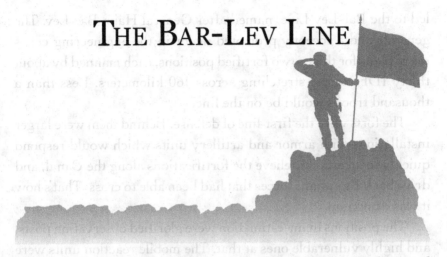

After the Six-Day War, a debate ensued in the public and government alike. What to do with the occupied territories of Judea and Shomron. The same arguments broke out over the Gaza Strip, Golan Heights, and Sinai.

The debate over Judea and Shomron, usually called the West Bank, continues to this day. Religious parties were especially exultant after the war and felt it was Israel's destiny to rule over Judea and Shomron – and other lands too. The exultation continues and it has shaped the country's politics for a half century now.

It would be fair to say that since the heady days of 1967 the occupation of the West Bank has often been quite harsh. This has hurt respect for Israel in the world, though many religious and political figures and their followers do not believe this. This is one of the worrisome divides in our nation. Wars are never truly over.

With greater security and confidence in the land, businesses flourished. We exported fruits and grains, technology and weaponry. The IDF invested more and more in modern weapons and high technology. Though the Arabs were defeated soundly, they were rebuilding their armies with Soviet help.

There was another debate: how to defend the Sinai Peninsula. Ships patrolled the coast to the north, aircraft flew reconnaissance missions, but the eastern side of the Canal had to be defended. This led to the Bar-Lev Line, named after General Haim Bar-Lev. The generals and a recently promoted major in the engineering corps made plans for thirty-two fortified positions, each manned by about thirty IDF troops, stretching across 160 kilometers. Less than a thousand troops would be on the line.

The forts were the first-line of defense. Behind them were larger installations with armor and artillery units which would respond quickly to an attack, relieve the fortifications along the Canal, and drive back Egyptians forces that had been able to cross. That's how it was drawn up.

The positions in my estimation were glorified observation posts, and highly vulnerable ones at that. The mobile reaction units were too small to provide an adequate response. Generals Ariel Sharon and Israel Tal were of the same mind. Higher-ups got their way, perhaps out of budgetary considerations.

The Egyptians fired repeatedly on our positions on the eastern bank of the Canal and even launched occasional commando attacks. We returned fire and conducted command raids of our own. These engagements became known as the War of Attrition. Each side tried to inflict sufficient casualties to force the other to relent. Amid this, the forts had to be constructed.

General Bar-Lev himself came to the Canal to discuss the proposed system. We stood crisply at attention when he entered the makeshift command center, and saluted dutifully. He returned the salute casually and took on a friendly demeanor. He asked me to call him "Haim". I did, even though it felt awkward.

"So you are the engineering expert who will build the line bearing my name!"

Receiving an affirmative reply, the general went over the two-tier system and outlined which generals supported the various aspects of the system. Clearly, he and Sharon were at odds. That was well known inside the army, probably outside it as well. Bar-Lev opened maps of the Canal and blueprints for the forts, including communications networks, power supplies, trench systems, and comfortable bunk rooms, at least by the less than demanding standards of army bunkers.

"After all, our boys will have to spend many hours in them," he said.

We went over the plans in considerable detail then settled into friendly conversation.

"You know, in my boyhood I wanted to be a veterinarian. Helping animals. That still appeals to me. Good for the soul. Animals are true friends. They don't have ulterior motives the way we humans do. A dog will do anything for you. Yet here I am in a general's uniform. Ah well."

After a moment of wistfulness, he asked how I came to Israel and a brief account followed.

"I was fortunate to have gotten out of Europe before hell came down. During the war I served with the Palmach in the British army. We're better organized now, more professional and all that. But war is still the same. Take a position, defend a position."

As he stood to leave, a photograph fluttered from his map case onto the table, intentionally, I think. It was a professional photograph of himself.

"Ah, those things! They gave me a stack of them when I became chief of staff. Souvenirs, I suppose."

He inscribed one and handed it to me.

"Now, Zvi, let's build the forts that will bear my name!"

Work began. I was to direct the construction teams but not go up on the line myself. I didn't like it but when generals tell a major what to do, after he has expressed demurrals, the major must comply.

Every morning I'd go over the day's work with a crew of forty, all quite young. I told them to do exactly as ordered and not to spend any more time up there than needed. The Egyptians could easily see our bulldozers and cranes on a stretch of the Canal and direct accurate fire upon them. IDF guns replied but the construction sites were dangerous places. I told my men to retreat if fire came in too hard. The young men, however, were determined and fearless, and took casualties because of it. Oz was one of them.

He was fresh out of engineering school and thought he knew all there was to know, from putting up a berm to defending the nation. He irritated many people, including myself, on more than one occasion, but no one could fault his abilities. I came to see a decent young man who wanted to do well for Israel. It's part of an officer's job to understand his troops.

"Oz," I asked one evening, "why do you always have to be a pain in the neck."

"I don't know what you mean."

I gave the young man a look of concern.

"Of course you know what I mean. Why do you interrupt everyone, express your superiority, insist on having your way, even at the most trying times?"

He offered no reply.

"Look, I understand that you want to excel in everything, and that's good. But we can't needlessly put off others along the way. You'll not have too many friends. Life is hard, Oz. So is our work here. No need to make it any harder."

"I try to control my ego but can't. I need to be the best at everything. That's who I am. Yes, I know it costs me friends along the way but I truly think that after initial learning, I know best how to get things done."

I urged him to share his great knowledge in a more helpful manner. And with that, our conversation ended and Oz returned to his bunk.

The next day I sent a team to complete a fortification about five kilometers west of the command tent. A young man named Ethan was in charge. Oz was to operate a bulldozer leveling the ground nearby and the rest would place iron plates between concrete layers of the bunker, which would allow it to withstand almost anything.

Hard experience told me the team would come under artillery fire and as quick and accurate as our counter-battery fire was, there'd be casualties. We'd lost about twenty-five killed and wounded thus far. It was hard to sit back there in the command tent.

Several loud explosions came from the distance. I got on the radio to get word from Ethan. He stated as calmly as he could that the team was under heavy fire and taking casualties. I repeated my order to pull back when the fire got too heavy. Oz got on the radio net and said he'd drive his dozer to the bunker and help finish the job. "It'll only take another hour," he insisted.

Ethan discouraged this as the Egyptian fire was intense. He repeated the casualties.

"I'll be there in five minutes."

Such a quandary. We wanted the fortification finished and that meant casualties. That's how it was on the approaches to Jerusalem and the Syrian border. That's war. Unfortunately, in this part of the world it's peace too.

I authorized Oz to work on the fortification, adding to pull back if casualties mounted. I asked him pointedly if he understood my orders and he replied in the affirmative. He was remarkably calm. True to his word, Oz was there in a few minutes and he and Ethan set to work. I forced myself to envision the crew placing steel plates as round after round came in. In an hour, darkness would come and the artillery would slacken.

The operators of bulldozers and cranes were reasonably safe inside the vehicles as sheet metal surrounded the driver's compartment. It was not especially thick and would only protect against shrapnel from an impact ten or more meters away. Anything closer meant trouble from blast and shards of hot metal.

Trouble came. Ethan reported a round had hit nearby, badly injuring his legs. He couldn't bring himself to look but the pain was great and his legs were sticky from blood. Furthermore, the impact caved in the protective plates around the vehicle, trapping him. He was near panic. I tried to contact Oz but could not raise him. Maybe he too was badly wounded or worse.

I sent in a small team to help Ethan out of the cab and get everyone back. I anxiously sat by the radio awaiting word as the team made its way up to the Canal. In twenty minutes or so, the leader of the relief team called in.

"You won't believe it! Oz pried open the cab and got Ethan out. He's not as bad off as we feared."

Hearing more shells screaming in and exploding, I told them to get out of there immediately. A few minutes of painful silence followed.

"Oz won't leave. He's working on the bunker. He says ten more minutes."

"Tell Oz I do not authorize it! The work can be finished another day!"

"I understand, but Oz is still out there."

I could hear more explosions and the rumbling of Oz's dozer over the radio, as I ordered the mike to remain keyed. After thirty minutes my man reported that Oz had lowered the last plate into position. An especially loud screeching sound came, followed by a startling crack. The radio went silent. Moments later the sound wave reached me. Static came on intermittently, then the click of a transmission.

"Direct hit on Oz's vehicle. Nothing left but twisted metal. He's gone. Gone. We're heading back now."

I acknowledged the transmission. Oz had it his way. It saved Ethan's life but cost him his own.

Months later, I was present as General Sharon gave Oz's widow a medal. She sobbed as she held her young daughter. The general spoke, then the major did.

"We don't know how much we care for people until they are gone. I worked with Oz on the line and can tell you he will be missed. His spirit, wit, and courage. He'll always be with us. May he rest in peace."

About eighty men under my command were killed or badly wounded during the construction of the Bar-Lev Line. The IDF promoted me lieutenant colonel. It was considered a solid line of defense. Many of us knew it wasn't. That became clear to all in the fall of 1973. My work with Shin Bet had increased significantly by then.

WRATH OF GOD

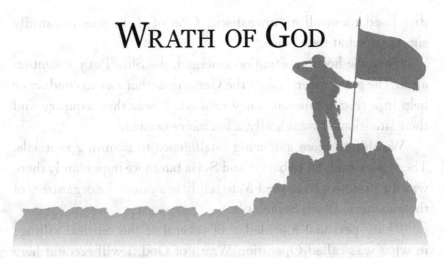

Everyone remembers the Munich massacre. Everyone of a certain age, that is. The rest have heard the stories or read the books or seen the movies. It was 1972 and our best athletes traveled to Germany to participate in the Olympics. The old Germany that held so many dreadful memories was being put in the past and a new one was going on display. That's how Germany saw it.

Many of us in the army and security bureaus were worried. It was our job to worry. We worried while people shopped and dined in Tel Aviv. We worried when our children went to school. And we worried when our sons and daughters traveled to foreign countries.

Events gave us every reason to be concerned. Sabena Flight 571 had been hijacked in May of 1972. Our special forces took it back. Two future prime ministers, Ehud Barak and Benjamin Netanyahu, took part in the rescue operation. Only a few weeks later the Japanese Red Army, recruited by the Popular Front for the Liberation of Palestine, opened fire and hurled grenades inside Lod Airport. Twenty-six people were killed.

A month before the Olympics opened, an Israeli Paralympic team traveled to Germany. A Shin Bet detail was allowed to accompany them. Not the case when the other games began.

Word spread inside Shin Bet that security at the site was thin. German authorities had hired a consultant to come up with terrorism scenarios. He came up with twenty-six. The authorities dismissed them all as unrealistic. One of them was uncannily similar to what took place.

Once the hostage situation emerged, the Shin Bet pit went on alert. The government asked the German authorities to conduct or help in a rescue mission. They refused. It was their country and their situation. It went badly, a massacre ensued.

We shifted from gathering intelligence to planning reprisals. There were raids in Lebanon and Syria but more importantly there was the directive from the PM to retaliate against the organizers of the massacre, Black September.

I have personal knowledge of several of the reprisal killings in what was called Operation Wrath of God. I will recount here what is permissible, intermixed with open source material. Mossad presented Golda Meir with a list of major Black September figures and she authorized assassinating them. Several teams of fifteen were sent to various parts of Europe. Each team contained two men who would do the actual killings. The rest performed supportive roles such as getting the assassins out of the country as soon as possible.

More than eliminating leaders of Black September, we wanted to instill fear in their minds. We planted stories in newspapers about the deaths of certain members a few days before we actually killed them. The message was clear: they couldn't stop what was coming.

Wael Zwaiter lived in Rome. On the night of October 16 1972, he entered his apartment building on the Piazza Annibaliano and called the elevator. The sounds of a piano wafted down through the elevator shaft. When the car reached the ground floor, two men stepped out and fired several rounds into Zwaiter. The pistols were equipped with silencers. The two men exited the building calmly, got into a car, and drove to a location where another vehicle awaited. They were out of Italy in hours.

Black September got the message: they were being hunted. Many of them went underground, changed their names, or moved to new cities. Some did all three. They could no longer live normal lives.

Mahmoud Hamshari lived in Paris with his family. He took exceptional measures to protect himself. He used to visit coffee shops, dine out, and enjoy Paris. No more. He stayed at home. We learned that he was sure we would not risk killing family members. True but not relevant.

The Mossad team had to be patient. In time, they were able to plant an explosive device inside his dwelling. A team member called Hamshari at home and asked him to identify himself. When he did, explosives in his phone went off, severely wounding him. He died a few weeks later.

Hussein Abdul Hir went to sleep in the hotel Olympia in Nicosia. A bomb had been planted in the bed. The blast killed him. His replacement was soon killed too.

Basil al-Kubaissi enjoyed a splendid repast at a Parisian restaurant on the night of April 6 1973. Availing himself of the good weather, he decided to walk home. He neared a man and a woman at an intersection when a prostitute in a car propositioned him. After negotiations, he climbed into the car. Less than an hour later he was dropped off nearby and the man and the woman fired several pistol shots into him. The woman was actually a male Mossad agent in female attire. It's unknown if al-Kubaissi realized it.

On April 10 1973 our special forces and paratroopers raided a PLO-Black September complex in Beirut. It was called Operation Aviv Neurim (Spring of Youth). Having experience in Beirut by then, I helped plan it. Forces commanded by Ehud Barak and Amnon Lipkin-Shahak came into Beirut by boat and were met by Mossad personnel who'd rented cars to transport them to the complex. Some of the Special Forces troops were dressed as women to help them get as close as possible.

Muhammad Youssef al-Najjar was the chief target, though we knew other Black September principals were also in the complex. He was awakened by the commotion and explosions. He ran for his weapon and was shot to death. The Special Forces troops made absolutely certain he was dead. Kamal Nasser was similarly awakened and killed. The same for Kamal Adwan.

Moussa Abu Zayyad took extra caution over the last few months at the Hotel Aristides in Athens. He locked himself in his room, ate his meals there, and didn't leave save for short walks. On April 11, he went on one such walk to get the morning paper. For one reason or another, he scurried back to his hotel. On the way, a stranger bumped into him and asked questions in a tongue unknown to him. Zayyad said he didn't understand him and after more futile attempts at communication, he excused himself. It was a ruse that gave a Mossad team more time. Early the next morning, Zayyad received a phone call asking his identity. When he replied, an explosive charge hidden in his bed killed him.

Mohamed Boudia was difficult to find. Many leads were run down and considerable time was spent. A theater lover, Boudia liked to dress up as a different person almost every day. Sometimes he dressed as a woman. Women were his weakness. The rumor was that he romanced women sympathetic to the Palestinian cause, wealthy ones of course.

Sometimes rumors are helpful. Sometimes they help find people. June 2 1973, Boudia parked his car in the Latin Quarter in Paris and entered a dwelling across the street to spend the night with a woman. The next morning he left and went to his car, checking it carefully as usual. Despite the precautions, a powerful bomb exploded as he turned the ignition switch. He died instantly.

In July 1973 we received information that the head of Black September, Ali Hassan Salameh, was in Norway and planning more attacks on Israeli targets. This led us to a small Norwegian town

called Lillehammer. The team collected information and identified
a man they believed to be Salameh. Two of the team members shot
and killed him in front of his wife.

They killed the wrong man. They killed a Moroccan waiter
named Ahmed Bouchikhi who had no connection with Black
September or any such organization. Wrath of God was put on
hold.

Ali Hassan Salameh lived peacefully in Beirut and remained
an important figure in Black September. He was thought to have
been behind a bus massacre in Israel in 1978 after which the new
PM, Menachem Begin, wanted the hunt for Salameh to resume. I
was with Shin Bet in Beirut permanently at the time.

A woman who went by the name Erika Chambers rented
an eighth-floor apartment overlooking a fashionable Beirut
neighborhood. She wasn't terribly sociable, except to stray cats. She
went out onto the streets and fed them every day. Neighbors were
amused that she spoke at length with them. A harmless eccentric,
they thought. Local color.

Ms Chambers' apartment had a lovely view of the city. It
afforded her the opportunity to note the comings and goings of
people in the neighborhood, including those of Ali Hassan Salameh.

In January of 1979 a man left the Hotel Mediterranean, parked
a rented Volkswagen Golf on Madame Curie Street, then took a
cab to the airport.

The next day Erika Chambers did not go outside to feed the
cats. She remained at her apartment window and waited for several
hours until two cars appeared. The two vehicles traveled down
Verdun Street, then turned onto Madame Curie Street. When
they reached a certain spot, she pressed a remote control button.
Twenty kilograms of explosives in the VW Golf exploded, creating
a large fireball. Ali Hassan Salameh, the head of Black September,
the person who planned and directed the Munich Massacre, was
gravely wounded. He died shortly later.

BETWEEN WARS

I t was odd being in the army at times. Only my commanding officer, Colonel Yagodnik, knew of my intelligence work. My wife didn't, nor my children. They only knew that I went away for several days and returned with gifts that could not have come from Israel. My absences were explained to the guys in the engineering battalion as due to higher-ups calling me away for special assignments. No one inquired much. I brought them an occasional bottle of liquor and mentioned travel to the continent. Everyone let it go at that.

I came to learn about intelligence sources and operations along northern borders, also about helpful agents in Lebanon and Syria, even in the Syrian capital of Damascus. I got to know the roads and restaurants and joked to myself about writing a travel guide for Arab countries – in Hebrew. I got to know European cities too. Posing as a European man of business, I had a goodly amount of money which allowed me to stay at the better hotels and even enjoy a night at the theater. All this for a poor boy from Romania.

I managed to go into strange cities, perform assignments in increasingly dicey situations, and return home without lingering fear or anxiety. My colleagues would grin and wonder how I'd developed nerves of steel. I wouldn't have used that description, but whatever ease I had while undercover probably stemmed from an early introduction to and acceptance of danger.

Egypt's Nasser died in 1970 and Anwar Sadat became the new president. Though part of the regime since the 1950s, Sadat was an unknown commodity but wasn't considered as strong-willed and wily as Nasser. Our military and government felt confident in our security, at least as confident as we could expect to feel.

Shin Bet was more circumspect. We devoted a considerable amount of our time and energy to gathering information on the armies around us. Egypt would not accept the loss of Sinai, nor would Syria forget we controlled the Golan Heights. Their eagerness to overcome the losses of 1967 was intensified by the humiliation of such a swift and overwhelming defeat. It was a source of irritation and embarrassment to the entire Arab world.

The Six-Day War also changed our international support. France and Britain had once been stalwart allies, providing us with arms and even fighting alongside us in the 1956 war. No more. The threat of oil boycott was too much and no country marches knowingly into economic catastrophe. The US, however, stepped up. We had American armaments and the proximity of the Sixth Fleet.

Before heading to Lebanon on intelligence jobs, I'd fly to Europe, usually Prague, then board a plane for Beirut where I'd check into the Phoenicia Hotel. I became a regular. The desk clerk and bartender were glad to see me and I exchanged pleasantries with them. This wasn't a bad thing. They knew me as a businessman from Europe, not a mysterious figure from who-knows-where.

"Sam" also worked with Hussam. He was CIA and quite good. We learned from one another and looked out for one another. I got the better part of the arrangement by far.

Hussam was helpful in gathering intelligence on Syrian and Egyptian armies by means of a contact in the Arab League and another source or two. One of them was a Russian named "Vitali". His sources were nebulous. The USSR was worried about contacts between Sadat and the US. It thought that increasing military support and perhaps even pressing for a war of revenge would secure its influence. Strange world.

Anyway, I was to meet Vitali at a restaurant in a neighborhood quite far from the Phoenicia, in both distance and elegance. The exterior did not impress. I found a table and looked about the ramshackle interior. The elderly proprietor saw my unease and came over.

"Please do not let the humble surroundings cause you to think the food here will be anything less than sumptuous!"

His smile revealed rows of teeth darkened by years of smoking the pungent tobacco of the Middle East. He handed me a menu but quickly noted, with little if any remorse, that many entrees were unavailable. He suggested I begin with hummus and tahini, to which I was amenable. He furtively asked if I'd be paying in Lebanese money. I was.

A stout man in a dark jacket entered and looked about. There were only a few people there but he was looking at the doorways and windows. He brushed away the proprietor and stood beside me awkwardly.

"The air in Lebanon is invigorating, like that in the foothills of the Swiss Alps."

"Much warmer, but just as invigorating," I replied.

I started to bid him to share the appetizer. His hand was on the pita before my lips could move.

"I'll lead you to the paperwork after we eat."

That didn't sit well with me but he did open with the designated passwords about invigorating air. He ingested the pita and hummus as though his last meal had been in Russia and the next one was in doubt.

With my guest sated, I paid up and followed him to an empty factory where he rapped on a metal door which was quickly opened then quickly closed behind us. We walked down a hallway to a room with old chairs and a worn sofa. Every step brought more unease.

As soon as I seated myself a man as stout as Vitali asked me for the names of people I worked with in Lebanon. His voice was nonthreatening and even pleasant. I responded in a voice at least as pleasant as his that I knew nothing of such matters and that I was simply here to pick up some paperwork for my agricultural implement business in Hungary.

He smiled. It was not a comforting smile by any means.

"You are to provide us with the information we require. Your Vitali will no longer be of use to you. We also know of Hussam's network and the great efforts they've made for you. They will be of no further use to you, either."

Vitali made plain where his allegiances lay by tying my arms behind my chair. I thought of my Shin Bet training and a few movies and braced myself.

"My business here is with agricultural machinery. I really don't understand the meeting in this charming building, let alone the ropes."

"I repeat. We'll need the names of your contacts in Lebanon."

Again that smile. I started to repeat my cover story when Vitali's fist slammed into my face. *Wham!* Blood trickled from my lower lip.

"I paid for your meal!"

"I don't pay for meals."

Wham!

Another blow and my tongue felt a tooth come loose. I quipped about a visit to the dentist but neither Vitali nor his accomplice was amused in the least.

"You are not in a game – at least not one you can participate in competently, let alone win. You can disappear without a trace. You work for the Israelis. Yes, we are certain of this. Tell us the names we require and your part in the game will come to a close."

The man drew a pistol and attached a silencer to the muzzle. A 9mm of some sort, probably a Makarov, though my attention was understandably fixed on the muzzle.

I'd come close to death more than once before. It was nothing new. Nor at this point was it frightening. I say that without bravado. I'm not sure it's a good thing to be so calm in the face of death.

Footfalls came from outside and the door opened suddenly. Two men barged in, pistols at the ready. One shouted something in Arabic with a heavy American accent – one that would have been comical in other circumstances. Vitali and friend were unwilling to engage in a gunfight in an abandoned factory. The Russian dropped his pistol on the cement floor. The metal clang reverberated in the near empty room.

One of my liberators untied me and handed me his handkerchief for my bloodied mouth. I was puzzled by his unshaven face and garish Hawaiian shirt. He looked like a slovenly American tourist. It dawned on me – CIA.

He looked at my swollen mouth and shook his head.

"A little sherbet will help soothe that. Let's go."

His colleagues took Vitali and friend away and my new friend and I walked a few blocks to get medical attention at the nearest Italian ice shop.

That was Sam. I can only presume that he'd been tailing me as part of his own intelligence gathering. Yes, spies spy on one another, as will be clearer anon. Sam eschewed the more typical appearance of intelligence officers and donned touristy attire and tried to blend in as someone there to buy souvenir hats and pottery before searching for a hamburger joint. Naturally, I mean that in a kind way.

Sam and I encountered one another not long thereafter at Hussam's dwelling. His taste in clothing had not improved. As Hussam and I sipped shockingly strong coffee from small cups, Sam helped himself to a mug of the brew.

"So, Zvika, what's the situation in the north these days?"

I wondered how he knew my nickname. He continued.

"Egypt and Syria are building up their armies, and the Soviets are backing them. There's lots of support from other countries. I hope you guys aren't S-O-L!"

Hussam added that it was only a matter of time until war came.

"We're aware of what our neighbors are up to. And the disposition of the Soviet Union isn't unknown to us. Gentlemen, please give us some credit."

"Perhaps you boys in Shin Bet and Mossad know this, but your government is complacent. It rests on the piles of laurels it harvested in the '67 war. You won't have the element of surprise like you did then. Soviet eyes are all over you. They watch every move of every reserve unit."

I again indicated that we were aware of those things.

"The Russians are training Egyptian engineers to put down bridges across the Suez Canal. The Syrians and the Egyptians have built an elaborate multi-layered air defense system. You won't have an easy time getting air supremacy. And two can play the surprise-attack game."

Well, in this business a little trading of information is in order. It helps both sides and builds trust. I mentioned that we had bolstered the forts along the Canal with high-pressure hoses to fend off assault forces and attempts to lay down pontoon bridges.

"We know – and that's good. Your main problem is overconfidence and insufficient intelligence. Or maybe you have the intel but aren't paying close attention to it. Zvika, we both know that Egypt and Syria are moving troops near the Canal and Golan."

"They move troops up regularly. We believe they're simply exercises."

"The big shots think they're just exercises. And the big shots think the Arabs are too awed by your military to attack. Well, I think the big shots have it all wrong."

Sam was stating something that many of us worried about. We were too quick to assume troop movements were routine. Too quick to assume the other side calculated the chances of success exactly as we did. Too quick to assume that the other side's desire to retake territory and honor didn't sway their thinking and make war seem winnable.

Sam finished his coffee and said, "War is coming. I suggest you prepare for it day and night, day and night."

THE YOM KIPPUR WAR (1973)

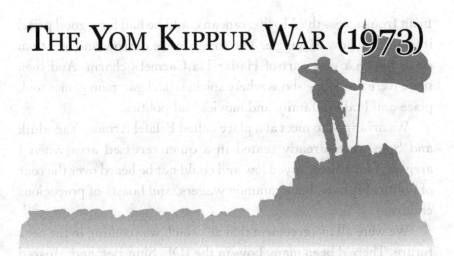

I sent my thoughts up the chain of command in both Shin Bet and the IDF. Both bureaus, however, held fast to the interpretation of routine training exercises. They'd seen several such exercises in the last six months. This was just another one.

Colonel Akiva Goren gave me a fair hearing but then sighed and did his best to put me at ease. He insisted that we were watching the movements closely and saw no sign of imminent war. He went on to remind me that the IDF had been placed on alert six months earlier and stayed that way for over a month. Nothing happened – nothing but the costs of mobilization and lost productivity.

"Paranoia is expensive, Zvi."

"So is misjudging an enemy."

I went on to say the Arabs may have conducted exercises in the past simply to watch our moves, then planned an attack when we'd been lulled into a sense of security. Colonel Goren didn't budge. He insisted that the IDF was always ready. Mobilizing our reserves could be done expeditiously – less than twenty-four hours. I noted that Arab troops could reach Tel Aviv in that time.

One Friday afternoon I lunched with Colonel Yagodnik and Sam in a Haifa neighborhood called Hadar Ha Carmel. Small shops and carts lined the streets. The smell of kabobs and spices and the shouts of shopkeepers praising their goods were all around.

Fruit from across the Mediterranean could be had for a good price, if you knew how to haggle. The streets were narrow and less than clean but that was part of Hadar Ha Carmel's charm. And then there were the coffee shops where spirited backgammon games took place amid talk of family and movies and politics.

We arranged to meet at a place called Falafel Armon. Yagodnik and Sam were already seated in a quiet recessed area when I arrived. Our voices stayed low and could not be heard over the roar of political debate, backgammon wagers, and boasts of precocious children.

We were all in agreement that an attack was coming in the near future. There'd been many boys in the IDF, Shin Bet, and Mossad who'd cried wolf in the last few years only to be proven wrong. Prime Minister Golda Meir did not want to mobilize the reserves for fear this would be seen as a sign that we were about to strike first, as in 1967.

Yagodnik summarized a meeting he'd attended with the prime minister and Mossad chief Zvi Zamir. Mossad was convinced that Egypt could not expect to regain lost territory through war, and Syria was simply not strong enough to take us on.

Our food arrived and we dug in. Sam, ever in tourist garb, was drinking Coca Cola. Sometimes he seemed like a caricature, though a discerning and likable one. He was in agreement and urged us to ignore world opinion which in his estimation was trivial and short-lived. He did not reveal how widely-held his views were back in Langley. He did say that new American weapons could prove useful to us when war came. He looked at his Timex and said he had to get back to the embassy.

Yagodnik and I went over mobilization plans and the Bar-Lev Line. Everything depended on rapid mobilization of the reserves and getting them across Sinai. Silence followed as we pondered the prospect of the reserves reaching beleaguered forts in a timely manner.

We looked around the room. All the tables inside and outside were taken and a dozen people were awaiting seats. Yagodnik said we should have become restauranteurs not soldiers. The pay's better, the hours shorter. After more levity he had to get home.

I was stuck with the bill.

Two weeks later I was in Beirut again, this time to get information from a Czechoslovakian agent. He arrived from Prague and was to meet me in a restaurant. Mindful of my unpleasant experience with Vitali, Shin Bet had two colleagues tail me.

I sat down in a seafood restaurant. Off to one side were my two colleagues who'd arrived before I did and were enjoying a white wine, probably an inexpensive one if I know anything about Shin Bet accountants. I wore a black sport coat and casually looked through that day's edition of *Pravda*. Both were arranged signs.

A man with light brown hair came over and asked, "Is there any news out of the Soviet Union?"

"Nothing out of the ordinary."

The gentleman placed another copy of *Pravda* on the table with a brown envelope peeking out. I shifted the newspaper a bit and rested a hand on it. The envelope wasn't empty.

"I see you also read *Pravda*."

"Yes, my favorite paper," he answered coolly.

I took his newspaper with the envelope, folded it, and stood. He took my paper and did the same.

"Thank you. Enjoy your stay in Beirut."

He bowed and left.

Back in my hotel, I looked through the papers and was impressed – and concerned.

I showed the material to Hussam and Sam. That wasn't unusual. As noted, we often shared sensitive data and exchanged thoughts on them. After all, raw intelligence is just that – raw. And often highly so. It had to be interpreted before it was of any use to the big shots.

Hussam read through it and sat back.

"It seems the Soviets are telling their people to prepare to get their families out of Cairo and Damascus. That's an ominous sign.

Alas, we do not have a date for departures. We have a stronger case for war, but no precise date. Your bureaus will not be swayed. I can only hope your forces are ready."

"We have lightly-manned fortifications along the Canal. Behind them are reinforcements." I did not offer numbers.

"Can the generals and politicians be persuaded to send more troops to Southern Command? Something short of mobilization, of course."

I shrugged my shoulders.

"We've built sand berms along the Canal. Twenty-five meters high. This will slow the Egyptian assault. We're also developing a pipeline to pump oil into the channel. It will be ignited. *Poof!* It's not operational yet, unfortunately."

Sam ran down the upgrades to the Egyptian and Syrian armies. New tanks, new surface-to-air missiles, new anti-tank weapons. The three of us pondered the correlation of forces and wondered when the trouble would begin.

Upon return to Israel I once again pressed my superiors on the matter. Once again, I got nowhere.

"Go home, Zvi," one said. "Tomorrow's Yom Kippur."

October 6 1973, the High Holy Day was at hand. Observant Jews and secular Jews alike respect it. Stores are closed, streets silent. Most Israelis were at home and fasting. The more pious went to temple in the morning.

I was at home with my family when the phone rang. It was two pm. No one would be calling on Yom Kippur unless....

"Egypt and Syria have attacked," Colonel Yagodnik said quietly.

I packed my war bundle and in less than five minutes I was driving toward the base. I saw many other military people hurrying to their units. Colonel Yagodnik gathered us in a conference room. The friendly exchanges of previous gatherings were absent. The boss looked worried, even frightened.

"We've been attacked on two fronts – Sinai and Golan. Egyptian and Syrian aircraft have struck our airstrips and command centers. The damage, fortunately, is not especially bad. Egypt unleashed a heavy artillery barrage on the Bar-Lev Line, bridges are being built across the Canal and infantry and armor are preparing to cross. Our reserves are mobilizing as quickly as possible. Major battles are coming on both fronts."

There were many unnerved faces that day. As noted, after the '67 war, a sense of invincibility had set in. Some of us were unsurprised. Concerned, yes, and deeply so. It wasn't the time for boasts or recriminations. Israel was in danger.

Hours later, the Egyptians were using powerful hoses to wash away the sand berms we'd built. Assaults on our forts were underway. There were only five hundred IDF troops on the Bar-Lev Line that day, and a few thousand behind it. One by one the fortifications fell with heavy losses. By the second day only one was still in our hands – the "Budapest" position at the north end of the Canal.

Our air force went after the Egyptians on the Canal. The American-made F-4 Phantoms and A-4 Skyhawks were superior to anything the Egyptians had. However, the Egyptians had a dense array of SAM batteries awaiting them and our losses were appallingly high. Golda Meir forbade Moshe Dayan from telling the country of the casualties or the danger.

Once our reserves were fully mobilized, a counterattack began. General Bar-Lev returned to active duty and became overall commander. He was instrumental in imposing calm on the bickering generals of Southern Command. Sharon commanded one of the armor divisions and pushed his troops hard as they crossed Sinai.

A few days in, Egyptian infantry and armor had crossed the Canal in numbers. This, paradoxically, gave us an advantage. The Egyptians were bottled up in areas along the eastern side and vulnerable to airpower. The attack was blunted and we began a counterattack.

Sharon convened a meeting in a spacious but crowded command tent. There before us was an impressive array of food from his mess detail. Even in the desert, amid a difficult war, Sharon got what he wanted and that day he wanted a buffet. Drinking Coca Cola straight from the bottle, he bade us to dig in. It was a welcome departure from the canned beef we'd been eating the last few days.

The general was calm and determined, though ire occasionally came through as per his reputation. He was headstrong and ever willing to exceed the directives of commanders when he thought it best. He often did. He spoke as he ate.

"We've been losing the war until now. I want to turn the tables and I'll need the help of your engineers, Zvi. I have an armor division and a detachment of paratroopers, but I need to get them across that damn Canal!"

His fist came open hard on the table, sending plates bouncing about. Through luck or calculation, not a morsel was lost.

"You've practiced putting down bridges for years. Now put that practice into action right here and now. With your bridge, I can crush the Egyptians in a few days."

I told him that indeed we knew how to put down bridges and that my equipment would arrive in a few hours.

"So you can begin," he looked at his watch, "at 1900 hours."

I nodded.

In a tent about twenty kilometers east of the Canal, I gathered my men. They were young, some fresh from civilian jobs building houses and roads. Most were in school back in 1967 and had never been under fire. That would soon change. The sounds of convoys heading west and the occasional fighter jet overhead made them appreciate the gravity of what lay in store.

I told them that we were about to conduct one of the most important operations of the war. We were to build a bridge across the Canal that would allow Sharon's armor to isolate the Egyptians on the eastern side.

"This will be the turning point. Once we're across, the war will be over. Who knows," I added for a little encouragement, "maybe we'll dine in Cairo tomorrow night. But be careful up there, guys. Let's not add any more names to the casualty lists."

Heartened but sobered, my boys went into their first war.

Construction began under heavy Egyptian artillery fire. That was to be expected. They'd fired on us as we built the forts along the Canal, they'd fire on us when we tried to cross it. Our artillery did their best to knock out the Egyptian guns, and met with considerable success, but from the other side's perspective the bridge had to be prevented or all was lost. When one gun fell silent, another took its place. When a fighter was shot down, another took off.

A detachment of paratroopers rowed across the Canal and armor followed on makeshift ferries. They secured the other side and reduced the direct fire on us. My unit suffered twenty casualties in this preliminary operation alone. Then we set to work on the bridge.

Heavily-armored tanks would haul polyurethane and iron segments into place one by one, then cranes would connect them the same laborious way. Segments had to be carefully positioned as they bobbed and drifted in the water until the entire 200 meters had been spanned. When the first bridge was completed, we'd set to work on a second. Then our armor could pour across.

As with the construction of the Bar-Lev Line, I was to supervise from the rear. I looked at the young men entrusted to me and doubted very much that I'd sit back in a tent this time.

Casualties mounted and replacements went up. Many would be wounded or worse in a matter of hours so I tried not to send men with wives and children. I sent one young man named Gal and watched the work proceed through powerful binoculars. To my dismay an artillery round scored a direct hit where he was working. Gone in a violent flash.

I ordered another young man, Yoav, to take his place. A look of fear came across his face for a moment, but he nodded and headed up. He did well, connecting a few more segments. "Quickly,

quickly," I found myself whispering. An incoming round killed him too.

There was about twenty meters left to go on the first span. I had five men left who knew bridge construction. Why was I different? My life was no more valuable than those of Gal and Yoav. Yes, I was an officer and had been in other wars, but at times rank and age do not make someone more valuable than anyone else.

Climbing into a crane mounted on a raft I set to work with my team. Behind us, our tanks fired round after round into the Egyptian side. Incoming roared overhead. Loud cracks like those of a nearby lightning strike sounded as they impacted. The sheet metal around me rattled and groaned from the blasts. I maneuvered the rig until I could position the steel connectors into the last few sections. Two hours passed. An artillery round shrieked in and destroyed a few sections. Quite a setback.

The last pin went in around midnight. The bridge was now complete. Sharon tested it with a few vehicles and they made it. His armor and infantry dashed into Egypt. With the other side more secure, construction of the second bridge could proceed more quickly.

I sat in a crane and watched tank after tank, truck after truck, cross the Canal. The incoming eased but didn't end. A round ripped through the air with the sound of a huge piece of canvas tearing down the middle. As it became louder, I knew it would be close. A fatalistic notion occurred that a chunk of metal mined in the Urals and shipped to the Middle East was going to end my life. There was the beginning of a loud noise then I went deaf and numb. A brief stench of explosives then unconsciousness.

RECOVERY

Consciousness returned some time later, slowly and painfully. I was in a clean hospital room – not an aid tent near the front, not in an afterlife of some sort either. That was a relief. In a few minutes a young nurse was pleased to see her newly-awakened patient.

"And how are we today?"

"Terrible headache. Can't move. Besides that, we're fairly well. Thank you."

"You've undergone four surgeries. That explains some of the pain. As for your lack of mobility, you have several broken bones in your legs. The healing process will be a matter of weeks, not days. You are a very fortunate man, Colonel Rittman! Oh, you're in the Tel Ha Shomer hospital in Tel Aviv."

"Are we fortunate enough to get something to eat?"

"I can bring you juice and yogurt. No solid food yet."

She fluffed my pillow and off she went. After the sumptuous repast I went back to sleep. Images of the Canal fight kept coming to the fore. A few hours later, Colonel Yagodnik came in.

"You should see that crane, Zvi! It's amazing you lived through that one. How do you feel?"

"Exactly how I look – terrible. I'll survive. I'll be back on the job soon enough."

He paused a moment.

"Your wife and children will be here in a few hours. They're anxious to see you, as you can imagine."

I had mixed emotions about their seeing me in my present state, but their anxiety must have been tremendous.

"What about the war?"

"We got three divisions across the Canal on the bridges you and your boys built. They routed the Egyptians on the western side and isolated those on the eastern side. It was touch and go for a while, but it's over. We won, Zvi, we won."

"Glad it went well."

I hurt too much to be effusive.

"Some people are upset because you disobeyed orders to stay away from the Canal. Some want an inquiry. Don't worry about it. No one's going to discipline a hero. You're getting a medal!"

I wasn't terribly interested in either bureaucratic procedure just then. Yagodnik said he had to get back to the unit, shook my hand gingerly, and left. A figure stood in the doorway a while later. The flower shirt and pastel shorts alerted me that my sartorially-challenged CIA colleague had learned my whereabouts. He was good at that.

"I knew my favorite colonel would pull through!"

"I had some doubts, Sam. I had some doubts."

After a little idle conversation he asked what sort of work I'd pursue once I was back on my feet. The implication was clear, even to someone newly reacquainted with consciousness. I wouldn't be able to be a combat engineer any longer. My army career was over. It took a few moments to come up with even a semblance of a reply.

"I don't know yet. First I need to recover. Lots of broken bones, they tell me."

Sam suggested the intelligence field full time.

"Will I have to dress like you?"

"Maybe, but the food's better."

Recovery was slow and frustrating. Early attempts to sit up brought pain and disappointment. Regular visits from my wife and children helped speed the process and encourage me. As pleasant as the visits were, they made me think that those who died in the war also had loved ones.

THE CAPUCCI INCIDENT

After twenty-six years in the Haganah and IDF, and a slow recovery, I retired and went to work for Shin Bet full time. The transition wasn't jarring as I'd been spending more and more time in the intelligence field ever since meeting with that Tel Aviv grocer in Yagodnik's office.

I initially worked counterterrorism in the Jerusalem area. We had a slew of Arab agents who gathered information on Fatah and other groups that were emerging after the '67 and '73 wars. Naturally, they didn't help us in the name of peaceful relations, they did so for money. Not everyone, however, was in it for the pay.

One of our more useful agents was a Palestinian teacher. He came to work with us after a severe auto accident in which he lost a lot of blood. There was no luck finding a match from hospital banks and donors. A search of IDF records identified a soldier with that type and he agreed to a transfusion.

The Palestinian recovered nicely and was deeply moved by a Jew saving his life, so much so that it took very little persuasion to get him to work for us. We let it be known in certain circles that we thought him complicit in a few acts of terror. He wasn't, of course, but it gave him some respect with Fatah. One might say we gave him "street cred" on the West Bank. He became part of the Fatah network which stretched into Beirut and Damascus. He provided timely information about caches of arms and explosives.

I sat down with him one day and listened to his report. Sensing vagueness in his words and nervousness in his person, I pressed him. He gave in and said he had critical information but if we acted on it, we'd give him away. That, of course, would mean a dreadful death. I assured him we'd act in a way that protected a prime intelligence asset.

He'd seen a car in a Damascus garage with a cache of explosives being hidden in several compartments. All in all, 200 kilograms of RDX, a common military charge. The car was a Mercedes – a pretty ritzy car to blow up. He went on. A man would drive the Mercedes into Jerusalem where the explosives would be transferred to another car, presumably a less expensive one. The transfer would be done at the driver's house.

"Who's the driver?"

"Archbishop Hilarion Capucci."

"Knowingly?"

"Yes, knowingly."

Well, Capucci was well known in and out of intelligence circles. He was an important figure in Israel's Christian community and in much of the Middle East as well. I dug around for more information about him. Born in Aleppo in 1922, poor family, seminary schools, ordainment. Not your typical Fatah operative.

A little more digging revealed that he was a gambler and had a way with women. In the latter pursuit he romanced Christians, Jews, and Muslims. A highly ecumenical fellow. He threw elegant soirees at his Beit Hanina home, not far from Jerusalem, where even a few Israeli ministers raised a glass or two. One of his women was an IDF officer. She had to be told to drop the relationship, not because of suspected terror ties, but because of his flamboyancy and politics.

Along with his social life came dalliances with the Palestinian cause. Hence, our informant's allegations did fit in with his profile. It was known that he opposed the occupation of the West Bank and supported the emerging Palestinian movement. His support was apparently shifting from words to bombs. Most vexing, his position in the region's religious hierarchy gave him diplomatic immunity. That meant we could not check his car when it crossed into Israel.

I brought the information to higher-ups and it reached Shin Bet chief Joseph Hermelin. He in turn apprised PM Yitzhak Rabin, who authorized us to arrest Capucci, but only if we were positive there were explosives in his car or dwelling.

Capucci drove the Mercedes from Jordan into Israel over the Allenby Bridge without incident, then proceeded to his church and parked. A colleague and I walk about the church as German tourists. We spoke German as we walked about and took pictures of one another. Capucci's Mercedes was in the background of most of the photos.

We handed the camera to a fellow agent inside an adjacent gift shop and the photos were quickly developed and scrutinized. The car's suspension and tires were under strain. It was carrying something heavy.

Our informer thought Fatah agents would meet Capucci at his home and remove the explosives. So, a team watched the place. One night Capucci drove the Mercedes into Jerusalem and we followed in a rental – less luxurious than a Mercedes, I assure you.

Capucci drove recklessly, even in parts of the city with rough roads. This, according to our profile of him, was highly unusual. The Mercedes bounced wildly at times, causing us to worry of a crash that might detonate his souvenirs from Jordan. We radioed the information to the team commander who ordered a Shin Bet team in a civilian police car to stop him.

The archbishop protested and urged our people to contact the Jerusalem police chief – "a personal friend", he said. Meanwhile, one of the officers moved the car door back and forth and determined it was quite heavy.

Clergyman and Mercedes were taken to a police station where our explosives experts began to meticulously look through the car. Capucci remained calm, until two machine guns, several pistols, and large bags of RDX were removed. Under interrogation he insisted he had no knowledge of the contraband, but soon confessed to collaboration with Fatah. He even admitted to smuggling other weapons over the years. Most importantly, he divulged how the transaction was to unfold.

The operation shifted from Capucci to his Fatah accomplices, those who would take possession of the arms and use them. We dressed one of our people to resemble the archbishop and repacked the Mercedes with harmless materials of roughly the same weight. The accomplices were easily nabbed.

For his cooperation, Capucci was let go, but of course we had suspicions about him and kept him under surveillance. He reverted to his ways and we arrested him once again. He was tried, convicted, and sentenced to twelve years imprisonment. Pope Paul VI requested his release and Capucci was set free after serving three.

He continued his support of Palestinians in legal ways, possibly only because he knew we were watching him closely. He was aboard a Turkish ship that tried to reach Gaza but was interdicted by IDF troops. Capucci died in early 2017.

ENTEBBE

Sunday June 27 1976, I was looking forward to a short trip to Eilat in a few days. The five of us would soon be basking in the warm sand of the Gulf of Aqaba not far from the town that TE Lawrence and his bedouin bands seized from the Turks in the First World War.

The chief informed me an Air France plane had been hijacked on its way from Athens to Paris. Many Israelis were onboard as the plane had originated from Tel Aviv earlier in the day. Plans for quaffing a few beers on the sunny beaches of Eilat were gone. In such situations a group of Shin Bet, Mossad, and IDF personnel gather to monitor events and brainstorm.

A colleague named Rami briefed us. Air France Flight 139 was an Airbus 300 with 248 passengers and a crew of twelve. We knew nothing of the hijackers' numbers, organization, or objectives. We were assigned to gather whatever information we could to aid Unit 4 of AMAN, the military intelligence directorate which oversaw our Special Forces teams. They trained for many situations – planes filled with hostages among them. We knew the night would be long.

The chief soon apprised me I would not be spending that long night in Haifa. He sent me off to France. The following morning I followed the situation on television in a Paris hotel and awaited orders as the situation developed. The plane was headed for Benghazi, Libya. A pregnant nurse was released and taken to London where I was to debrief her or those who had.

"Keith" took me to a building of uncertain affiliation where I went through security checks before being led to an office. "Allen" had debriefed the nurse and I got the information we wanted. There were four hijackers – two German, two probably Arab, all armed with automatic weapons, pistols, and possibly hand grenades. The passengers were extremely fearful. A secure line to Shin Bet was established.

Back in Israel we learned the plane had left Benghazi and landed at the Entebbe airfield south of the Ugandan capital of Kampala. The Ugandan army was taking up positions around the airfield, probably to defend the terrorists. We collected information about Entebbe. IDF personnel who'd been to Uganda in recent years provided information on security and what went on in various buildings.

The two Arab hijackers, we learned, belonged to the Popular Front for the Liberation of Palestine (PFLP), an organization run by Wadie Haddad and George Habash. We were using diplomacy to reach a peaceful conclusion but prepared to use other methods.

The hijackers released all non-Jewish passengers and our concern of course grew. The French passengers that were released were brought to Paris and debriefed. One of them, a painter, sketched the hijackers and the interior of the terminal where the hostages were. Three more terrorists joined the original four at Entebbe.

There was a procedure to separate Jews from non-Jews – a selection, one might say. Long after the destruction of the Third Reich, there was a selection. The French crew refused to leave the passengers. Brave, honorable people.

A rescue mission was planned. Army officers Dan Shomron and Ehud Barak worked with the joint Mossad-Shin Bet team. The Special Forces (*Sayeret Matkal*) were given the information we'd brought back from London and Paris. A mock-up of the Ugandan airport was rapidly assembled and the commandos practiced their mission over and over. A young officer named Yoni Netanyahu would lead the mission.

Ehud Barak convinced the Kenyan government to allow us to use their airspace and to land for refueling. Prime Minister Rabin asked Rabbi Ovadia Yosef to offer dispensation for our soldiers to work on the Sabbath. He consented. One of our people flew to Nairobi, rented a civil aviation plane, and performed what one might call aerial reconnaissance of Entebbe. It was a Cessna, not a U-2, but all the same we got helpful shots of the airport and the Ugandan troops around it.

The most recent negotiations brought nothing but an ultimatum from the terrorists: they would begin killing the hostages, two every four hours. That was it.

The operation began midday Saturday, July 3. Four C-130 cargo planes were in the air over Ethiopia when the government gave the go-ahead. Back in the pit, I listened to the radio traffic between our planes and the operational headquarters. The C-130s mixed in with ordinary air traffic and began to land shortly after a scheduled British cargo plane touched down. The first plane's troops secured the field for the following three. The second plane contained our special forces, who approached the terminal in a convoy with someone dressed like Ugandan leader Idi Amin. Amazing.

As they entered the terminal, two Ugandan soldiers were killed with Berettas equipped with silencers. One soldier, however, got off a few shots which alerted other soldiers and the terrorists. One of the shots killed Yoni Netanyahu.

Our troops stormed the terminal and shot down the seven terrorists. Two hostages were killed, one by a terrorist, one by friendly fire. Out on the airfield a sharp firefight opened up between our paratroopers and Ugandan soldiers. The paratroopers did their jobs.

We heard the message that the hostages were free and in the air. To top it off, the mission was completed on July 4 1976 – the 200th anniversary of America's Declaration of Independence. No fireworks, but champagne glasses clinked in the pit.

SADAT COMES TO ISRAEL (1977)

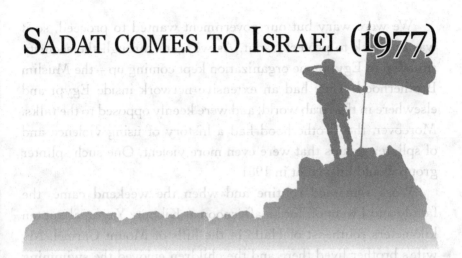

Egyptian sources apprised us that Anwar Sadat wanted to negotiate a peace agreement with Israel. This would mean a break from the Arab world – one quite risky for Sadat. Many of us were circumspect. "Too good to be true" is sound advice for consumers and intelligence officers alike.

In time, however, Sadat announced his peace initiative. He even offered to come to Israel for talks and Prime Minister Begin accepted. We worried about the details of an agreement and also about Sadat's safety while here. Many Arabs deemed him a traitor and yearned to see him die in Israel, or at least be embarrassed by an act of terrorism.

Many in Shin Bet and Mossad remained suspicious of Sadat. After all, he'd ordered the attack across Suez only four years earlier and long despised Israel, swearing to forever oppose our existence. Suddenly he wanted to be our friend.

We went over the information we'd gathered since 1973, especially regarding Egypt's intentions in the Yom Kippur War. Sadat didn't think he could defeat us. He had the more limited and very thoughtful goal of retaking a portion of Sinai to obtain a stronger negotiating position. He'd regain lost territory and honor. That scenario had never occurred to our security organizations. The things you learn after wars.

We were wary but our government wanted to proceed, so it was our task to protect Sadat. As we went through the security situation in Egypt, one organization kept coming up – the Muslim Brotherhood. They had an extensive network inside Egypt and elsewhere in the Arab world, and were keenly opposed to the talks. Moreover, the Brotherhood had a history of using violence and of splinter groups that were even more violent. One such splinter group would kill Sadat in 1981.

Work remained routine and when the weekend came, the family and I went off for an afternoon at Kibbutz Yagur, about ten kilometers southeast of Haifa in the hills of Mount Carmel. My wife's brother lived there and the children enjoyed the swimming pool and petting zoo.

The Arab owner of an establishment knew me as a former army officer. He belonged to the PLO and was a good source for what the Palestinian man-on-the-street was thinking. We exchanged greetings and inquiries about the health of families. I sensed some disquiet and soon enough he asked a coworker to watch the till and motioned for me to follow him to the back.

"I hope for peace in the region. All good men do. But there are many others who burn with a desire to kill Sadat when he comes. I'll give you a name and phone number of a man who has good information, reliable information. Please call him. You can trust him, Zvi. On that you have my word."

He repeated that he trusted the man I was to meet. Very nice, but I would be the one out on the line.

That evening, back in the pit, I told the boss of the exchange. I gave him the phone number and name of the contact – Illam. There was little in the way of a background check we could do on short notice, so we had to take a chance. That is, a certain Shin Bet officer with a record of resourcefulness had to take a chance.

I called Illam from the pit and we agreed to meet the next day inside the old quarter of Acre. A tracking device and voice transmitter were placed inside a coat button so a team could keep tabs on me. Shortly thereafter, I was in a working-class part of Acre knocking on a less than tidy door that bore no name. A young man opened it and asked me to enter.

I sat down in a spartanly decorated room and was soon greeted by a man identifying himself as Illam. Hearty handshake, cold eyes. I was frisked and my wallet was taken and looked through. It was of course a "work wallet".

"We'll have to move to another location. It is a precaution that is mostly for us but it will protect you as well. This will require blindfolding you. Should you find this objectionable, I will understand completely and you will be free to leave. The choice is yours."

I weighed the matter briefly, then consented. I trusted the tracking device more than I did Illam. My hands were tied firmly behind me and a hood was placed over my head, briefly bringing back old memories of confinement. I was placed in the backseat of a car and whisked off for a twenty-minute drive. How much of it was going around in circles was difficult to judge. I was led out of the car, still blindfolded. The scent of old stonework and mildew suggested we were in the old city whose walls date back to the Crusades.

It occurred to me that the thick walls might block the radio waves the tracking devices relied on, and the winding passageways and dank basements offered many hiding places. I mused that Acre was a popular tourist spot. Down some steps, a dozen or more. A heavy door creaked open, then closed behind me the same way. Images of dungeons from old movies came to mind. These chaps knew melodrama.

The hood was taken off, revealing my presence in a bare, dark room with nothing but two chairs – mine and Illam's. No pita and hummus, no tea, no brightly-colored banner reading "Welcome Shin Bet".

"I apologize for the discomfort. I have to take security measures which may seem excessive. We belong to Islamic Jihad – a group that began in Egypt but with cells here now. Most of the organization opposes Sadat's efforts. In their estimation he is betraying the

Palestinian cause and they want him dead. Some of us disagree. It's possible negotiations on Sinai will lead to further negotiations on the West Bank."

It was intriguing to peer into the eyes of an enemy we presumed to know and see unexpected complexity and conflict.

"Islamic Jihad plans to fire a missile at Sadat's plane as it comes in to land. Your attention, it is hoped, will be drawn away by diversions at the Suez Canal. Two men will set up along the flight path with a Strella missile. The plane will become highly unstable and crash. Should that fail, there will be someone in Sadat's honor guard who will turn his weapon on him. Less spectacular, but the result will be the same."

As I was formulating questions that would give more detail, there was a commotion. The door opened and men armed with Kalashnikovs came in. An argument began and escalated. One of the men called Illam a traitor and delivered a blow to his face with the wooden butt of his rifle. Illam remained strangely composed, despite the blood flowing from a gash on his cheek.

A heated exchange between Islamic Jihad factions ensued. Accusations of poor judgment and faithlessness flew. Sadat was a great leader, Sadat was a lackey. We must strike now, we must wait. A few Kalashnikov rounds ended the debate and Illam's life as well. My turn was coming. No one would mistake me for an Islamic Jihad initiate.

"And who are you with?" the gunman demanded. "Mossad? Shin Bet? What did Illam tell you?"

My reply was that Illam didn't have time to tell me anything. Unimpressed, he struck me hard across the face.

"But who are you with?"

I had to make him think I was valuable. That would keep me alive a little longer. I didn't know if the tracking device was working in the old city but certainly my colleagues would have followed me as best they could. At any sign of trouble, a rescue would be put into play. Time was my ally, and the only in the room just then.

"Shin Bet," I said quietly. This, according to our manual, would intimidate some and get others to pause. Killing one of us would bring hell down on them. What happened to Black September would happen to them.

"It's good that you admit this. It will not save your life, though. Illam may or may not have told you anything but your silence can be assured. Your people will know we are without fear."

This fellow wasn't going along with the Shin Bet manual. He stared at me, looking for signs of fear or imminent confession. He saw neither and began to calculate his next move. Twenty minutes or so passed as they mulled their next move. A sudden blast deafened me and tossed me and the others on the ground like discarded toys. Men scurried about and gunfire flashed. Consciousness left me.

Haifa's Rambam Hospital. My section chief stood by the bed.

"They say you'll be fine soon enough, Zvi. The tracking device worked remarkably well. That's what saved you. We were able to follow you and hear what was going on, even in the old city. Had they taken you a little deeper, well, that might have been more difficult. We heard things go bad and sent in the Atlit guys."

"They did well."

"We're hunting for the team with the Strella missile. So far, *bupkis*. The cell might think the job has been compromised and called it off. We're still looking."

I insisted on getting back on the case but my discomfort must have been obvious. My section chief patted my shoulder and urged me to rest a while longer.

A day later I was back in the pit with one of the teams assigned to Sadat's visit. Informants were contacted, copious amounts of cash was spread out. Still *bupkis*. We reported up the chain until it reached the prime minister. Sadat's plane would take another approach to Ben-Gurion but the arrival date and time remained the same.

On November 18 we detected Egyptian units moving up to the Canal, just as Illam had said. This might have signaled that the Egyptian army wasn't pleased with the negotiations and was complicit in the conspiracy or perhaps seeking to raise tensions. When it was suggested we take the precaution of mobilizing reserves, Begin refused, insisting it might harm the talks.

Sadat arrived as planned. Millions of people in Israel and Egypt watched an Arab leader come to meet his Israeli counterpart. It was unthinkable only a few months earlier. The honor guard performed their duties flawlessly. Salutes were fired. Nothing else. A symphony orchestra performed in Sadat's honor.

An agreement was eventually reached. Tourists came and went across borders that had once seen tanks and planes locked in combat.

To this day we don't know what to make of the conspiracy Illam warned of. Was he wrong? Was he lying? Or did the conspirators think the mission had been compromised and call it off? In the intelligence field, many things remain unclear even many years afterward. How well did Egyptian intelligence know what lay ahead for Sadat as he oversaw a routine military parade in 1981?

THE ANGEL OF DEATH AGAIN

T he Nuremberg Trials took place shortly after the Third Reich's demise while I was living on the kibbutz. We had no access to much media or any classified dossiers, but word reached us. We talked about the trials while in the fields and back in the dining hall. Many key figures stood trial, were convicted, and hanged.

Two figures stuck in my mind. Adolf Eichmann oversaw the system that transported people from ghettos to camps. I rode his Death Express on more than one occasion, including one from Oradea to Auschwitz. The other was Josef Mengele – the Angel of Death. He oversaw the selection process on the platform and directed medical experiments that inflicted suffering and death. I was a subject in some of them.

In 1960, a fellow army officer named Channan informed me that Eichmann was living in Argentina and that Mossad was planning to kidnap him and take him back to Israel for trial. Channan had been detailed to the Mossad team planning the operation. He quickly added that this information was not to be shared, though I of course knew that. He went on to say, almost in passing, that there was another important figure living in Argentina who might also be seized – an SS doctor named Josef Mengele.

That name jarred me. Eichmann became secondary. He was an abstract figure, Mengele was not. I knew people who suffered and died at his hands. I told Channan that Mengele took me out of a group headed for death and placed me in his medical experiments. Channan read my eyes and told me that despite my keen personal interest, the team was already in place and assignment to it was impossible. He arranged for me to speak with Mossad personnel and I eagerly offered recollections in the hope that any bit of information might prove useful. In return, Mossad apprised me of what was known about Mengele, most of which is now available to the public. Later, while with Shin Bet, I was able to read updates.

In January of 1945, as the Soviets neared Auschwitz, Mengele fled to the Mauthausen camp, about 300 kilometers to the southwest in what is now Austria, which was then part of the German Reich. Mossad gathered this information from an American report drawn from a man who'd been part of Mengele's twins experiments.

In April 1945, with the Reich's end at hand, a German army doctor named Kaler, who had served earlier with Mengele in Russia, saw him. He was certain that Mengele was in a Wehrmacht uniform, not his SS one. Upon surrender, Kaler and Mengele were placed in an American POW camp.

The Americans inspected all prisoners for telltale SS tattoos but found none on Mengele. He had four fictional identities. One of them was Josef Mamling, a Bavarian painter of local fame, so he was not classified as an important prisoner.

Mengele was severely depressed and contemplating suicide. Nonetheless, he managed to escape. Mengele's wife Irena and son Rolf lived with her parents in Günzburg, about seventy kilometers northwest of Munich, but they were not thought to have concealed him or known his whereabouts. There were various reports of what he did before escaping to South America but none were reliable.

One said he'd been captured near Berlin. Another claimed he was in Polish hands.

In June 1949 Mengele boarded the *North King* in an Italian port and sailed to Argentina. His papers identified him as Helmut Gregor, a mechanic born in Italy. It's thought that the Red Cross gave him the papers, though not as part of an effort to protect him. Upon arrival in Argentina, Mengele obtained an identity card from local police and began working for the family agricultural machinery company founded by his father in 1871. The company is a going concern to this day. Its website makes no mention of him. Paradoxically, I posed as someone in the agricultural-machinery trade while undercover with Shin Bet.

Seven years later, Mengele appeared at the German Embassy in Buenos Aires and presented his genuine birth certificate. The embassy confirmed its authenticity and issued him an Argentine identity card. It bore his real name, real place of birth, and real date of birth. Mengele was living openly. When Israel asked the Argentine ambassador for an explanation, he replied there was no arrest warrant for Mengele and Germany had filed no extradition request.

Mossad kept track of Mengele's family in Germany. His wife Irena refused to join him in Argentina and divorced him in 1954. She remarried shortly thereafter. For his part, Mengele married his brother's widow. Another brother, Alois, was the father of twins – an obsession with Mengele.

There were several erroneous stories about Mengele in South America. *Ha'aretz* reported in December 1973 that unknown persons, probably Israelis, had killed him in Brazil. It wasn't true. Another German living near the Brazil-Paraguay border had been killed. The killers were probably not Israelis.

Mossad had reliable intelligence on those who knew Mengele after he fled to Brazil. He made the acquaintances of a few German emigrants and using the name of a Swiss man named Peter Hochbichler, became an overseer on the farm of an immigrant couple. He took no pay and kept to himself. It was probably only a matter of time until the owners came across a photo of so notorious a man. When they confronted their overseer, he admitted to being Josef Mengele and went on to say he was one of many Nazi fugitives in South America. The owners were inclined to have him leave but someone from the Mengele business offered money to let him stay. They agreed, perhaps because the farm wasn't faring well.

Mengele later left and stayed with an Austrian woman named Liselotte Bossert. She too accepted money from the Mengele business. The arrangement continued, despite occasional heated arguments between Mr Bossert and Mengele. The Bosserts were present on the Brazilian beach when Mengele drowned in 1979. They heard his calls for help as he was swimming surprising far out in the Atlantic. Her husband tried to rescue him, and almost died doing so, but he was only successful in bringing Mengele's lifeless body to shore.

Officials exhumed the remains in 1985 and dental records indicated it was indeed Mengele. Later DNA tests did the same. There was no doubt that Josef Mengele was dead. It would have been more fitting had he been nabbed along with Eichmann in 1960, but the Mossad leader thought going after Mengele as well would endanger the entire operation.

Over the years I read of Mengele's experiments at Auschwitz. Their cruelty and senselessness greatly exceeded what I'd known of them. Surgery was performed on children without anesthesia. Blood was transferred from one child to another. Bacteria and other toxins were injected into people. Sex change operations were conducted. When a lice infestation struck one of the blocks in

Auschwitz, Mengele coolly ordered the hundreds of women in it to a gas chamber. Simpler than fumigation, I suppose.

I met with Channan a few years ago at his farm in the Negev. After a meal and light conversation, my then-retired colleague and personal friend apprised me of information in the Mengele file that was still classified. He asked me to keep the information confidential until it was released to the public. I abide by his request to this day.

THE ISRAELI-LEBANESE CONFLICT

I became head of a joint team of Shin Bet and Mossad personnel charged with operations in Lebanon, Syria, and as far east as Iraq. This of course brought me into routine touch with the CIA's man, Sam. A good thing.

The position had me working out of a regular office for the first time in my life – desks, file cabinets, refrigerators, and coffee pots. Nothing like my previous work. Even while in the army I was out in the field at least as much as in battalion headquarters. The new surroundings were brought on in part because of injuries sustained at the Canal, in part because the growing outfit needed experienced people.

Office life made me feel ineffectual. Sending people into danger while remaining behind a desk never sat well with me. I told this to my superior, Menachem. He was fair-minded, listened to others, and was both sharp and judicious. His taste for vulgar jokes would never be tolerated today.

When asked about my injuries, I replied I'd never be in the Maccabiah Games but I was fit and able to work in the field. He didn't want me out there but neither did he want me to leave for another organization. Reluctantly, he authorized me to work more in Beirut. I strode out of his office a happy man.

It was good to be back at Hussam's. He was relieved to be working again with someone he knew and trusted. Intelligence work is more than swapping envelopes. It's often exchanging thoughts with colleagues over a meal. Who's reliable and who's not. What goes on at a certain base camp. Which group is likely to strike next and how?

Our network in Lebanon included prominent Maronite Christian families. They had sided with Jewish settlers since the Mandate days and their patriarchs stood at the head of large networks of kin and clients that stretched across Lebanese society, including the army, state, commerce, and police. Average Lebanese who kept their eyes and ears open in marketplaces knew that good information brought reward. The patriarchs of these networks received monthly retainers from us. Exceptional work brought bonuses.

The dispositions of Syrian and Iraqi troops were still important but after the '73 war, Palestinian militants became the priority. Fatah and kindred groups operated from southern Lebanon, so much so we called it "Fatahland".

There were four main groups in Lebanon: Shia Muslims, Sunni Muslims, Christians, and Palestinian refugees. The Syrians and PLO recruited Palestinians for their militias and terrorist groups. We worked best with the Christians, who did not want the Palestinians in their country, mistrusted the Muslim population, and loathed Syria. The Shia then were mostly poor and unorganized. That would change.

Hussam's daughter became quite ill so we supplied her with medicine from the US that was unavailable in Lebanon and even Israel. Yes, there was a practical aspect to this but I came to care about Hussam and his household. Intelligence work isn't always as heartless as thought.

Our partnership with the Maronite Christians was sound. We established a fairly peaceful border with them which was known as the Good Fence. The border was part of my turf, so to speak. We issued permits to many Maronites that allowed them to work in Israel. We set up medical outposts to help the sick and injured. And of course we trained their militias to patrol the border. More on the militias will come, I regret to say.

The border remained a dangerous place. Terrorists infiltrated across it. Katyusha rockets rained down on our villages from time to time. The tempo increased, requiring villagers to spend nights in basements and shelters. That's no way to live. We had to find answers.

In March 1978 eleven PLO terrorists rowed south in rubber boats and landed near a kibbutz not far from Hadera and Haifa. They immediately killed an unfortunate photographer, then hijacked a bus and directed it toward Tel Aviv, shooting wildly along the way. The episode ended with more tragedy when the terrorists detonated a bomb inside the bus. All told, thirty-seven people were killed and seventy-one wounded.

The nation asked how such a thing could happen and demanded firm action. My team and I met with Motta Gur, the IDF chief of staff. There were about twenty of us in the conference room as he summarized the situation, more calmly than expected, and said we had to see it didn't recur. The IDF was going into Lebanon in a few days and we were to gather as much intelligence as possible in the short time before zero hour.

We went into Lebanon that night and met with agents. We gathered information on the location of PLO training camps, weapons caches, infiltration routes, and the like. Sam handed me a trove of papers and said he expected to see Israeli F-15 fighters in the skies soon. He either knew of the impending IDF operation or rightly inferred one was forthcoming. Well, every cabbie in Beirut probably knew it.

The F-15s did indeed streak over Lebanon shortly thereafter. Their mission was to keep Syrian fighters at bay. Our planes, pilots, and weapons were superior to those of Syria. If Assad didn't know it, his pilots did.

The intel we provided proved helpful. But General Ehud Barak, second in command, had a more ambitious plan than a punitive incursion. He wanted to strengthen the Maronite Christians in Lebanon and increase our position against Syria. That proved complicated.

Amid all this tumult, I was afforded a brief respite. Sam invited me to tour an American aircraft carrier, USS *Nimitz*, which was paying a port call in Haifa. Who could turn that down? Certainly not me, even though over the years I'd had two ships go down beneath me.

A launch took us out a kilometer or so, as the warship was simply too large to tie up at the docks. We were given a grand tour including looks at the helm, CIC room, and reactor. I stood next to an F-14 Tomcat and chatted with a few pilots.

Soon enough, it was back to cases. The *Nimitz* didn't sink on me.

OPERATION LITANI (1978)

The Litani is a small river in southern Lebanon. You have to look closely on a detailed map to spot it. It gave its name to an IDF operation aimed at clearing PLO training camps from the area, though it was initially given a lengthier and more presumptuous name – Father of Wisdom. Litani began three days after the terrorist spree from Haifa to Tel Aviv.

My part was to return to Lebanon, as usual by way of Prague, and gather as much intelligence as possible on events that would follow once the shooting started. How were the Palestinians reacting? Were Syrian troops on the move?

I reached Hussam's house and found Sam there with the information Washington gathered. He made the case for striking the camps near Tyre. General Gur, however, had already rejected this. Tyre was too heavily defended and a small country like Israel must avoid heavy casualties if it can. The startling casualties of the Yom Kippur War, only five years earlier, were still fresh in everyone's mind.

Gur's concerns were justified. Not long after they crossed the border, our troops came up against fortified bunkers with interlocking fire. Progress was slow, casualties numerous. An armor thrust to Beit Yahoun proved easier.

Sam's people maintained that the villages of Kana and Capra held weapons caches, and training camps were nearby. So we headed for them and found this indeed was the case. We were taking casualties from roadside bombs. Fortunately, the US provided us with devices that detected explosives from some distance. They worked well and saved lives.

The action lasted eight days. We reached the Litani River, halted the advance, and established a buffer zone that would prevent rocket attacks on northern Israel. We organized and trained the South Lebanon Army, led by Saad Haddad. Operation Litani brought some relief to northern Israel, though not as much as hoped.

Every action in world affairs has unforeseen reactions. Operation Litani created a flood of Shia refugees. They in time would rally to Hisbollah. That Shia movement, backed by Iran, became our chief enemy and remains so to this day.

OPERATION OPERA (1981)

I raq's nuclear program came to our attention in the late 1970s. The program had been looked at for several years, ever since France signed a deal to build the two nuclear reactors called Osirak I and II near Baghdad. They were supposed to be for peaceful purposes but with a leader like Saddam Hussein, we had to be watchful. One of the reactors, according to experts, was capable of producing plutonium, which can be used to make nuclear weapons.

We tried through diplomatic channels to get France to stop the program. The US did the same. Nothing came of it. France was eager to have good relations with Iraq and as much of the Arab world as possible. Big markets. Quite a change from the 1950s and 60s when they staunchly supported us. *C'est la vie, c'est la guerre.*

The International Atomic Energy Agency was supposed to inspect the Iraqi sites and give detailed reports on what went on there, but we were convinced the Agency was being deceived. My team focused on the equipment France had provided: what could it do and how could we sabotage it.

French manufacturers received anonymous calls that firmly recommended not doing any more business with Iraq. Nothing came of that either. Posing as a European businessman, I visited one such plant and looked at their production line. Shortly thereafter, fires broke out at factory sites and in the cars of key personnel. Meanwhile in Iraq, Saddam's experts were killed.

Mossad sabotaged some of the equipment before it left the French manufacturers. In 1979 a team detonated a charge attached to a reactor core. Saddam simply poured more money into the project. Replacements were made, guarded better, then shipped to Iraq.

Late in 1979 Sam and I talked on a Tel Aviv beach. After small talk of his plans to go home for the holidays, I knew something was coming.

"So guys at your end are worried about those Iraqi nuclear sites."

We hadn't discussed the matter but things going on in France and Iraq could not have gone unnoticed. I might have nodded, perhaps I didn't. Either way, he went on.

"You're slowing things down, but the work continues. Saddam wants nuclear weapons. You may be running out of time and options. A military strike should be considered."

I started to run down our diplomatic efforts but he waved me off.

"I know, I know. They're not working and they're not going to. Saddam has oil money and big ambitions. Nukes will make him the leader of the Arab world, at least that's what he thinks. You'll have to go with a more decisive approach."

So, I was being given a semi-official assessment as we strolled a beach. His people were telling my people something. That's the way it worked sometimes.

"You have a good Christmas vacation, Sam. When are you coming back?"

"Oh, don't worry. They'll have me back before the Super Bowl. That's in January, Zvi. Come to think of it, isn't January 1 your birthday?"

"Yes."

"In the event I've celebrated too much the previous night, I shall extend warm and sincere birthday greetings right here and now."

I'd never told him my birthday. Maybe I should leaf through his dossier.

Sam became more helpful over the next months. He handed us a pile of photos and documents. Along with them came the CIA assessment that Iraq was determined to obtain nuclear weapons. After studying the material and forming a position, we passed a report up to Begin. He was alarmed and ordered a decisive operation.

We reviewed the situation soon thereafter in the pit. Mossad personnel looked around the nuclear sites as best they could. One option was to get inside and blow it up. That was risky and unpromising. A second option was to send commando forces in. That risked high casualties without sufficient prospect of success. The third option was an airstrike. That was judged the best course. The bombs would be reasonably precise, inflicting serious damage without severe damage to nearby neighborhoods.

We gathered information on air defenses, hours of construction, and adjacent civilian sites to determine the optimal time to strike. Others studied which bombs to use. It was decided to use Mark 84 bombs. They were dumb but quite heavy, 925 kilograms, and able to penetrate the concrete and steel around the reactor core.

We needed aircraft that could fly long distances while carrying those heavy Mark 84s. Our A-4 Skyhawks and F-4 Phantoms weren't up to it. The US F-16 Fighting Falcons were. We had several on order but wanted them fast.

Our man in CIA was apprised and he got back to me shortly later, at 2am. He joked about waking me up, I joked about being woken up. Then we got down to business. Iran had ordered several

F-16s but delivery was on hold after the Shah fell. They could be sent over in short order but the big shots in our governments had to arrange it. I sent word up channels, Begin asked Carter to expedite matters, and the F-16s soon flew in. CIA came through in other ways. We received electronic countermeasure gear (ECM) that was fitted onto the F-16s to defeat Iraqi radar.

Hussam's people were at work gathering more details about the sites. His network was all over the Middle East, mostly in Lebanon and Syria but elsewhere too. Elsewhere included a small number of people in Baghdad. He got valuable intel on the Osirak reactors twenty kilometers south of Baghdad. The twin reactors were virtually the same because one was a backup for the other.

The IDF, intelligence bureaus, and government rarely spoke publicly about the Osirak reactors. Occasional mention was made to express concern. But showing keen interest might have signaled a likely attack and Saddam would have beefed up defenses.

The plans were decided upon, the pilots trained. Delay after delay came. Some people in Begin's government and Knesset committees opposed the attack and put off the decision as long as they could. Shimon Peres, for one, was convinced the raid would worsen our standing in the world. The morning the mission was supposed to go off, he sent a strong note to the PM: "I feel this morning that it is my supreme civic duty to advise you, with all seriousness and national considerations, to refrain from this." Begin gave in, even though Peres was a political rival, or even enemy. The pilots stayed in the ready room. When authorization came at last, bad weather intervened.

Finally, however, on June 7 1981, the ministers and weather gods allowed the mission to proceed. Hussam's people took up positions to help with damage assessment. Eight F-16s took off to an altitude of one hundred meters and began the 1100 kilometer flight. Another eight F-15s flew as escorts to deal with enemy fighters and suppress air defenses.

Word of the launch reached the pit. Everything was well planned, but who knew what would happen in the next few hours. Plans are one thing, operations quite another.

We later learned that our fighters roared low over a yacht on the Gulf of Aqaba. The king of Jordan happened to be aboard, enjoying the day. He saw Israeli markings and notified his air command. They tried to warn counterparts in Iraq but we blocked the message and sent Jordan a false reply.

Our planes crossed into Iraq undetected. The pilots identified their target visually and increased their altitude lest bomb blasts damage their planes. Greater altitude, however, makes them more visible to radar and antiaircraft weapons soon opened up. The fire was light and ineffectual. The pilots dropped their bombs and turned west. A few hours later our planes, all of them, touched down back home. Someone in the pit uncorked a bottle of champagne. I downed a glass or two. It was becoming a routine.

The prime minister hadn't apprised the full cabinet of the mission until shortly after the planes took off. When they returned, he issued a public statement explaining the reasoning. He finished by saying, "If they try this again, we will attack again." And so was born the Begin Doctrine.

As expected, a wave of condemnation crashed down. Some came from our own politicians. The United States expressed dismay and President Reagan put delivery of more F-16s on hold. An American paper questioned Begin's sanity and asked what he might do next. Behind the scenes, however, American security and military people supported us.

Sam and I shook hands a few weeks later. He congratulated us on a well-planned and expertly-executed strike. "Ignore the bullshit," he said. "It'll all be gone soon enough." He was right.

Many years later, another Likud government became deeply concerned with Iran's nuclear program. PM Netanyahu insisted that the mullahs in Tehran were close to having nuclear weapons. No attack came. This was in part because of the greater distances to the targets, which would have created challenges for our air crews. But I also think there was greater opposition to an attack from within our own security bureaus, including Mossad. They simply were not convinced that Iran's program constituted a grave danger.

OPERATION PEACE FOR GALILEE

I n 1981 I learned more and more about the Gemayel family, a
wealthy clan with connections throughout the country. Pierre
Gemayel was the patriarch and his son Bachir would soon be
elected president of Lebanon. Bachir was assassinated before he
took office, probably at the direction of Syrian intelligence.

The Gemayels were Christians, Maronites to be precise. They
opposed Syrian influence in their country. We opposed Syria, so
we were allies. That's politics, in the Middle East and around the
world.

We were concerned with continued rocket fire from southern
Lebanon. The casualties caused fear and concern, and many
people questioned the ability of the government and IDF to defend
them. Minister of Defense Sharon, whom I'd met with during the
construction of the Bar-Lev Line and during the Yom Kippur War,
was developing a plan to secure the north. He was not one to go
about things delicately.

Some information comes through hard work with longstanding
agents. Other times, information just falls into your lap. In both cases
we have to be wary of erroneous information and double-crossing.

One day I flew into Beirut via Prague and dined at a restaurant
near the shore, as was my wont. The hustle and bustle of daily
routines were all about. Halabi, the elderly owner, recognized me

from previous visits and noted the simple lives of the fishermen we watched unloading nets filled with catch from shoals to the northwest.

"They wake up early and sail to sea with the tide. Then they return around noon. Soon they'll be back at sea for another few hours of it. Simple people, good people. No interest in politics or war or much else beside tides and weather and the prices of the day. They want only to raise their families and see them prosper."

"I wish there were more like them. Sometimes I find myself looking for more simplicity in life."

"But you are a businessman! You fly from country to country. The simple life is not for you."

"Maybe so, Halabi, maybe so. I have a friend who fishes the streams of Czechoslovakia and elsewhere. He recently did some diving in the eastern Mediterranean and found artifacts from the early nineteenth century. They are thought to have been from ships under Napoleon's command – swords, muskets, and coins."

"History. My family has a long history. Alas, I have no children. The proud line ends with me. But I've seen things, and I know things. I collect antiques."

"A splendid pastime. What do you collect?"

"Lamps, pottery, and coins of course. I even have a few rifles from the many armies that have marched through the Levant in search of one thing or another. You wouldn't know it to look at me but I am an avid reader of history. In fact I studied history and sociology at the American University here. Your friend was quite fortunate to find those artifacts. I'd love to know where they were found. Was it near Acre?"

"Yes, it was off the coast of Acre, not far from here actually. Napoleon broke down the walls of an ancient Crusader castle there."

"Yes, he did. Your friend is welcome in Israel, I suspect."

Odd question.

"He might be welcome there. He knows many Lebanese as well, and travels back and forth between the two lands on business."

"And you probably know people who work with America and Israel."

Odder question. I weighed my words.

"I know people from those countries. Some are well connected and appreciate learning new things."

He sat at my table and chuckled softly.

"It's been many months since I thought you were just a European businessman. There's a new thing I'd like you to learn. Something urgent. You know of the Abu Nidal Organization."

From antiques to terrorists. Quite a segue.

"Abu Nidal is about to do something extraordinary. I do not know precisely when or where."

"Abu Nidal is capable of such a thing. But, Halabi, there's nothing anyone can do with information so broad. Can specifics be learned?"

My nod suggested that money could change hands.

"Many people pass through my city. Sometimes they become acquaintances, sometimes they simply talk too much, especially after a few glasses of wine. I will serve wine, I will listen."

A few days later I returned to the restaurant and Halabi motioned for me to accompany him to the office. Evidently, he'd poured wine and listened well.

"My friend, I have information, timely information, which you must pass on as soon as possible. A figure in the PLO tells me that Abu Nidal will try to assassinate your ambassador in London."

I was taken aback when he said "your ambassador", but only slightly. When asked when this would take place he said, "Very soon. Possibly this very day."

An envelope changed hands and I headed for a safe house where the information was relayed along with my assessment of a moderate level of reliability. My section leader replied that the ambassador had been killed an hour earlier. A strong response would surely come from Begin and Sharon.

As it turned out, our London ambassador had only been badly wounded. Nonetheless, Abu Nidal's attempt would not go unpunished. Governments and their militaries plan a range of responses. That's an important part of what they do. It was a question of how indelicate the punishment would be.

The following day, IDF aircraft struck PLO targets in Lebanon. The PLO in turn responded with heavy rocket attacks on northern Israel and with small ground attacks across the border. A few days later the IDF crossed into Lebanon once again.

Halabi's restaurant was closed. I saw his nephew inside and tapped on the window. He sorrowfully told me that his uncle had been shot to death on a street a few days ago, probably in retaliation for divulging information to a foreign power. That was plausible. He handed me a manila envelope Halabi had intended for me. I offered to help with money and transportation out of Beirut, but he declined. His uncle had left him money and he'd make arrangements to live in a village well away from the dangerous streets of a city descending into civil war.

Back at a safe house I opened the envelope and read of the positions of training camps, arms caches, and launch sites. A few days later IDF Special Forces and paratroopers assaulted various positions. Some of them had been identified by Halabi, some by other sources, including CIA.

I was in on some of the operations to help destroy bunkers and ammunition supplies. As we moved through villages such as Damoor, Einav, Mata, we avoided contact with Syrian troops. They were backed by the Soviet Union and we had no interest in bringing them into what we wanted to be a limited conflict.

Sharon put off Begin's demurrals and extended the operation all the way into Beirut. A much admired general and Begin's defense minister, Sharon was difficult to restrain. The army found and destroyed scores of positions of the PLO and related groups. In Sharon's estimation, the city was an enormous nest of terrorists.

I returned to Israel for a few days and enjoyed a little time with my family. By early September, though, I was back in Beirut. It was not the Paris of the Mediterranean it once was. Raids, airstrikes, and bombings were taking a toll. The drive to Hussam's took me past scores of badly damaged buildings. Whole blocks lay in ruins.

Hussam expressed deep concern about the Falangist militias who were becoming powerful amid the chaos in and around Beirut.

"I tell you Bachir doesn't control all his lieutenants. They are untrustworthy and bent on building their own power, regardless of what the Gemayel clan wants."

I knew them to be under the loose command of Bachir Gemayel, a reliable asset. That didn't mean I admired or respected the clan's militias. When I said we were aware of problems inside the Falangists, Hussam looked at me with reproach. He said nothing, probably because he'd presented his views and knew that I'd given them a fair hearing.

Anyone in the intelligence game knows that as much information as they receive, there's always some they've missed. There's also the risk of taking consensus within the bureaus as a certainty. That was the mistake before the Yom Kippur War. It's best to operate in a realm of at least some doubt. Hussam counseled me to keep my eyes open.

Not long thereafter, Bachir Gemayel was assassinated. His brother Amine took his place. Beirut and all Lebanon was on edge. Everyone braced for the inevitable dire response, from the Gemayels and from Sharon.

I went to a Palestinian refugee camp called Sabra to get a feel for the situation and meet with a few people. Israeli soldiers patrolled the perimeter. We were an occupying power with delineated responsibilities under international law. In fact I had to pass through an IDF checkpoint to enter the camp.

Sabra was situated near another camp known as Shatila. Both were densely populated with an assortment of Palestinians, Lebanese, and Syrians. Things were tense. Most of the Palestinians were expecting to be transported, forcibly, to southern Lebanon. Gemayel's assassination worsened their fears. Sharon was certain such camps teemed with terrorists and ill-disposed to protect them.

An asset and I walked down narrow streets. On either side of us were drab concrete buildings, wooden shacks, small shops, and overcrowded dwellings. Laundry hung from balconies. Farmers led donkeys bearing baskets of wares and boasted of their high quality. Children played with sticks, rocks, and cans in debris-strewn alleyways.

We entered a house where I met with a source named Gamal, a Pakistani whose search for work had brought him to the Middle East. Inside were three older men seated around a table with a hookah pipe and a bottle of liqueur known as Arak.

Gamal introduced me as a European businessman. No one pressed for elaboration. We discussed the assassination and the fear permeating the camps. I was not in a position to offer reassurance, let alone help. They wanted me to pass on their concerns, presumably not to an agricultural-machinery business in Europe. As the meeting proceeded and the Arak flowed, I better appreciated their concern. No, it was more than concern. They feared a terrible vengeance was about to come down on them and no one was disposed to protect them.

On the way out of Sabra, I saw more children playing in the streets. It reminded me of my own boyhood when friends and I played in the streets of Oradea Mare. A girl of about seven came to me and said, "Eish, eish". Reasonably at home in Arabic, I knew she wanted bread. She said her name was "Nur" – a word that means "light". She had no parents and lived in the streets. Looking around I wondered how many other orphans were scratching out existences in Sabra and Shatila.

I took her hand and passed through the IDF checkpoint where I convinced a young soldier to give her a candy bar. Into my jeep and off we went to Hussam's.

Nur was mistrustful. Not so much of me but of the strange new place. Sabra had the attraction of being known to her. It was her home. Hussam and his family graciously offered food. Nur accepted only after considerable urging, and after a few bites she insisted on returning home. She did ask for more food, though. A good sign.

With regret I told her I had to leave. She wanted to come with me. I said my home was far away where people spoke a different language. She promised to learn it. She wasn't making it easy. But leave I did, though only after an ordeal of pleadings and promises. Her sweetness and frailty attracted the attention of all in the house. I knew she would be far better off at Hussam's than at Sabra or Shatila, even in the best of times.

Colleagues and I spoke of the vengefulness loose in the city and the vulnerability of the refugee camps. The most alarming thing was that the Phalangists had formally requested permission to enter the camps. Sharon's hostility toward the Palestinians was palpable, his latitude toward the Phalangists was known. We made it known up the chain that letting the Phalangists in would bring disaster.

I made a point of driving by the camps. Each had IDF checkpoints around it and I stopped at many of them, conveying my regards to the guys and asking where they were from. Soldierly exchanges. They knew me as a civilian with connections to the army and the mysterious world of intelligence. I had an aura about me and they respected and perhaps even admired me. Most of them anyway.

Some, including a few junior officers, hated the Palestinians. One of them, Lt Rafi, was especially hostile toward the people he was expected and legally bound to protect. He was the type who relished power and enjoyed war. They are in every army. It was unpleasant to see them in mine and disconcerting to see them responsible for the refugees.

I could not give them orders, only underscore my concern. Lt Rafi shrugged his shoulders and said the Phalangists were allies and should be allowed "to have some fun". I told him in unmistakable terms that no Phalangists were to be allowed in, adding that though not in his chain of command, I was respected by many who were.

Rafi nodded desultorily. I told him that if he received orders to allow the Phalangists in, he was to contact me. I scribbled down a number and did the same at other checkpoints.

The following day my chief sent an urgent message directing me to check the refugee camps immediately. I headed toward the camps and heard sporadic gunfire a half kilometer away. Rafi was at the checkpoint and showed no concern.

"Who authorized entry?" I demanded.

"I received orders to allow them in to search for terrorists. I obey orders."

There was more than a trace of smug defiance, despite the gunfire and chaos behind him. I reported back to Shin Bet and there was a scramble at high levels of army and state to find out who'd given the order. Meanwhile, the massacre was going on.

Only the following day were the Phalangists ordered out. We went in and saw scores of bodies – men, women, and children – lying in hideous positions, pools of blood around them, flies swarming. Exact numbers are in dispute. The carnage reminded me of atrocities I'd seen in my boyhood.

The Knesset formed a commission. I testified – and pointed out Lt Rafi's failures and words. He again insisted that he obeyed orders, and no charges were brought against him. One might have thought that so infamous a defense would have incensed most Israelis.

The committee recommended that Ariel Sharon be removed from office. He was, but he became minister without portfolio. Army chief of staff Rafael Ethan was criticized but not removed as his retirement was coming soon anyway. Begin himself was criticized but little came of it.

As occupying power, my country was responsible for the safety of the population, including Palestinian refugees. The massacres at Sabra and Shatila are stains upon Israel's honor and standing in the world.

TIMES OF CHANGE

The years after Sabra and Shatila were troubled. The Begin government fell. The IDF withdrew from Beirut, in part due to American pressure. We maintained a presence in southern Lebanon to limit rocket attacks across the border.

Work continued in and around Beirut. This kept me in touch with Sam as well as others who shall remain nameless. Our occupation of parts of Lebanon brought growing resistance, especially from the Shia. Small bands, then a large and durable social movement sprang up against us. Some resistance took the form of terrorism.

One such attack was nearby. In November 1983, about fifteen minutes after I left an IDF headquarters in Tyre, a powerful car bomb exploded. Islamic Jihad took responsibility. Once again good fortune was with me.

Another incident brought shame to our security bureaus. It was the IDF with Sabra and Shatila, Shin Bet with the Kav 300 event. Two Arab terrorists hijacked a bus and upon capture were taken to a field and executed. The killings were ordered by Shin Bet chief Avraham Shalom. The killings angered and horrified many Israelis.

The following year we lost Yigael Yadin, an esteemed general from the Haganah days. Resembling a professor more than a general, he embodied the early army leadership and contrasted markedly with many successors. Yigael was a friend and father figure. I miss him, and Israel misses his dignifying presence in public life.

Shimon Peres became prime minister. He had personal warmth and a generous nature that benefited the government and nation. Peres was deeply embarrassed by the massacres and wanted a better understanding of Lebanese society. His predecessors had taken the nation into a protracted and inconclusive war and Peres wanted sounder policies. I gave him personal briefings and we became amicable. I had the privilege of dining with him and his wife Sonia on a few occasions, all of them delightful. His party was my choice on election day.

Our intelligence network spread throughout the Middle East. It now comprised over a hundred agents. In February 1985 I awaited Sam's arrival at a Haifa restaurant. I scanned passersby for someone dressed in his manner but saw only a few actual American tourists. In a few moments a noisy, dented Studebaker Lark attempted to parallel park on the crowded avenue. After several futile efforts, it was reasonably well placed and a man in garish attire got out, ambled over, and sat down across from me. After hearty greetings, a one-sided discussion of the San Francisco Forty-Niners, and a few bites of food, Sam and I got down to work.

His team was working on a prisoner exchange that Washington wanted to see through. A pause told me that something tough was coming. No professional training for that.

"The PLO will release three of your guys for some of theirs."

The lack of immediate elaboration troubled me.

"Okay, Zvi, this is the deal. Three of your guys for eleven hundred of theirs."

"What? Sam, I'm not an accountant, my knowledge of math isn't great, but that sounds like a *very* bad deal for us."

"It does. I admit it. Nonetheless, the big shots in the US like it. Some in your country do as well. They want guys like us to work out the details and handle the exchange."

"Okay, we're soldiers, not politicians. I'm thankful for that. What's the arrangement?"

"You will release prisoners on Ahmed Fibril's list. I'm sure you're familiar with it and also know some reprehensible people are on it – people who've killed your people. On the other hand, the exchange will bring back three of your guys. They'll be reunited with their families and can serve their country again. Well, that's my two bits. Pardon the absence of deep conviction but like I said, this one comes from the big shots."

One figure on the list was Ahmed Yassin who would go on to found Hamas. I didn't care much for the unequal exchange but that was irrelevant. I wondered why Sam conveyed his personal view of the exchange.

Shimon Peres approved the exchange. This brought a great deal of criticism from the Right, especially from the ambitious new Likud leader, Benjamin Netanyahu. In coming years many of those we released went on to participate in further terrorist activities and also in the Intifada uprisings. Many were rearrested.

I was on the team that took our three figures from their captors and returned them to their families. The first part of the deal was sobering as I looked into the eyes of intent enemies. The second was gratifying as I saw families reunited. I thought we'd made the right decision.

The PLO continued to use camps in Lebanon to attack us. This went on despite my team's success in identifying and destroying many sites. On Yom Kippur, a PLO squad seized a yacht off Cyprus and killed the Israelis on board.

A meeting was convened. Peres, defense minister Yitzhak Rabin, and the heads of Mossad and the IDF were in attendance. So was I. Rabin was determined to strike back. We had to make it clear that our memory and reach were both long.

Rabin was motivated less by anger and vengeance than by the need to protect our people and principles. There was for him a time for war and a time for peace. He outlined a plan to strike inside Lebanon. Shin Bet was tasked once again with identifying targets.

We set to work. The pressure from the top was intense, our workload almost unbearable. Contacts had to be pressed. Money had to be spread around.

After a few weeks I managed to get back to Haifa for a few days with my family. A cabin at Achziv Beach beckoned. The warm sand and gentle waves had already drawn a thousand or two people. The kids were splashing and paddling in the surf as my wife looked for a good place to dine. I'd finally gotten away from the cramped safe houses and apartments of Beirut.

Off to my left strode a man in a beige sombrero. I half expected to see a Studebaker parked behind him – with the same muffler and a few more dents.

"Nice place, Zvika. How come you never told me about it? No matter. I had to stop by to give you a little news. Not the weather report, I assure you. Can I get you something to drink?"

I shook my head, sensing something was afoot.

"Zvika my friend…."

Now I was sure of it.

"Disagreements come about in even the happiest of families. Husbands and wives, brothers and sisters. They argue, they fight. Nothing out of the ordinary with that."

"Sam, please get on with it."

"Alright, alright. We've found a spy in our navy. He was working out of Maryland, just outside DC."

I remained uncertain where this was going but the reference to "family disagreements" gave me an idea.

"Looks like he works for you guys."

"Didn't know of it, Sam. Was he Mossad?"

"No one's quite sure. As you might suspect, the guy's not exactly forthcoming with names and pay stubs. But it's going to cause commotion. Lots of ruffled feathers back in Langley. The info he gave up must have been good stuff. As for me, I'm a practical guy.

We spy on enemies, we spy on friends. And of course, our friends spy on us."

"I presume you have a name."

"Jonathan Pollard. Funny thing about the guy. He wanted to work for the Company but we rejected him. The navy in its infinite wisdom hired him as an analyst and over the years gave him increasingly sensitive material."

I knew what was coming.

"Zvika old friend, have you ever seen or heard information coming from Pollard or our navy?"

"I haven't. I'm up in Beirut eating Arab chow and dodging Arab bombs. You know that."

"Well, even if you find something, don't let me know." He looked to the sea. "It's nice here. Reminds me of Cancun. Enjoy your holiday with the wife and kids."

He gave me a pat on the back and walked away.

Pollard later confessed, on the record, that he'd been a spy for Israel. His work must have been known by only a handful of very high-level people. Nothing changed between Sam and me. I'm glad for that.

The following Monday we worked on the details of Operation Wooden Leg – a retaliatory strike on the PLO headquarters in Tunis. My team gathered information on buildings and supportive sites such as training camps and arms caches.

A woman on the team by the name of Ayelet passed around satellite and ground-level photos of a few such sites. They were remarkably clear, not the sort of thing that came from a passing car or plane. I marveled at the quality and asked their provenance. She hesitated, then said a contact named Amir had given them to her. He'd gotten them through an information exchange program with the US. That didn't make sense so it was time to question Amir. He was evasive but I pressed him. At length he said he found the photos in a parcel stuffed into his mailbox.

I naturally wondered if they'd come from Pollard and tried to imagine the arcane pathway that got them into a Lebanese agent's mailbox. Well, Sam said he didn't want to know anything I might learn from Pollard, so I didn't mention the matter to him.

The photos were checked against other information we had on the PLO in Tunis and judged to be accurate. The airstrikes went ahead. Months later a member of the Knesset intelligence committee said, behind closed doors, that the photos had indeed come from Pollard.

The Tunis attack itself was initially planned for naval vessels and commandos. Assessments, however, foresaw steep losses so it was decided to use aerial bombardment, as with the Iraqi nuclear site. F-15s had greater range and ordnance capacity than F-16s and were picked for the mission.

Ten F-15s would each carry one laser-guided smart bomb. Aerial refueling would be done by two Boeing 707s. Our pilots were instructed to drop their ordnance only after positively identifying their targets, as tourist areas were nearby.

The F-15s took off on October 1 1985, refueled without incident, encountered no interceptors, and destroyed the targets. We estimated sixty PLO personnel were killed. Tunisian authorities reported conflicting numbers, including many innocent civilian casualties.

The operation was widely condemned. The US criticized but didn't out and out condemn it. The operation made Arab countries rethink hosting terrorist organizations on their land. Tunisia ordered the PLO out.

Less than a week later terrorists took over the cruise ship *Achille Lauro* and murdered American citizens. Shortly later, a Tunis policeman, a brother of someone killed in the Tunis strike, opened fire in a synagogue, killing three people. Also that year, the Abu Nidal Organization struck – according to them, in retaliation for Wooden Leg.

It was back to more day-to-day intelligence work. Something was always coming up, though. In late 1986, during an IDF airstrike on a weapons cache in Lebanon, an F-4 Phantom was badly damaged by a secondary explosion. The pilot and navigator had to eject. The pilot was rescued by one of our helicopters, but the navigator, Ron Arad, fell into the hands of a Shia organization called Amal. We pressed our agents for information.

Try as we did, we got nothing. His captors sent proof of life photos and letters from him, but the captivity went on. We tried contacts in Syria, Iraq, and Iran. Nothing. The effort continued for years. We came to believe that Arad was dead. Deeply concerned with his fate for many months, I came to think of the poor guy as a family member. A sign of advancing years, perhaps.

BEIRUT DESCENDS

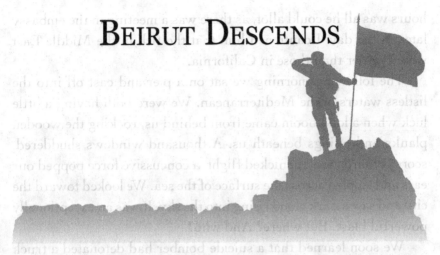

April 18 1983, breakfast with Sam at Hussam's. Our Lebanese colleague was concerned, more so than usual. Beirut was racked by violence from various militias – Christian and Shia ones foremost. He warned that attacks on Israeli and American targets were likely. Major ones.

Sam shrugged and said there was nothing new about that. Hussam agreed but went on to say there was specific information. He showed us transcripts of radio traffic his people had intercepted. Indeed, there was something afoot against "international forces" in Beirut.

"These men are capable of horrible acts, gentlemen. There is no defense against those who have no hope in this world."

"Agreed," Sam said. "That's why we have to kill them first."

There was a bit of John Wayne in that guy.

I had a bad feeling, because I'd come to respect Hussam's bad feelings. There wasn't much to go on, though. No specific targets, no specific times. I took it more seriously than Sam did, but there was little to do but pass the information to higher-ups, along with my assessment that its credibility was high. I'd put out feelers in my networks. Sam would do the same in his.

Conversation turned to the more pleasant topic of fishing. We exchanged boasts of prowess with rod and reel and agreed to settle the debate manfully in the early morning. No more than a couple hours was all he could allot, as there was a meeting in the embassy later in the day. I cautioned him that the fish in the Middle East were craftier than those in California.

The following morning we sat on a pier and cast off into the listless waters of the Mediterranean. We were both having a little luck when a loud boom came from behind us, rocking the wooden planks and pilings beneath us. A thousand windows shuddered, scores of birds took panicked flight, a concussive force popped our ears and rippled across the surface of the sea. We looked toward the city and saw a dark cloud rising into the sky. It was an exceptionally powerful blast. But where? And who?

We soon learned that a suicide bomber had detonated a truck bomb just outside the American Embassy. The entire front of the building was destroyed and sixty-three people killed, including several of Sam's colleagues. Odds enough, an investigation revealed the truck had come from Texas.

A few months later, two suicide bombers drove their trucks into a compound holding American marines and French troops, killing 305 people. Both attacks, according to Hussam's people, came from Iranian-backed groups. Things were only getting worse in my second home.

TWA FLIGHT 847

I t's rarely a good sign when a section chief comes into your office with worry written on his face. It was June of 1985 and an American airliner, TWA Flight 847, scheduled to fly from Rome to Boston then Los Angeles, had been hijacked.

The group assembled in the pit and the questions flew.

"Who are the hijackers?"

"Don't know. They diverted the flight to Beirut. They'll land shortly."

"Any Israelis on board?"

"Yes and no. I'll get to that. But there are Jewish Americans aboard."

"Is the US going to do something?"

"Not sure, but they have rescue teams just like we do. Sam will be here in a few hours."

"Good. Now what's the thing you're going to get to?"

"Ah…. One of our guys is on board. Mossad. Undercover as a German citizen. German papers only. No one aboard knows. He was on his way to a job in Rome. Don't tell Sam a word of this. Not yet."

I objected. My CIA colleague should know everything I did. Trust. My chief said it would take some time. It did take some time, just not as much as the boss hoped. I'll get to that.

More info came in. Flight 847 had left Cairo on the morning of June 14 and arrived at Athens without incident. A fresh crew came aboard and they were off for Rome when the plane was taken over. The Beirut tower wouldn't allow it to land until the pilot made it absolutely clear the hijackers would detonate a grenade if they didn't land. The tower gave in.

Nineteen hostages were released in exchange for fuel. The Mossad fellow was not among them. Some in the pit thought the whole episode was designed to capture him, but there was no sign he'd been singled out. The plane took off from Beirut and headed for Algiers.

Sam arrived late at night and spared me the usual light talk. We exchanged information, including the recent news that the hijackers were Shia, probably with Hisbollah or Islamic Jihad. When asked if his side had an operation in the works, he said nothing was imminent.

I quickly read an updated report and told Sam that another twenty hostages were released in Algiers. I added that "our man" wasn't among them. There's no rewind button in life.

"Your man?"

Sam was putting things together.

"Well, yes. Mossad."

I told him what we knew and of our intermittent concern that the hijacking had been designed to capture an Israeli intelligence officer. He shook his head.

"These guys aren't that bright. It's just bad luck for your man, though maybe it'll turn out to be good luck for all of us."

"Except for the hijackers."

"Yeah."

Soon enough, the plane was back in the air and headed back to Beirut. That was bad news. The airport isn't secure and it's surrounded by Shia neighborhoods where Hisbollah and Islamic Jihad have supporters, networks, and plenty of places to hide.

That night the hijackers singled out an American sailor, shot him, and tossed his lifeless body onto the tarmac. This raised concern that more killings would soon follow. We all agreed that they were targeting Americans, at least for now. Another seven Americans with Jewish names were taken off the plane and taken to a makeshift prison somewhere in Beirut. The hijackers appealed to their fellow Shia to persuade airport authorities to refuel the plane.

We worked on a rescue plan, the Americans did the same. Our Special Forces and American SEALS were on alert. But the plane moved from location to location unpredictably. It was headed for Algiers in a matter of hours, this time with a few more terrorists aboard.

Sixty-five passengers were released in Algiers, only forty remained. The plane lifted off for Beirut. Our man was still aboard and debate erupted once more about his importance. Sam insisted that if he were known, they'd have killed him, not the sailor, or proudly announced to all the world they were holding so prized a hostage as a Mossad officer.

The hijackers demanded the release of the Kuwait 17, who pulled off the 1983 bombing of the US embassy in Kuwait, the release of 766 Shias in Israeli prisons, and the withdrawal of all Israeli forces from Lebanon. They further demanded international condemnation of Israel and the US. Sam shook his head and asked for a Coke.

Our special forces were preparing to go in by sea. Going overland would bring them into contact with Shia militias. We would not proceed without American approval as TWA was an American carrier.

The Greek government released Ali Atwa, who was being held on suspicion of complicity. The hijackers then released eight Greek citizens, including musician Demis Roussos. The remaining forty hostages were taken off the plane on June 17 and taken to a Hisbollah district of Beirut. One passenger developed heart trouble and was released. Thirty-nine passengers remained in Shia neighborhoods. Yes, one was our man.

Storming a plane is straightforward compare with searching Beirut neighborhoods block by block, cellar by cellar. Plans were formed, but no authorization came.

Sam came into the pit late one night and announced that the hostages would soon be released. Puzzled faces abounded. When I asked if there'd been a deal, he simply said, "Political pressure from all around."

My stare must have conveyed that I thought he was withholding information. He sighed and with a haggard look said, "Let's just say that a few governments have arranged for the hostages to be released safely. It'll be over soon and we can get some sleep, maybe do some fishing." He patted me on the back and left, his exhaustion plain.

On June 30 the hostages were transferred to Syria and from there to West Germany aboard an American plane. Over the next few weeks Israel released more than 700 Shia prisoners, all the while claiming that the move had been planned long ago and had nothing to do with the hijacking. That one will still makes me roll my eyes.

Sam and I dined a few weeks later in downtown Haifa. I told him he looked positively rejuvenated, and he replied that he'd needed rest and that a short vacation had worked wonders. He even insisted on footing the bill for a change. I asked if there were details about the end of the hijacking that we hadn't been apprised of.

"The food's great," he replied.

A few minutes passed and he asked which passenger was the Mossad agent.

"The food's great," I replied.

We laughed and finished the meal. The food really was great.

RETURN TO AUSCHWITZ

In 1985 I went back to the Auschwitz camps. Friends, some of them Holocaust survivors, had gone there over the years and some suggested I do the same. I always declined. There was nothing to see or learn. For reasons unclear to me, I finally decided to go. My wife and a few friends accompanied me.

The plane landed in Krakow and I thought back to a train ride with my Oradea family. We hired a driver to take us the thirty kilometers to Oświęcim, the Polish village whose name was Germanized into the name of the death camp.

There above the gate was the infamous inscription *Arbeit Macht Frei*. Recognition of a familiar sight usually elicits positive thoughts; it's part of how our minds work. But on seeing those words and the buildings and fields behind the gate, I fought off an unexpected sense of confinement. No one noticed.

How many times had I come here? Yes, this was my third time.

I entered the gate and walked into the main camp. Along the way, I passed a million souls marching the other way toward Birkenau. There were dirty uniforms, emaciated bodies, and terrified and hopeless faces. I saw Aunt Catalina, Yanosh's wife and children, and others whose names I could not recall or never knew. On and on they marched. I looked for a youth.

All around were the fences with their arrays of grotesque electrodes and L-shaped posts, where people chose to go out on their own terms.

The buildings had been well maintained. They cast somber shadows on neatly-trimmed grass. It could be mistaken for an old but not unpleasant historical site. Signs, enlarged photographs, and articulate young guides conveyed who'd been there and what went on there. They were instructive. The visitors learned.

In Birkenau we came upon the building where we ate our meager rations before hurrying off to appell and work assignments lest we be beaten. After a few wrong turns, I found among a number of trees the block where I lived upon arrival. I walked inside, my companions just behind. The old wood had been preserved with varnish – a better smell than the one that came to mind on entry. The wood was cool and smooth to the touch.

Stumbling briefly, I walked down the center and pointed out one of the bunks to my wife and friends. "This is where I slept." They could only stare.

At the north end of Birkenau were the gas chambers and kremas. Both seemed unchanged. On entering the anteroom of one of the gas chambers, the shoes and clothes of dead people are all around. It smelled of cold cement. The kremas were strangely quiet, as they'd been unused since early 1945 when the Russians got close.

We walked to where the trains once arrived. The tracks were still there, but the platform was gone, replaced by a walkway and long grassy stretches. That's what my wife and companions saw. I saw cold spotlights, rifles crashing down on helpless people, snarling dogs, and families torn apart.

Tired and somber, we headed out, exiting through the railroad track opening with the forbidding tower atop it. Coming in were a group of young visitors, one carried the flag of Israel.

I'd come to Auschwitz three times. I'll never go there again.

MORDECHAI VANUNU

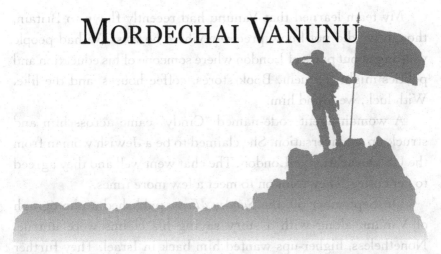

In late 1986 we again gathered in the pit for a special briefing. They weren't uncommon. The boss ran down the basics.

"There's a fellow outside the country offering information about our nuclear program. The *Sunday Times* is trying to verify his information. He's an Israeli – Mordechai Vanunu. He emigrated to Israel from Morocco when he was nine years old. Military service, IDF engineers. Education, physics. He started to work at Dimona in 1976 and sometime later snuck a camera in and snapped photos. That's highly illegal, as you know."

We leafed through Vanunu's dossier. He belonged to Israel's communist party and held very strong pacifist beliefs which caught the attention of his employers at Dimona. They judged him a security risk and let him go. He wasn't pleased.

He traveled about the world and came in contact with a journalist with the *Sunday Times* who convinced him to reveal what he knew about Israel's nuclear weapons. This didn't sit well with Peres or Rabin. They instructed us to find out what material Vanunu had and if warranted, nab him and return him to Israel for prosecution.

The Kanyuk Operation began. Two teams comprising both Mossad and Shin Bet personnel were assigned to it. One went to Australia, which was where Vanunu was living at some point. The other deployed to Britain, which was where he might be now. I was in charge of the latter unit.

My team learned that Vanunu had recently flown to Britain, though we did not know precisely where he was. We had people walking about parts of London where someone of his education and politics might frequent. Book stores, coffee houses, and the like. With luck, we found him.

A woman agent code-named "Cindy" came across him and struck up a conversation. She claimed to be a Jewish woman from the US on vacation in London. The chat went well and they agreed to get coffee. They went on to meet a few more times.

On September 30, the *Sunday Mirror* published a photograph of Vanunu along with a story saying his claims were untrue. Nonetheless, higher-ups wanted him back in Israel. They further decided that his seizure must not happen on British territory. Peres did not want to upset a collegial relationship with Margaret Thatcher.

That evening, Cindy found our target very upset. She became closer to him and invited him to get away with her to a sister's apartment in Rome. He accepted. We'd be waiting there. All was going well but there was a possibility that Vanunu would get cold feet. A British journalist had warned him against leaving the country.

The next day, however, Vanunu and Cindy flew to Rome and as they arrived at the apartment, our people nabbed and sedated him. He was taken by car to a boat which sailed out to sea where he was taken aboard a cargo ship bound for Israel. I received a phone call with a coded message that all had gone well. The team was happy to be going home.

Shortly thereafter, the *Sunday Times* published Vanunu's information and photos and proclaimed them as proof Israel had nuclear weapons.

Vanunu was held and interrogated for several weeks. He was never told how he'd come to be in Israel. He only knew that he'd been kidnapped in Rome. He was clever enough to convey this to the public via a message scrawled on his hand.

In 1988 he was convicted of espionage and treason and given a prison sentence of eighteen years. He served sixteen. To this day, he is not allowed to meet with anyone in the media.

I didn't feel entirely good about this one and had to give it a great deal of thought over the years. I've concluded that although our nuclear capacities were fairly obvious long before Vanunu's information came out, he had nonetheless disseminated state secrets and illegal photographs. Further, I am convinced that Vanunu's actions were based less on high principle than on a yen for self-aggrandizement.

IVAN THE TERRIBLE

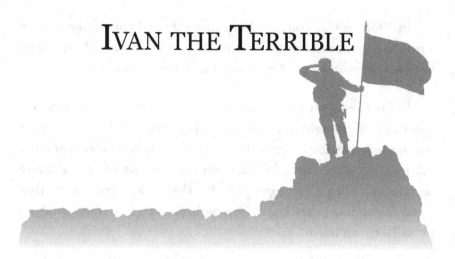

In February 1987 a retired auto assembly worker named John Demjanjuk was deported from the United States to Israel to stand trial for crimes committed during the Holocaust. It was alleged that Demjanjuk was "Ivan the Terrible" – an infamous SS guard at the Treblinka death camp in northern Poland.

On our own, not part of the investigation, colleagues and I compared images of Ivan the Terrible and the aged auto worker. We could not say with certainty that they were the same person. Could I recognize anyone from Auschwitz or Dachau forty years later? In most cases, probably not. There was one face – more specifically, a pair of cold, fish-like eyes – I could surely recognize. However, Mengele was dead at that point.

Demjanjuk was put on trial and all Israel watched the proceedings, as they had the Eichmann trial in the early 1960s. The proceedings were long. Demjanjuk insisted that he was not Ivan the Terrible. He admitted to having been a guard at Treblinka, Sobibor, and Majdenek, but insisted he'd been forced to do so and had committed no crimes. Eleven survivors testified they were positive the man before them was Ivan the Terrible. A former SS guard even testified that it was him. Demjanjuk was found guilty and sentenced to death.

He appealed. Israeli law gave him that right. A prosecutor traveled to the Soviet Union to look through archives for further evidence against him. Instead, he came back with doubts. In time, as the gears of justice turned, Demjanjuk was cleared. The witnesses had been positive, they'd also been wrong.

Demjanjuk was not Ivan the Terrible but neither was he an innocent figure. He indeed had been a brutal guard, one guilty of many war crimes. The Israeli judiciary, however, decided not to prosecute Demjanjuk again. He was sent back to the United States where courts stripped him of citizenship for lying about his past on his immigration request.

He was sent to Germany, put on trial, found guilty, and sentenced to five years in prison. He died in 2012 while his case was under appeal. In a convoluted and imperfect way, justice was served. However, I can never forget the absolute certainty of witnesses.

The identity and fate of the Treblinka guard known as Ivan the Terrible have never been determined.

LEBANESE ROULETTE

Little changed along the northern borders. We tried to stop the attacks and met with success. The other side didn't give in. They trained more diligently and planned more carefully.

One bright spot in Lebanon was Nur, the little girl I took from the Sabra refugee camp and placed with Hussam. I saw her when at his home from time to time and it was clear she'd become a member of the family. It pleased me that something good had come out of that.

In October 1987, Hussam and I sat on a wrought-iron seat behind his house. The morning was cool and calm. It was a shame we had to talk shop. He said more attacks inside Israel were coming. It wasn't just rumor. The streets and cafes of Lebanon teem with people who claim to know important people and have knowledge of big things. They rarely do. Hussam was my filter. One of them, anyway. The best one beyond a doubt.

Naturally I asked for specifics but he could only determine that the attacks was planned by Ahmed Fibril's Popular Front for the Liberation of Palestine – General Command, and that one would take place near Kiryat Shmona, an Israeli town right on the border. The precise date was unknown, but such things rarely follow a tight schedule anyway.

I asked Hussam if he felt safe where he was. He'd been an asset for so long that word was out. He and everyone in his household was in danger, even though his dwelling was well-guarded and what little traveling he did was under guard.

We'd long discussed moving to Israel. He'd even mentioned how much he liked a Druze village named Dalyat El Carmel. But this was only an idea we'd bandy about after work. I didn't think he'd ever leave Lebanon. I looked out on his orchards and wondered where I'd be in ten or twenty years.

Not long thereafter, I prepared to meet a Lebanese named Buchris. He was a food merchant, an occupation which saw him in and out of Syria. He knew many people in the Levant and many of them spoke freely with him. He provided Shin Bet and CIA with useful information, for which he was handsomely compensated. Sam and I discussed precautions.

Buchris and I arranged to meet in a crowded Beirut market where the din would make our hushed conversation more private than might be thought. I parked my car and headed for the cafe. He arrived at the appointed time and after coffee and light conversation, we got down to business. He handed me an envelope with a number of documents. The top ones specified seafood items and prices by season and we spoke casually of them as I riffled through the relevant papers.

My head suddenly felt heavy. My hands moved awkwardly and words came out slurred, as though I was suffering a stroke. Buchris too was disoriented. He looked down to the food and coffee in dismay. The restaurant had become empty. As they say in gangster movies, we'd been had. Buchris slumped over, I did the same.

In those gangster movies people in my position either don't wake up or they do so in a dark room. The latter scenario was granted me. I was on a sofa in a rundown room with a small table and chairs. On a far wall was a banner in Arabic. I was in the less-than-genteel hands of Amal. My memory was working well enough to know that Amal was a Shia group thought to be holding our airman Ron Arad.

But who set me up? Buchris? I didn't think so but neither could I dismiss it. Interrogation awaited me. What else? I was brusquely tied to a rickety wooden chair.

"Do you know about Amal?"

I shook my head and said I was a confused European businessman. He held up the papers that Buchris had given me showing PLO positions in southern Lebanon.

"Do you work for Israel or America?"

Those papers undermined my cover. I had a backup, of course, and it would at least buy time, though I didn't have anyone tailing me that day.

I told him in German that I was with the BND – West Germany's equivalent of Mossad and CIA. The backup was based on the premise that groups like the PLO and Amal had enough enemies without bringing another one down on them. To my astonishment the interrogator asked in heavily-accented German what the BND was doing in Lebanon.

"We're a large organization, always gathering information. The Middle East is not so far from us, after all. We think we can be helpful here."

"Hah! You Europeans think you can help us? You think that sitting back in your office in Germany you can find a solution? Such arrogance you have!"

His last words were hurled in great anger but I held to my story and kept personal views on German-Arab relations to myself. When asked about Buchris I said he was a local businessman who earned a little extra money by acting as a middleman. He knew nothing of the people on either end of the transaction.

As he paused to think things over, presumably my fate among them, I asked a question.

"Is Amal holding the Israeli airman Ron Arad who was shot down last year?"

He was taken aback but intrigued.

"We captured him."

His face showed pride. I wasn't sure of my fate or that of Buchris, though I had suspicions. If I was to go into the long night, I wanted at least to know what happened to Ron Arad, even if word of his fate wouldn't reach his family, any more than word of my fate would reach mine. He was amused by my boldness.

"Why am I to discuss this matter with a man tied to a chair?"

"As I said, my country wants to gather information and find solutions here. Maybe we can start by gaining the release of the Israeli airman in exchange for an amount of money that can be negotiated. It would likely be a lot."

"We don't care as much about money as Europeans do, especially the burghers of Germany. We want our country back. Besides, when did Germans start caring about Jews? They didn't like them forty years ago."

I kept my mouth shut and listened. It was another opportunity to peer into the mind of an enemy.

"We know your friend Buchris worked for the Americans. They are worse than the Israelis because without them Israel could not exist. One day both countries will suffer great defeats and we'll have our land back. I promise you that."

His thunder reverberated in the bare room.

"So you don't want German money? It can help you get weapons, cars, food – a lot of things. I'm talking about what the Americans call 'serious dough'."

Gears were turning in his head. He wasn't just another hothead.

"You'll never give me money. We both know that. Anyway, the Israeli you talk about was transferred to Hisbollah. Your fate will be the same. Maybe worse."

Buchris was dragged into the room in bad shape. A severe beating had left him with bruised, closed eyes, and a blood-soaked shirt. Why had they beaten him and not me? Maybe they believed my German intelligence story. More importantly, Buchris hadn't given me up.

The interrogator drew a small revolver. It was a cheap one, not a Colt or Smith & Wesson. His colleagues trained a Kalashnikov on Buchris and a Glock on me. He opened the revolver and let five of the six bullets drop into his hand. He spun the cylinder and snapped it back into place with a swift wrist motion. He'd done it before.

"Spin the chamber again if you like, then aim at your friend and pull the trigger. Only once. Then it's his turn. Maybe."

My hands were freed from the ropes and feeling came back to my hands. The Glock was pressed close to my temple in case a moment of audacity came over me.

"We may need Buchris in the future. I can arrange a large amount of money in exchange for his life. Millions of dollars for you. Straight into your bank accounts. Swiss accounts, if you prefer. All Europe can be yours – Paris, Rome."

The pause was welcome and intriguing. A conversation went back and forth in rapid, hushed Arabic. The interrogator motioned to the pistol and told me to proceed. The Glock remained at my temple.

"The money can be wired to you this very day. If you don't have a Swiss account, we can set one up for you in moments. For all of you."

"Proceed!"

Buchris lowered his head as I raised the pistol. I slowly squeezed the trigger and felt the spring pulling back.

Snap!

"Since your friend here is unable to perform his role in the game, I shall extend my assistance."

The interrogator spun the cylinder, snapped it back into place, and aimed at my chest. Let it be quick, I thought to myself. I stared straight ahead and waited.

Snap!

"Your turn."

I took the pistol with more hesitation and slowly began to squeeze the trigger as Buchris looked downward.

Footfalls in the hallway distracted my captors. I renewed my offer to make them rich but they looked at each other in confusion.

An explosion blew in the door and bullets flew. The Arabs went down hard but the firing continued until there was no doubt. There was a man in a cheap hat. The Prince of Langley had once again galloped to my aid. Spies do indeed spy on one another.

I had to take leave and undergo a series of medical examinations, including psychological ones. SOP, they said. It was modern bureaucratic fuss that would not have crossed the mind of anyone who walked out of Dachau or fought on the roads to Jerusalem. Everything went well, there were no signs of trouble, and I returned to regular duty.

Sam and I met not long thereafter and I thanked him for looking out for me once more. My suspicion was that he was tailing Buchris for one reason or another, but he offered no explanation. He only apologized for his tardiness. Strange, I thought his timing was excellent.

TOWARD THE FIRST INTIFADA (1987-91)

Hussam warned of an impending operation along the border and we increased security. Nonetheless, on November 25 1987, two guerrillas from the Popular Front for the Liberation of Palestine - General Command took off from inside Lebanon on motorized hang gliders and crossed into Israel. One came down just across the border and was immediately killed by an alert IDF patrol. The second landed near Kiryat Shmona where he attacked IDF personnel with a Kalashnikov and grenades, killing five and wounding seven before being killed.

The public was outraged. The government had to do something. The general responsible for the Lebanese border was fired. We looked into installing low-level radar systems that could detect hang gliders. Deputy chief of staff Ehud Barak promised a strong response. One came.

Hussam looked ill on our next meeting and made no effort to elide my questions. He had liver trouble, the legacy of a bout with mononucleosis. Turning to business he said that anger was rife among Palestinians in Lebanon, the West Bank, and Gaza. West Bank settlers had their own ideas of justice and were roughing up Palestinians. Sometimes the beatings were severe. Settlers indeed did such things and our courts did not always punish them in a manner fitting their crimes.

"An uprising might be at hand. Not a riot, an uprising."

Hussam knew the mood of people in the area – Maronites, Shia, and of course Palestinians. In December 1987 riots broke out in a Gaza marketplace. Disturbances spread to other occupied areas, including Jerusalem. We'd entered a period of protracted rioting – a general uprising, if you will.

Our task was to prevent the flow of arms to the tumultuous areas. Stone-throwing mobs are one thing, armed insurgents another. I began to work closely with Ehud Barak. We sought to interdict the flow of arms and prevent rocket attacks from Lebanon. Barak and I became friends and remain so to this day.

The Intifada went on for years and many people died, most of them innocent civilians. I'm sorry to say that it's part of war and part of the Middle East.

I was in my sixties and my family wanted me to put in retirement papers. I'd spent enough time in the army and Shin Bet. It was time to enjoy life with my family. I stayed on, though. In part because of colleagues, in part because of a sense of duty. I spent less time in Lebanon and more in the pit.

When offered a promotion, I declined. I wanted to reduce my work and ease into retirement. That was my intention anyway. The Middle East has a way of upsetting plans, especially my own. This time the trouble came not from Egypt or Syria or Lebanon. It came from Iraq.

THE FIRST GULF
WAR (1990-91)

Iraq, still led by Saddam Hussein, invaded Kuwait in the summer of 1990. The US organized an impressive coalition to liberate it and a large-scale war began the following spring.

Israel was not part of the coalition, nonetheless Saddam threatened to attack us with Scud missiles armed with either conventional or chemical warheads. This, he calculated, would elicit a response from us which would anger Arab countries. Their armies would no longer fight beside western ones, the coalition would collapse, and Kuwait would be his. The scenario was given a great deal of analysis but few of us thought it likely. Still, we had to prepare for Saddam's missiles.

Shortly after the coalition offensive began, I was at home in Haifa and sound asleep when explosions sounded in the distance. They were larger and more numerous than the ones I'd practically come to ignore in Beirut. Sirens wailed, I switched on the radio, my phone rang. Iraqi Scuds were slamming into Israel.

We were surprised but not unprepared. I'd worked along with Barak in the planning for civilians. Shelters were prepared and gas masks issued. We'd also planned retaliatory strikes on Iraq. IDF chief of staff Dan Shomron, following the urgings of the US, recommended refraining from retaliation and allowing the coalition to destroy the Iraqi military and its Scuds.

Sam said there was debate in Washington on how much effort should be placed on Scud-hunting. General Norman Schwarzkopf wanted the airpower to concentrate on Saddam's ground troops. Defense chief Dick Cheney wanted the planes to stop the Scuds. Cheney won out and American aircraft hunted down Scuds in the desert of western Iraq. They destroyed as many as possible.

The attack created a great deal of anxiety but only a little panic. Our casualties, however, were quite low. The Arab population of Israel and the occupied territories cheered the incoming missiles. This did not trigger any meaningful acts of violence. The war was over very quickly.

GOODBYE, OLD FRIEND

The next time I saw Hussam he was quite ill – visibly so, terminally so. His face brightened on seeing me, then sank back down into acceptance. He waved off attempts to encourage him and said his time was at hand. As he put it, it was time to pay the light bill. Those words were witty and wise – a welcome lift to a sad moment. When I asked if there was something my outfit could do, his eyes became alert.

"I'd like to accept your kind offer of settling my family in Israel. They'll be safer there. A house somewhere in the countryside. Someplace peaceful would be appreciated."

I promised we'd see to it.

"My daughters, including Nur, must go there. They will sell everything here and that will allow them to live comfortably there. And please, if you can, look in on them from time to time. But I want to be buried here. My parents, my wife – they await me."

Again I promised.

"But before my bones are lowered into the ground, let us enjoy good company and good food."

Hussam died in June 1992. His funeral was well-attended by mournful family and friends. I was present but stayed in the background.

We relocated his family to a Druze village named Daliat el Carmel. It's only a short drive from my house, and I keep in touch as best as possible. They are Israeli citizens, college graduates, and accomplished people. Unfortunately, they do not value our meetings as much as their father and I hoped. Nonetheless, I enjoy seeing traces of my old comrade on their maturing and happy faces.

Nur too grew up well. She studied art and married an architect. There's so much to build and rebuild in the world. I wonder what the family knows about their father's work with me. Perhaps not much, as he did not have the time to jot down his memoirs.

INTERNATIONAL SERVICE

My path took me from Shin Bet to the diplomatic service – a military and intelligence attaché in European embassies. This naturally strengthened my ties with Mossad.

My three children were grown and off on their own, and the idea of living abroad appealed to me. I knew German, Hungarian, and Romanian and could go out on the town. Prague is much safer than Beirut and though it doesn't overlook the Mediterranean, it nonetheless has majestic architecture that managed to survive a dozen or two wars. I'd seen some of it after taking my leave of Dachau.

It had been forty-five years since I'd left Europe for Mandatory Palestine. Many times I wondered what became of childhood friends. Many must have perished in the Holocaust. Some must have gotten through it.

I came across an old friend by complete chance. Having enjoyed a bowl of heavily-spiced goulash, I sent my compliments to the chef who came out to thank me. It was Alfred. We'd known each other in Oradea where we played sports together. We met up after work and talked of the many things that had happened since childhood, good and bad. We focused almost entirely on the good.

On a later meeting I mentioned that I dabbled in the culinary arts. He let me use the kitchen when the place wasn't too busy. There before me were knives and seasonings that no Rittman kitchen ever held. A few weeks of experimentation followed. When I offered Alfred a bowl of couscous, he asked me to put together a batch of it and hung a sign out front – "Tonight's Special: Couscous from Chef Zvi". The customers seemed to enjoy it and Alfred asked me to prepare a dish every week or so as my schedule permitted.

One evening I was a diner, not a chef, enjoying an espresso and taking in the aromas of the various meals around me. Anyone who was ever in the intelligence field is always looking around and listening in. Two men were speaking Russian. It's not a language I know but a few words are imported from English or German or a Slavic tongue. And I knew that "ubiystvo" meant "kill".

They were in their mid-thirties and had the dour, suspicious countenances of Russian security apparatchiks. I inserted a hearing aid-like device and turned my head for optimal reception. The conversation turned to their country and they expressed scorn upon Boris Yeltsin, the president of Russia who would visit Czechoslovakia soon. They went on to talk about a plan and a colleague. When their plates arrived, conversation shifted to the lousy restaurants of Moscow.

Approaching their table, I introduced myself, in Hungarian then German, as one of the chefs and inquired if everything was to their satisfaction. Congeniality came quickly and falsely across their faces. They expressed satisfaction and went on to praise not only the food but the service and ambience as well.

"Prague is filled with pleasing accents. I've come to acquire a hobby for identifying them. Would I be wrong to say you gentlemen are from Russia, perhaps Moscow?"

They looked at each other for a moment before one answered. "We're from Kazan."

"I've never had the privilege of visiting Kazan, though I'm sure it has many attractions. My name is Herman and I come from Oradea, as my accent might reveal."

That was part of my cover. It was the city I grew up in and knew reasonably well.

356 | Zvi and Danny Rittman

"We are visiting relatives here."

"Ahh. Family visits. How delightful. Are you here long?"

"Only a week."

In my most ingratiating voice I invited them to come back another evening. Back at my table I overheard mention of a later meeting. They soon left and climbed into a gray Russian Fiat. I scribbled down the license plate.

The Mossad chief at the embassy was intrigued and set up a detail to look into the men and tail them and their car. Two days later, a pair of Mossad officers equipped with sophisticated listening devices followed them into a restaurant. The Russians, along with a third man, sat in a recessed area. Mention was made of Bratislava and Brno. One of our people tailed them back to their hotel room. Later, when they went out in the early evening, he bugged it. The Mossad chief and I sat in a nearby room and listened in.

Yeltsin was coming to Bratislava. There were two assassination teams. One would leave from Prague and pick up a colleague in Brno. A second would come from Budapest and join the first in Bratislava, two days before Yeltsin's arrival. The president would dine in a restaurant where gunmen would shoot him, dispose of their weapons, and disappear into Eastern Europe.

I flew back to Israel and sat in on a meeting in the pit with Mossad leader Shabtai Shavit, Ehud Barak, and Yitzhak Rabin. What to do, what to do. We could do nothing and let Yeltsin be killed or at least face grave danger. We could inform Russian intelligence. But what if they were involved in the plot or if word somehow reached the conspirators? The decision was made to relay our information to Washington which we believed would pass it on to someone in Moscow.

We cannot be sure of what happened to the would-be assassins but Boris Yeltsin had an uneventful visit to Bratislava. I received a commendation for my astute eavesdropping. I got nothing for my cooking.

FAREWELL, SAM

S am usually showed up out of thin air, whether on a warm
Israeli beach or a dank Beirut cellar. Our paths didn't cross
much since I began pulling embassy duty. My beat was Europe, his
remained the Middle East. One of our last meetings took place on
the Haifa beachfront. He was retiring. Time to focus on the 49ers,
the football team in his hometown of San Francisco. He wanted to
see as many games as possible and devour a hot dog or two at each
of them.

He sighed and said he'd miss Israel – the sea, the arid inland,
and the architecture of Jerusalem. He sighed all the more when
he mentioned that he'd long thought of retirement but didn't think
it would ever come. Life would be less demanding, though less
interesting too.

"When you retire, you feel old. It comes right up and grabs you
by the lapels as you hand in the paperwork. When you sign your
name, you might as well write 'Old Guy' next to it."

"Old guys can still come to Israel every now and then, Sam.
Many of the Israelites were old when they got here from Egypt. You
might need an authentic passport for a change, though."

He smiled wistfully.

"My health isn't that good anymore. In fact, it's slipping away."

My heart sank.

"Don't worry, Zvika. I can still make a few trips. Company men aren't easy to get rid of, and doctors are often wrong – at least as often as we were. But one thing I definitely want to see. I want to see you in San Francisco. I want to take you to a football game – American football, of course. The hot dogs are on me."

"Hebrew National, I hope."

Sam sent tickets not long thereafter. A stop in Europe then over the pole to California. Sixteen hours – the longest flight I've ever taken. Sam was waiting at San Francisco International. His attire hadn't improved with retirement. He showed me around town – Fisherman's Wharf, trolley-rides up and down steep hills, and a museum or two whose names I've forgotten. We even took in a nightclub. Two old guys in a California nightclub.

When I expressed how much I enjoyed the city, he assured me the best was yet to come. The following Sunday we went to a 49ers game where I threw caution to the wind and ingested a hot dog of undetermined composition. Afterwards we went to the docks and watched seals frolic in the lazy tide. People tossed scraps to the gentle creatures. The more gifted ones caught the treats in midair then expressed gratitude. The practice was against the law, but seal and man alike enjoyed it.

On the way home, Sam made a confession.

"You know, Zvi, before I started working with you I read the Company file on you. Your past in the Nazi camps, Haganah, and the army – you are one tough hombre. Not sure I could have stood up to all that."

"I was too young to know better."

"The Holocaust was a disgrace, and for all the world. I hope nothing remotely that horrible ever takes place."

"That's my hope as well, Sam."

"Not sure if you've read up on me, but you might as well hear it straight from me. The stuff in dossiers isn't always right, whether it comes from CIA or Shin Bet. I was in the marines for a few years – Vietnam. Then I went into CIA. Tough things, lots of them. Nothing like Auschwitz."

"We both dedicated our lives to our countries and saw good and bad."

"That's for damn sure."

"You must have been a young man in Vietnam."

He recognized the implicit invitation. A door opened.

"Well, I could tell you about this and that but it's the bad things that stick out. One day we got intelligence about a Viet Cong camp where American POWs were held. So, we put together a rescue operation. As our Hueys neared the camp we caught a lot of fire. Dushkas and PKs. Tracers everywhere. Some close.

"Well, we silenced the guns and got the rest to *di-di mau*. Two of our Hueys were shot up and had to limp home. On landing, we found a hut packed with our guys. Some had been dead for days. Others were in very poor states. They looked at us uncertainly. Were we rescuers or a new batch of prisoners? They were too exhausted to know.

"'Americans? Americans?' one said over and over in a quavering voice. One of his eyes was swollen shut, his face and body clearly showed signs of torture but he was able to murmur a few words. Well, we didn't have room for all of them. Someone had to decide which ones got rides out, and which didn't."

"You had to decide."

"Affirmative, Zvi, affirmative. How do you do that? How do you select who lives and dies?"

I'd seen such decisions made by far less compassionate people, but I let Sam continue.

"Who was most likely to survive? Time was pressing and I pointed to nine of them. One of the others asked if we'd come back for the rest. I said we would but I'm not sure anyone believed me. He gave me the name of his girlfriend in Rochester and asked me to tell her of his fate. I told him he'd see her again.

"So we fly out with the nine and make it back to the base camp. We refuel, rearm, and head back. A mile or so out we see smoke and as we start to come down, everything's ablaze, including the prisoner hut. The place had been doused with kerosene or something and the poor guys were burned alive. We took them back. Pretty sure the boy with the sweetheart in Rochester was one of them, but the fire had done its work. I see its work at night."

"Those images never leave us, do they. They cause doubt about the idea of a higher power looking over us. I don't believe in any of that."

"I used to be the same way but late in life now, it's coming back. Slowly. I wish I'd been able to take another boy or two out, especially a certain one."

"You did well, Sam. We don't always get good deals in life. You saved my life twice. And I want to see you in Israel sometime soon."

"I hope so, Zvika."

That was the last time I saw Sam. Six months later I received a letter from his wife saying that he'd passed away from an illness she didn't specify. Enclosed with the sad letter was a photo of Sam and me in Haifa. I attended a memorial service for him at the American embassy in Tel Aviv.

ASSASSINATION ON MALTA

I returned to embassy duty in Prague. An important part of embassy work was arranging security for visiting officials. All in all I was working in an office, not spiriting in and out of distant airports, hideouts, and safe houses. I put on a chef's hat from time to time.

In September of 1995, "Ronen", a Mossad officer in his thirties, met with me in an embassy conference room.

"Are you familiar with an Islamic Jihad leader named Fathi Shaqaqi?"

"I know the name from my days in Beirut. He's a medical doctor of some sort, though more importantly for our interests, he's engaged in terrorism."

Ronen nodded. He would have been keenly disappointed had I not known the name.

"We deported him in the mid-1980s and since then he's become increasingly active in terrorism. Getting better at it too."

"Ronen, you aren't here for idle conversation about terrorism and its practitioners. You're planning to kill Shaqaqi. How may I help?"

Ronen grinned and cut to the chase.

"Shaqaqi will arrive here from Libya next month. Our team will greet him. Afterwards, we'll need help getting them out. You know the city."

"I'll get them out."

Things change rapidly and unexpectedly in our craft. In October we learned that Shaqaqi was not coming to Prague. Instead he was going to Malta, the small island between Sicily and Tunisia. We flew into Valletta, the capital. Mossad planned the operation from Atlit, just south of Haifa. New escape routes had to be made, but an island affords the opportunity to use small boats from any number of places, including fishing harbors and quiet coves.

Word reached me that Shaqaqi would arrive by ferry at Sliema, a town rich in history just across the bay from Valetta. I moved to the Diplomat Hotel where Shaqaqi would stay and later breakfasted with two young men who'd just arrived from London. We chatted about this and that, then took in the sights. Especially memorable were the old churches and castles. Conversation was light. No mention of work. It's odd how you can build trust for something as bold as an assassination by simply walking around town and having a meal.

I was sitting in the Diplomat lobby reading the local paper when Shaqaqi and a bodyguard checked in. I'd studied the grainy black-and-white photos we had of him. Glasses, beard, high forehead merging with a balding top. He smiled courteously at the desk clerk. I called the operation leader and said, "Arrived".

Shaqaqi went to his room, then came back down and went out into Sliema. No bodyguard. I followed about 150 feet behind. A motorbike with two men darted out from a side street. The passenger drew a pistol and fired several shots into Shaqaqi. He fell to the ground motionless. The motorbike sped away. I walked down another side street and bought a handful of souvenir postcards. Sirens blared minutes later.

I'd apprised the assassins of escape routes. The primary one worked well and I watched from afar as they boarded a fishing vessel. One of them looked back in my direction for a moment. He might have nodded. The fishing boat would rendezvous with a Zodiac boat that would then take them to a freighter bound for Israel. I headed back to the Diplomat.

The street returned to normal in a short period. I sat in a cafe and looked around at tourists and shopkeepers exchanging pleasantries and haggling over prices. A man had been shot to death an hour earlier, but business was back.

Shaqaqi's assassination wouldn't bring back those he'd killed, but it might save others. Maybe. You never really know. You might call it a faith you have to have for that line of work. But who am I to invoke the idea of faith. A replacement would be made soon enough and it remained to be seen how well he could direct Islamic Jihad.

I was not an assassin, just part of a team. But that didn't make me feel good about the operation. Killing an armed enemy in war is one thing, shooting someone as he strolled down a street to get lunch is another. There was something coldly instrumental about it. I wondered if the actual assassins felt that way, or were they too young and too enthralled by their organization's mystique.

It was good to get back to the kitchen in Prague and prepare another meal for the patrons. I was getting old.

ASSASSINATION IN JERUSALEM

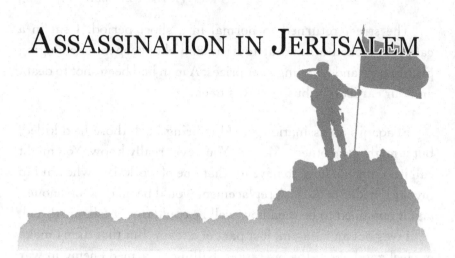

I n November of 1995, Israel was close to an agreement with the Palestinians. It was close to something else, too. A lone assassin named Yigal Amir killed the architect of the agreement, Prime Minister Yitzhak Rabin. In a sense he was a lone gunman, but that does not take into account the passions and politics of the day.

The Oslo Accords were the most divisive issue the country had ever seen. The Center and Left welcomed it as a step toward peace in the region. The Right, however, especially the religious elements who'd settled on the West Bank, saw it as a betrayal. They demonstrated in large numbers and with palpable anger, some with deep hatred. Posters depicted the Rabin in the uniform of an SS officer. Some ultra-Orthodox Rabbis saw justification in killing him. Crowds called for his death. This for a founder of the Israeli military who'd served in every one of his country's wars.

Shin Bet recognized the mood on the Right, but we were far more concerned with the Palestinians who opposed the agreement. Also, it wasn't long after Shaqaqi's assassination on Malta, so we worried about revenge attacks. We urged Rabin to wear an armored vest. He declined.

After the assassination, we learned about Yigal Amir. He was a young law student and follower of the Religious Right. He owned a Beretta 81, told family members of his intention to kill Rabin, and followed him about Israel. He came close to him on more than one occasion but for an unknown reason, did not draw his pistol.

Shin Bet conducted an internal review and found there'd been leads that should have been followed up on. Several people lost their positions. Amir was sentenced to life in prison. Accomplices received shorter terms.

Rabin's assassination marked a turning point in Israel's history. Violence and terrorism had been parts of the nation since its inception. But there was now a new source of death, and it came from among our people – from our most religious and nationalistic people.

THE LAST OPERATION

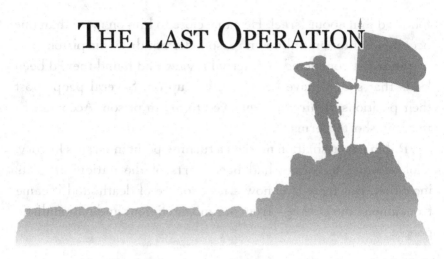

Terrorism did not decrease with Shaqaqi's death, even though his outfit, Islamic Jihad, fell into disarray. Rocket fire from Hisbollah positions in the hills of Lebanon continued apace. We worked on more plans to fight back. On and on.

My recommendation, and that of many others in the intelligence bureaus, was to use naval fire, airstrikes, and Special Forces operations to destroy camps and arms caches. The attacks soon took place but without the hoped-for effect. Over 700 Hisbollah rockets crashed into northern Israel the following year.

Hisbollah used densely populated areas and even schools to hide their positions. Retaliatory efforts were bound to cause civilian casualties. In one case, the results were horrible; many women and children were killed. International pressure forced us to suspend the strikes. Shimon Peres held a press conference in which he stated resolutely, "We are very sorry but we do not apologize."

Not long afterwards, just after a bombing in Jerusalem, I was called to Tel Aviv. Digging around usually revealed something about such meetings, but this time my shovel got nothing.

"You'll know when you get there, Zvi."

The room had special people there that day. Danny Yatom, the head of Mossad, made a few introductory remarks then got to the point.

"We're facing yet another threat – Hamas. It's responsible for the Jerusalem market bombing. Prime Minister Netanyahu has directed us to retaliate. We are to assassinate Khaled Mashal, and do it in a manner with plausible deniability."

Another stalking, another killing. The room was packed with eager faces.

"Mashal lives in Amman, so the operation will be more complicated than those elsewhere. Yes, there are problems and risks, but nothing that sound planning can't handle."

I pointed out that Jordan is a friendly country and that as carefully as we might plan, blame will be placed at our feet. Even if Mashal was hit by a drunk driver or a bolt of lightning, we'd be blamed.

"You're right, Zvi, you're right. But we have to respond. Now let's look at the plan. It's a good one. Quite different in approach from previous ones. We've been rehearsing on the streets of Tel Aviv."

Yatom looked over to one of his lieutenants who stood and began a presentation.

"We've had the target under surveillance. Naturally, such people vary their daily activities in case people like us are watching. There will be no car bomb or shooting in the streets. We've developed an innovative way of doing the job and we're very proud of it. Let's take a look.

"Two agents will approach Mashal. One will use a plastic syringe to spray him with a powerful opioid. It's a poison but doesn't kill instantly. It takes hours to do its work. It will be difficult or even impossible for anyone to determine the cause of death. And if they do, our people will be far away by then. In the unlikely event that the poison inadvertently comes into contact with our people, the team will be equipped with an antidote."

Yatom's lieutenant looked around the room and took in the appreciative faces. I asked how long Mashal had been under surveillance and how predictable his activities were.

The young man said, "A few weeks".

I asked of escape plans.

"There will be several."

I asked when the operation was to take place.

"Two weeks. Escape plans are being worked on now."

He went on to sketch the escape phase of the operation. I would be a "ghost operator", one of several. Not even the assassins would know us.

Folders were handed out with details, photographs, and maps. We were instructed to look through the material while in the room and not take it with us. The details written out in crisp prose, the folders and documents were tidily assembled, but the operation itself was slapdash. I requested time in Amman to study the assassination site and escape plans, one of which after all I'd be responsible for.

"Sorry. No time for that."

A few days later I asked Yatom to take me off the Mashal operation. I didn't like it – not in general, not in specifics. The whole thing came from political pressure, not careful thought. Yatom asked me to stay on despite my reservations, but my mind was set and he honored my request. I was out.

I looked at the people in the hallway leading from Yatom's conference room. So young. Most of them avoided eye contact. It was best to go back to Prague and do some cooking.

The Mossad team successfully sprayed the poison on Mashal. That part went well. But they were quickly nabbed by Jordanian authorities and forced to hand over the antidote. We had to release scores of terrorists to get our people back. The disaster was covered on European television over the course of several days. I watched for a while but soon turned it off and stared at the ceiling.

Embassy work continued. Two years in Prague, two more in Bucharest. The tours were interesting but I felt myself distancing from it. I traveled about whenever possible. I visited Oradea, where I grew up. The ghetto was gone and that was fine by me. The station where we were packed into cattle cars and sent to Auschwitz was still there. A train groaned to a halt before moving on again.

I returned to Israel and filled out retirement papers. I was officially an old guy. No more IDF, Shin Bet, or Mossad. They occasionally sought my ideas on certain matters. After a year or two the calls became less frequent.

EPILOGUE

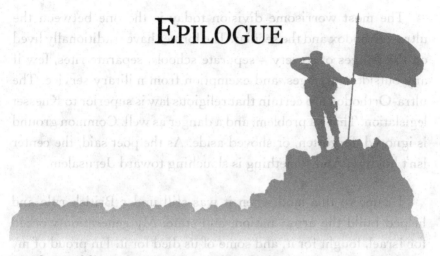

The Middle East is more tumultuous than in centuries, perhaps more so since the days of princes and emirs fighting for mastery of Jerusalem. Syria, Libya, and Iraq have ceased to exist and the number of hostile armies has gone down. A slew of presidents, warlords, and self-proclaimed emirs battle one another. Only Egypt and Jordan remain intact. They're friendly toward us for now. Vicious militant groups operate around us, but that problem has existed since the days of the early settlers.

The Palestinian problem is more urgent than ever. Our governments allow more and more settlements on the West Bank and put off negotiations on the two-state solution which they all profess to support. Terrorism follows, then more repression. I don't have a solution, but neither do I see our leaders searching for one. Shimon Peres and Yitzhak Rabin are gone, one from old age, the other from a settler's bullet. Meanwhile, our standing in the world is in decline.

There are deepening divisions in our society – observant Jews and secular ones, Ashkenazim and Sephardim, rich and poor, Right and Left. Some conflicts began thousands of years ago. Others are more recent. A portentous one began at the birth of Israel when Jewish militias fought each other and when a secular prime minister gave religious authorities permanent positions in the state.

The most worrisome division today is the one between the ultra-Orthodox and the secular. The former have traditionally lived on the fringes of society – separate schools, separate rites, few if any outside marriages, and exemption from military service. The ultra-Orthodox are certain that religious law is superior to Knesset legislation. That's a problem, and a danger as well. Common ground is ignored, forgotten, or shoved aside. As the poet said, the center isn't holding. And something is slouching toward Jerusalem.

I came to this land when it was still under British rule and helped build the army, nation, and state. My generation worked for Israel, fought for it, and some of us died for it. I'm proud of my service, fiercely so. I'm not the first old guy to think young people don't know what his generation went through.

It's said that when an old person dies, an entire library is lost. From boyhood in Romania to retirement in Israel I've seen great things and encountered remarkable people. They haven't all been good, of course. Some saved my life, others wanted very much to end it – with a bullet, artillery round, or a cloud of Zyklon B.

Good and bad, they all made me who I am and who my children are. That's why I've put together this memoir. It's for friends, family, and those who wish to learn and remember.

I've changed in regard to religion since the end of World War Two when I told a naive American reporter at Dachau that I couldn't believe in a higher power guiding us. "Look around!" I told him with unexpected ire. In the past decade I've become more accepting and inquisitive, perhaps because the light bill is coming due. I do not, however, think religion holds all the answers to private or public life and remain skeptical of those who think it or any ideology does.

I have three children. Two boys born in the 1960s, a daughter in 1970. My wife passed away in 1999. After a decade or so, I was fortunate to again find someone to share my life with. A brother and sister have died in recent months, as has my second wife now.

But a brother lives in Florida and a sister is not far from me in Israel.

My children have children. That Romanian boy is a grandfather. I take my grandchildren to the old kibbutz in Galilee and to Jerusalem, though we do not walk the hills to the west. I hope to take them to Sam's grave someday in California. Anyway, I'll encourage them to go there and keep him in their thoughts. Reading this, they'll know why.

My work is done and I'm ready to go on. Israel is in the hands of the young. May they guide and guard her well.

In spite of everything, I still believe that people are really good at heart.

– Anne Frank

Mementos

Herman (Shuly) – One year old in Focsani, Romania.

Herman in school uniform, age 11,
with Uncle Joseph and Aunt Catalina in Oradea, 1941.

Herman, age 8, with Uncle Joseph in Alba Julia, Romania.

Hermina and Solomon, ca 1910.

Front row: siblings Viorica, Rosy, Motzu.
Hermina Rittman is holding her baby, Herman. Solomon Rittman is to the right.
The other three women are Hermina's sisters.

Yanosh and Zvi, 1989, Los Angeles.

Yanosh, his wife, and Zvi, 1989, Los Angeles.

Zvi and his mother Hermina, 1986. She passed away in 1989.

Zvi and the IDF Soccer Team, 1975.

Zvi Rittman with grandchildren Bar and Noa, 2014, Netanya.

Motzu, Zvi, and Lucian, 1995, Prague.

Lucian, Motzu, and Zvi, 2013, in Netanya.

Zvi with sons Danny and Alon, 2014, in Netanya.

Merav Rittman with father Zvi, 2015, Haifa.

Zvi and grandson Daniel, 2015, Netanya.

Kibbutz Kfar Giladi

Haganah Identity Card

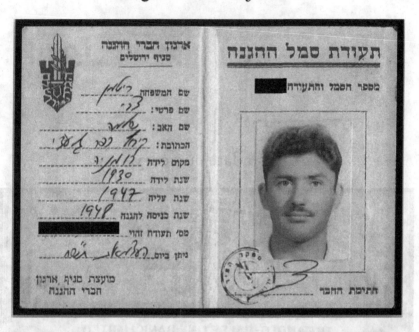

Mandate currency

Relief convoy in Jerusalem

INS Eilat

Beirut in war and peace

"Sam"

Hussam

Awards and Decorations

Haganah Service Ribbon

Six-Day War Ribbon

Six-Day War Medal

Moshe Dayan in Jerusalem Medal

Three Generals Medal

Carmeli Division Medal (Haifa, 1968)

Intelligence Medal

Distinguished Service Medal

Moshe Dayan Peace Medal

Special Engineering Operation Medal

Printed in the United States
By Bookmasters